CRITICAL CONTENT ANALYSIS OF VISUAL IMAGES IN BOOKS FOR YOUNG PEOPLE

Extending the discussion of critical content analysis to the visual realm of picturebooks and graphic novels, this book provides a clear research methodology for understanding and analyzing visual imagery. Offering strategies for "reading" illustrations in global and multicultural literature, chapter authors explore and bring together critical theory and social semiotics while demonstrating how visual analysis can be used to uncover and analyze power, ideologies, inequity, and resistance in picturebooks and graphic novels. This volume covers a diverse range of texts and types of books and offers tools and procedures for interpreting visual images to enhance the understandings of researchers, teachers, and students as they engage with the visual culture that fills our world. These methods are significant not only to becoming a critical reader of literature but to also to becoming a critical reader of visual images in everyday life.

Holly Johnson is a professor at the University of Cincinnati, USA.

Janelle Mathis is a professor at the University of North Texas, USA.

Kathy G. Short is a professor at the University of Arizona, USA.

CRITICAL CONTENT ANALYSIS OF VISUAL IMAGES IN BOOKS FOR YOUNG PEOPLE

Reading Images

Edited by Holly Johnson, Janelle Mathis and Kathy G. Short

Routledge
Taylor & Francis Group

NEW YORK AND LONDON

First published 2019
by Routledge
52 Vanderbilt Avenue, New York, NY 10017

and by Routledge
2 Park Square, Milton Park, Abingdon, Oxon OX14 4RN

Routledge is an imprint of the Taylor & Francis Group, an informa business

Library of Congress Cataloging-in-Publication Data
A catalog record for this title has been requested

ISBN: 978-1-138-38705-8 (hbk)
ISBN: 978-1-138-38706-5 (pbk)
ISBN: 978-0-429-42646-9 (ebk)

Typeset in Bembo
by Taylor & Francis Books

MIX
Paper from
responsible sources
FSC
www.fsc.org   FSC™ C013985

Printed in the United Kingdom
by Henry Ling Limited

CONTENTS

PART I

Research Methodology and Analytical Tools

1

CRITICAL CONTENT ANALYSIS OF VISUAL IMAGES

Kathy G. Short with the Worlds of Words Community

As a community, we are excited about the potential of critical content analysis as a means of bringing a critical lens to our work as researchers and educators, defining critical as a stance of locating power in social practices to challenge conditions of inequity. Our initial efforts to identify useful procedures focused primarily on the analysis of written language in global and multicultural literature (Johnson, Mathis, & Short, 2016). We recognized, however, that we needed other analytical tools to effectively use critical content analysis to examine the visual images that are so integral to meaning-making in books for young people.

This chapter provides a description of critical content analysis as a research methodology that includes tools for examining visual images, specifically the illustrations in picturebooks and graphic novels. Throughout the book, researchers share studies in which they used various visual tools within a theoretical lens to engage in critical content analysis of a particular text(s). By sharing a range of research studies to show the different ways in which this methodology can play out, the flexibility of critical content analysis becomes apparent as does the usefulness of the analytical tools. The final chapter highlights the ways in which we are taking this work into our own teaching and our interactions around literature with teachers and young people.

Our Inquiry into Critical Content Analysis

Our understandings of critical content analysis began several years ago and grew out of inquiring as a community about the processes and procedures because we wanted to use this methodology in our research. We talked with literary critics who engage in critical content analysis such as Clare Bradford, and read literary critics such as John Stephens, Perry Nodelman, and Mavis Reimer. We also read critical content analyses by educators who focus on representational issues, power relations, and language as a postcolonial tool, particularly seminal studies by Rudine Sims Bishop (1982) and Joel Taxel (1986), along with research by Vivian Yenika Agbaw, Wanda M. Brooks, Carmen Medina, Maria Botelho, and Masha Rudman. We revisited content analysis within the field of communication to understand the history of this methodology and engaged in our own research. In addition, we met as a group over several years, discussing published critical content analysis studies, and developing descriptions of the methodology from our readings and research studies. We proposed sessions and a study group on critical content analysis at the Literacy Research Association's annual conference to engage in conversations with other researchers. This inquiry was pulled together by writing a book about the methodology to share our understandings of the procedures we found most useful with each of us writing a chapter to share our research (Johnson, Mathis, & Short, 2016).

No inquiry is ever final, however, as new questions always emerge, so we soon found ourselves struggling with how to more effectively analyze the meaning-making processes within the visual images of illustrations in books. We read about illustration and visual image, examined published studies of illustrations and books on visual methodologies, and talked with other researchers in our search for analytical tools to examine visual images within a critical frame.

Connections between Content Analysis and Critical Content Analysis

Content analysis is an umbrella term used to indicate different research methods for analyzing texts and describing and interpreting the written artifacts of a society (White & Marsh, 2006). The content of texts is interpreted through coding and identifying themes or patterns, with the actual approaches ranging from impressionistic, intuitive, and interpretive analyses to systematic quantitative textual analyses (Hseih & Shannon, 2005). Since content analysis involves making inferences from texts to the contexts of their use by using analytical constructs derived from theories or research, researchers adapt content analysis to their research questions and develop a range of techniques and approaches for analyzing text (Krippendorff, 2003).

Content analysis has a long history but is particularly associated with communication studies and includes both quantitative and qualitative approaches. Quantitative approaches are used in fields concerned with mass communications (Neuendorf, 2002), while qualitative content analysis covers methods such as discourse analysis, social constructivist analysis, rhetorical analysis, and textual analysis. Krippendorff (2003) sees content analysis as a "research technique for making replicable and valid inferences from the texts to the contexts of their uses" (p. 18), while Hsieh and Shannon (2005) argue that this approach reflects a focus on "the characteristics of language with attention to the content or contextual meaning of the text" (p. 1278).

Content analyses of children's books were initially quantitative, counting the presence and images of a specific cultural group or phenomena (Galda, Ash, & Cullinan, 2000). Current research is qualitative, with researchers taking a theoretical position that frames the development of research criteria for text analysis based on an understanding of texts and readings of these texts in the social, cultural, and political contexts in which they are considered (Short, 1995).

Content analysis reflects a hermeneutic, reader-response oriented research stance. Meaning is not in the text but in the reading event, which is a transaction between a researcher and a text (Rosenblatt, 1938). Texts thus have multiple meanings that are dependent on the researcher's intentions as a reader and the context of the study because the purpose for the reading influences the meanings that are constructed as research findings. Analysts read to draw inferences from texts to apply to the context of the study, thus to make sense of something outside of the text. The texts do not speak for themselves but are read to inform another context.

Since content analysis is a stance, one option for researchers is to take a critical stance. What makes a study "critical" is the theoretical framework used to think within, through, and beyond the text, and so involves a specific critical theory such as postcolonialism, critical race theory, or queer studies. Adding the word "critical" in front of content analysis signals a political stance by the researcher, particularly in searching for and using research tools to examine inequities or resistance to inequities from multiple perspectives. Researchers who adopt a critical stance focus on locating power in social practices by understanding, uncovering, and transforming conditions of inequity embedded in society (Rogers, 2004). This critical consciousness challenges assumptions within thought and in the world that privilege some and oppress others (Willis, Montavon, Hall, Hunter, Burke, & Herrrera, 2008).

Critical content analysis differs from content analysis by prioritizing a critical lens as the frame for the entire study, not just in discussing the findings or citing scholarship in a literature review. In critical content analysis, the researcher uses a specific critical lens as the frame from which to develop the research questions, select texts, analyze the data, and reflect on findings. Since the researcher takes a political stance based in issues of inequity and power, some researchers believe that this positioning is subjective and unduly influences the research. Freire (1970) points out that all research is political and is always conducted within the subjective stance of a researcher. Critical content analysis makes the researcher's stance explicit and public to readers of that research.

Freire (1970) states that the world and texts are socially constructed and read through perspectives that differ from one reader to another. Each person conditions or transacts with a specific text in unique ways based on their lived experiences, value systems, and cultural understandings (Rosenblatt, 1938). Texts are never neutral as readers can revise, rewrite, and reconstruct texts to shift and reframe meaning. Texts are also written from a specific perspective to convey certain understandings of the world by positioning readers toward certain meanings through the language and visual images of the text and the use of narrative strategies. Because of this positioning of text and reader, the perspectives of each should be questioned. The concept of critical therefore requires a questioning stance when reading the word and the world (Freire & Macedo, 1987).

A critical stance focuses on social issues and the ways language and images are used to shape representations of others in relation to the intended audience. Language and visual image can impact readers' perceptions of specific groups of people and influence the power that people within those groups may or may not have within a society. A critical stance questions the concept of "truth" and how it is presented, by whom, and for what purposes, along with whose values, texts, and ideologies are privileged or considered normative. A critical stance thus focuses on voice and who gets to speak or be seen, whose story is told, and in what ways. Groups marginalized due to gender, language, race/ethnicity, sexual orientation—anyone labeled as "different" by mainstream society—are often the focus of a critical lens (Luke, 2012).

Freire (1970) argues that a critical lens involves:

- Critique (questioning what is and who benefits).
- Hope (asking what if and considering new possibilities).
- Action (taking action for social justice).

A critical lens thus moves from deconstruction to reconstruction and then to action. Freire points out that in everyday life many people stop at critique (deconstruction), which often paralyzes them with guilt or overwhelms them with the enormity of societal problems, unsure how to take action. In critical content analysis, the focus is on critique, on a critical examination of stereotyping and misrepresentation in literature, a deconstruction of books and the societal issues reflected in representations of marginalized groups. Freire makes it clear that we should also engage in reconstruction to look for the ways texts can position characters as resistant to existing stereotypes and representations. These counter-narratives offer new possibilities for how to position ourselves and others in the world. Based on critique and hope, researchers act by publishing for a broader audience and engaging with teachers and students in their own critical analyses and use of these texts.

Analysis of Visual Images

In this book, we focus on the critical content analysis of visual images in picturebooks and graphic novels, formats in which both words and illustrations are *essential* for readers to create meaning. The visual images do not just enhance a story told in language or provide some additional information, they are integral to the reader's experience and understanding of a book. Graphic novels add an additional visual element through the use of frames in addition to words and visual images.

Books with strong visual images hold special appeal and meaning because children are immersed in a visual culture in which images are integral to their experiences and interactions. A visual culture is one in which images are central to how meaning is created in the world. Duncam (2002) argues that more than any time in history, "we are living our everyday lives through visual imagery" (p. 15). This visual way of life influences what children know and how they think and feel about the world.

Visual image is no longer limited to a specialized form of expression in an art class, museum, or picturebook, but is instead an essential form of daily communication reflecting multiple ways of knowing. Duncam (2002) notes that this visual culture offers new freedom of expression and a willingness to play at signification, but can also be self-referential and depthless with an emphasis on immediate, short, intense sensations. This shift in visual culture has increased the significance and influence of picturebooks and graphic novels in the lives of youth of all ages and led to more extensive integration of visual images into middle grade novels and more focus on book design.

Our search for strategies for analyzing visual images began with Molly Bang (1991/2016) and Perry Nodelman (1988), whose work is grounded in art theory. Bang's work provided an easy entrée into basic art principles related to the composition of images and how the elements of art can provide the power to tell a story, particularly in the use of color, line, shape, and space. Nodelman's pioneering study of the narrative form of picturebooks deepened our understandings of the interplay of word and image to create a rhythm in which words and images "define and amplify each other" (p. viii). He focuses on how illustrations engage with words to tell stories. Pulling from art theory and semiotics, Nodelman particularly draws from Arnheim (1974) and Moebius (1986) to discuss how the visual choices of style and codes, along with the communicative elements of visual images, such as color, texture, shape, movement, and the positioning of objects, create a tone that supports readers in meaning-making. His book continues to be the standard in literary criticism on the picturebook as a distinctive art form.

Another significant influence is *How Picturebooks Work* (Nikolajeva & Scott, 2006), a book that analyzes the interplay of word and image through the relationships between pictures as complex iconic signs and words as complex conventional signs. Their analysis offers tools for analyzing the text created by the interaction of verbal and visual information to create setting, characterization, narrative perspective, time and movement, mimesis and modality, and figurative language, metafiction and intertext. Sipe and Pantaleo (2008) engaged in close analysis of metafiction and intertext in picturebooks, especially those considered postmodern, and offer insights into how these devices create meaning at multiple levels across images.

The work of Kress and van Leeuwen (2006) on multimodality and a grammar for visual design brought us a new way of thinking about visual images and picturebooks. Their influence has been widespread for many working in the field of picturebooks. Serafini (2014) points out that texts in the world today are no longer dominated by written language but have opened up into multimodal ensembles that integrate "visual images, design elements, and typographical features to communicate and represent ideas" (p. 2). He offers a range of tools and strategies for teachers and students in understanding visual images and multimodal ensembles that revolve around the elements of picturebooks, picturebook codes, and text–image relationships. Albers and Harste (2007) argue that educators need to consider the contributions of multimodality and new literacies for defining text and building on the social and literacy practices learners bring to the classroom. Albers (2008) combines multimodal theories with art to create what she calls a theory of looking and seeing to describe the "codes that exist in visual representations across time and space" (p. 167). She identifies a range of schematic or representational codes that she argues allow the visible to become recognizable to readers/viewers, developing a theory and a set of strategies she then applies to a set of picturebooks.

We were particularly drawn to Kress and van Leeuwen's (2006) work on visual grammar but struggled with applying their analysis to picturebooks that rely on a sequence of images instead of a painting that stands alone and does not depend on other images for meaning. When we found *Reading Visual Narratives* by Painter, Martin, and Unsworth (2013), we were intrigued by their approach, which combines visual grammar with Halliday's (1978) systemic-functional linguistics to create a complex, yet accessible, model for the social semiotics of picturebooks. The nuanced complexity of their work became evident as we sat down with a stack of picturebooks and gradually worked our way through their model, diligently examining the illustrations they were using to describe each tool and trying to see what they saw. The interweaving of reading their text, talking with each other, and examining illustrations in the picturebooks they were referencing brought us increased understanding and excitement.

We quickly recognized that their analytical tools could be used within a critical theory framework, a tension we struggled with in exploring other models for visual analysis. We each went off to try out the tools with other picturebooks, and these further explorations brought more confidence in using these tools. Writing these chapters to share our analysis of visual images in books for young people was another step in pushing ourselves to more deeply understand their use in supporting a critical stance. The underlying theoretical frames for systemic-functional semiotics and the tools within those frames are described by Clare Painter in Chapter 2 of this book, and the specific tools are described in more depth in each chapter.

In addition to these sources on the analysis of visual images, research studies on children's responses to picturebooks examine how children think about and respond to illustrations. These studies offer insights into the strategies that children bring as meaning-makers of visual images, and so are an important source of possible tools for examining visual images (Arizpe & Styles, 2003; Arizpe, Colomer, & Martínez-Roldán, 2014; Evans, 2015; Kiefer, 1995; Sipe, 2008). Edited books on new directions in picturebook research include research studies by leading scholars, and so are another source of theoretical frames and analytical tools (Colomer, Kummerling-Meibauer, & Silva-Diaz, 2010; Hamer, Nodelman, & Reimer, 2017). Finally, several books on visual and multimodal approaches to research were useful for our work (Norris, 2004; Thomson, 2008).

Critical Content Analysis of Visual Images as a Research Methodology

Critical content analysis involves bringing a critical lens to an analysis of a text or group of texts to explore the possible underlying messages within those texts, particularly as related to issues of power. At a practical level, we developed a shared understanding of the processes, procedures, and tools that we engage in as researchers when using this methodology, recognizing its flexibility for a researcher within a context (see Figure 1.1)

Note that in this book, the texts we are examining are books for young people because those are the texts that most interest us. Critical content analysis as a methodology, however, can be used with many kinds of texts, including documents as

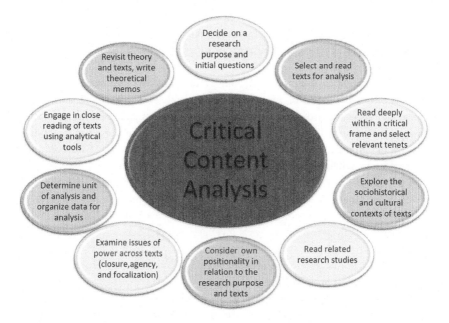

FIGURE 1.1 Engaging in the Process of Critical Content Analysis

well as texts within other sign systems, such as a piece of art, a musical composition, a dance, etc. Text for us is any chunk of meaning that has unity and can be shared with others (Short & Harste, 1996). Examples of studies in which researchers use critical content analysis to look at other kinds of texts include Satori (2018) who analyzed Peace Corp posters through a critical whiteness lens, Utt (2018) who analyzed the training manuals for school resource officers through a critical race lens, and Croce-Zimmerman (2018) who analyzed representations of diversity on websites of historically white colleges through a critical whiteness lens.

Our approach to critical content analysis is through the perspective of educators. Our intentions as researchers are based in our commitment to, and knowledge of, children, adolescents, teachers, and classrooms. This commitment influences our reasons for selecting a specific research focus, critical theory lens, texts, and tools for analysis, as well as our reflections on the implications of our research. We are also interested in the ways in which our research strategies and tools for analysis can inform classroom practice, both in teacher education and in K-12. The findings from our research provide critical perspectives that can inform educators by providing perspectives on global and multicultural books being used in classrooms. In addition, the strategies, tools, and questions used within research can be adapted as strategies for critical reading by teachers and students.

Decide on Research Purpose and Questions

Critical content analysis is embedded in a tension, a compelling interest in exploring texts around a focus that matters to the researcher and, because we are educators, that matters to young people. We research something because our interactions with young people and teachers in classrooms or other contexts indicate the significance of that focus for young people's perceptions of themselves and the world.

Sometimes research questions arise out of our work in classrooms, particularly concerns about the kinds of representations available of marginalized and under-represented groups and the impact on children's identities and their understandings of classmates' diverse lives. Desiree, Susan, and Megan note the small number of picturebooks that depict depression and the need to examine the nature of those representations, while Mary and Tabitha call attention to the same issue in books on families with same-sex parents. Several researchers focus on the underlying ideologies of books labeled as culturally diverse to demonstrate how these ideologies can be uncovered and challenged. Hee Young and Kathy examined a Caldecott Award winner to reveal the problematic ways in which this picturebook reflects dominant discourses and ideologies, while Carmen and Denise analyzed a retelling of a Mexican folktale that reinforces colonist ideology by erasing the contributions of Indigenous communities to Mexican culture.

These concerns led several researchers to examine books that could serve as counter-narratives, offering representations of a cultural community that resists and speaks back to mainstream depictions. Desiree and Wanda look at how Black illustrators portray Black children to bring a more textured and humane under-standing of Black children's lives to challenge antiblack racism.

Sometimes the questions arise from current events and media portrayals that affect the lives of youth. Seemi's concern about media portrayals of violence and conflict in the Middle East led her to research graphic novels written as memoirs by immigrants from those regions. The same concerns about negative media portrayals and social discourses about immigrants led Janine, Julia, and Jeanne to explore the visual depictions of Latinx immigrant journeys in picturebooks.

In any qualitative study, the researcher begins with a tension and an initial set of research questions that are transformed through interactions with the data, in this case with the texts and their interplay within the theoretical frame. We start critical content analysis with a research purpose and broad questions, but the specific research questions emerge as we immerse ourselves in the texts and theoretical frame.

Select and Read Possible Texts for Analysis

The selection of texts is based on the purpose of the study and often involves a careful process of researching many possibilities before deciding on a specific text or set of texts for analysis, based on specific criteria. Sometimes the tension relates to a set of texts, which occurred for Holly in reflecting on her participation in an award committee to recognize outstanding international books, and her tension about the kinds of representations promoted in these books. Carmen and Denise selected a book they felt was problematic and engaged in close analysis to uncover why they felt those tensions.

Although critical content analysis is often associated with a negative critique of representations in a text, researchers can also select texts that offer positive por-trayals or potential insights for readers. Janelle selected a book she believed por-trays the significance of agency in a child's life, while Angeline selected a book she viewed as a counter-narrative created by an Apache author/illustrator in an act of decolonization, or resistance, to mainstream narratives of Indigenous life. These researchers use critical content analysis to uncover the specific strategies used to offer representations in books that resist stereotypes.

Sometimes a broad range of texts related to the research focus are gathered, from which texts for analysis are selected based on specific criteria. Desiree, Susan, and Megan gathered many books that focused on children labeled with a range of disabilities, and from this larger set selected four books depicting depression. Holly gathered 82 picturebooks that had been named to an award list over a three-year period and used criteria to select 59 books for close analysis. A small number of texts might be selected for in-depth analysis as with the books on depression, or a larger set of books, such as the award books, can be examined to look for patterns across books rather than engaging in a close analysis of the contents of each book. Botelho and Rudman (2009) offer many examples of analyzing patterns across large sets of books.

The first step of analysis after selection is immersion as a reader, rather than as a researcher, in the texts. The focus is not to analyze the texts and take them apart but to respond to the whole text as a reader. We find it useful to read each text at least twice, once completely through to engage with the story and then writing a reflection to capture our initial response. The second reading is still a response to the text but involves making notes as we read, either in the margins or on post-its or in a journal, about passages, words, and visual images that catch our attention.

This first reading is in keeping with Rosenblatt's (1938) admonition to initially read from an aesthetic stance, to immerse ourselves in the experience of the story, rather than standing back to observe the story and get information, a more efferent stance. Much of critical content analysis involves an efferent stance, so we first want to "live within" the experience of that text as a reader—to experience and understand the whole before we start analyzing parts.

Select and Read Deeply within a Critical Theory Frame

One of the most important steps we take as researchers is to read deeply in the critical theories that seem most relevant to our work, to ground ourselves in that theory. There are always many possible critical stances, including critical race theory, critical feminism, postcolonialism, green theory, Marxism, New Historicism, queer theory, critical disability studies, and childism. Reynolds (2011) points out that scholarship in children's literature has benefited from adapting the critical theories used in literary, media and cultural studies to support investigations into written and visual narratives for children. Which theory or combination of theories is used depends on the research purpose and the set of texts.

This significant immersion into reading critical theory is a key insight that we gained from literary critics. As educators, we too often quickly locate a theory and spend most of our time with the data. Theory is cited in the initial frame and final discussion of the research but is not woven throughout our thinking. We have learned to instead spend large chunks of time reading theory until a frame for analyzing the texts becomes integrated into our thinking as a constant lens through which we interact with data.

Jackson and Mazzei (2012) argue that researchers are often taught to analyze qualitative data through mechanistic coding that reduces data to categories and does little to capture or critique the complexities of social life. They argue for thinking *with* theory by reading the data while thinking about theory, instead of waiting to apply the theory in the discussion of the findings. This movement of "plugging in" and making new connections is a transactional process that creates knowledge out of chaos. Both the data and the theory are essential in this transaction and both are changed to create something new. Theory is used to turn data into something different and data is used to push theory to its limit. This complete interweaving of theory and data moves us out of the complacency of seeing as we always have and into thinking with theory in more integral and complex ways.

We search for a critical theory or set of theories that have the most potential to provide an effective lens from which to critique texts based on our research purposes. Some researchers use the same theoretical lens across many studies, focusing on different aspects of that theory as relevant to their work. Clare Bradford (2016), for example, often uses a postcolonial lens for her analyses but selects different aspects of that theory depending on her research focus and combines postcolonialism with other critical theories as needed. Using the same theoretical lens allows a researcher to develop more complex understandings of that theory with each study. Other researchers bring different theoretical lenses to each study, enjoying adding new perspectives to their existing understandings. Still other researchers combine critical theories to develop a lens for their work. Botelho and Rudman (2009) drew from theories such as critical anthropology, cultural studies, political criticism, critical literary criticism, poststructuralism, critical discourse analysis, New Literacy studies, and critical pedagogy to develop what they call a critical multicultural lens to analyze sets of books.

To broaden the critical theories that we consider, books with chapters on different theories, such as *The Routledge Companion to Critical and Cultural Theory*, edited by Malaps and Wake (2013) and *Critical Theory Today* by Tyson (2015a), have been extremely useful. In addition, Gillespie (2010) and Tyson (2015b) summarize different critical theories and recommend ways of engaging students with these theories. These books provide overviews of critical theories so that we do not just fall back on the theories that are already most familiar to us. These sources help us identify theoretical perspectives that might be the best match with our research focus and provide references to pursue for in-depth understandings of theory.

Junko and Yoo Kyung found that postcolonialism, particularly the concept of imagined community, provided an effective frame to look at national ideologies in World War II books from Japan, while Carmen and Denise used decolonizing theory from an Indigenous perspective to recognize the devastation of colonialism on culture and the action and resistance to that colonization. Others used a range of theories, like Deanna who found that critical multicultural analysis integrated the range of theories she needed to analyze a book app and picturebook, and Holly created her own combination of theories from critical pedagogy, positioning theory, critical discourse analysis, and gaze theory as her critical frame.

Research the Relevant Sociohistorical and Cultural Context

Given our research focus and the selected texts, we search for sociohistorical and cultural sources to understand the broader social context within which a book is embedded. This framing of our research has taken on increasing significance to help us identify ideologies and social discourses from a specific sociohistorical context that are embedded in the texts we are analyzing. In our initial work with critical content analysis, context was only occasionally included but has since become integral to our work as researchers.

Seemi needed to understand the time period of her selected texts as one of instability and violence in the Middle East in order to evaluate memoirs of authors who were children in that time and place. Sometimes the context is broad, such as the examination by Janine, Julia, and Jeanne of immigration patterns in the U.S. as a context for analyzing Latinx immigrant books. At other times the context is specific, as in Mary and Tabitha's history of the different editions of a picturebook and Janelle's history of luche libre within Mexican culture. When analyzing a large set of books, the context takes a different focus around the purpose behind the text selection. In Holly's analysis of international picturebooks, the context is the specific award list and the processes and criteria by which books are selected.

Another purpose for careful research is to challenge our own perspectives and biases. Deanna found, as an outsider to Bengali culture, she had to engage in extensive reading of Bengali traditional literature and consult with multiple informants about their insider responses to the book and app she was analyzing. Angeline defined the sociohistorical context as the significance of oral traditions within Indigenous cultures, knowing that her valuing of these oral stories as the source of her knowledge and actions as an Apache woman would not be understood by scholars and researchers, who are outsiders reading her research.

The sociohistorical context and the discourses generated in that context are especially significant in studies that focus on uncovering hidden ideologies in books. Junko and Yoo Kyung took a close look at Japan's history of aggression and colonization of other Asian countries and the different forms of Japanese nationalism to undercover nationalist ideologies in Japanese picturebooks about the atomic bombing in Hiroshima and Nagasaki. Hee Young and Kathy provide a detailed description of the context and social structures that contributed to the protests and riots in LA after the Rodney King beating and the social discourses that were generated from this context. These discourses and social structures are embedded ideologies that play out in visual images and written language in a picturebook set in that context.

Select Theoretical Tenets to Frame the Analysis

Reading broadly within a critical theory provides an overview of the theory but can also overwhelm the researcher with knowledge about too many different aspects of the theory, making it difficult to apply the theory into the analysis. What we find most productive is to identify a specific set of theoretical tenets from our reading that relate most closely to our research questions. The additional step of synthesizing our reading of theory into 3–5 theoretical tenets of most relevance for our specific research focus and texts refines and deepens our analysis. Those tenets do not become categories or themes for the findings that emerge from the analysis but provide a clearer lens for reading and analyzing the texts through a critical theory lens. .

Listing the most relevant theoretical tenets for a study provides a way to vary the use of the same critical theory lens for different research studies. In addition, identifying the tenets provides an important opportunity to revisit the research purpose and the research questions, to make revisions in the purpose and to shape more specific research questions. Each research chapter provides examples of how researchers selected specific tenets to use as a lens for their analysis.

Read Related Research Studies

Another body of reading focuses on locating related research studies that either involve an analysis of a similar set of texts or use a related research purpose or the same theoretical frame. Sometimes other researchers have engaged in critical content analysis of books directly related to our research focus and so their findings inform our analysis. Mary and Tabitha found studies that examined the same picturebook they were analyzing, while Desiree and Wanda located studies that analyzed the depictions of Black children by Black illustrators.

Other times researchers have used the same critical theory frame, even though the focus differs, and the ways in which they use the theory to think with their data can inform our research processes, such as when Janine, Julía, and Jeanne examined studies using critical race theory as a theoretical lens for analysis. Junko and Yoo Kyung found research where the analysis focused on World War II and representations of war victims, as well as studies using postcolonialism as a frame for examining national ideologies. These studies provide useful insights from findings as well as possible theoretical frames and research strategies.

Examine the Texts through Close Reading within the Theoretical Frame

In-depth theoretical and contextual research provides a more effective and complex frame from which to do a close reading and analysis of the selected children's or adolescent texts. A number of processes are involved in this close reading, including reflecting on our positionality as researchers, considering broad issues of power, determining our unit of analysis, preparing the data for analysis, and doing close analysis of selected images and words/passages.

Reflect on Our Own Positionality as Researchers

Taking an explicit critical theory stance on research involves taking a position and making that stance clear to readers. Another aspect of stance is being explicit about our own positionalities as connected to the specific research focus and texts. Sharing our positionalities makes public the biases and experiences we bring to the analysis. In analyzing Japanese picturebooks about World War II, Junko and Yoo Kyung bring differing experiences, and sometimes opposing perspectives, because one grew up in Japan and the other in Korea with strong feelings about the Japanese occupation of Korea. Angeline's positionality as Apache, the cultural setting of the picturebook she analyzed, supported her in-depth insights into the cultural symbolism embedded in the visual images. Deanna is an outsider to Bengali culture in India and her recognition of this outsider positionality led her to engage in much deeper research in original sources and with Indian informants than she had initially anticipated. Positionality can also be significant due to specific experiences, such as Holly's membership of the award committee.

Making sure we are explicit about our own positionalities was not a regular aspect of our initial work with critical content analysis. With the benefit of time and experience, we realize the importance of making our positionalities explicit for readers, because that positionality alerts them to possible biases in our analyses. By making our positionality clear, we are also challenging ourselves to become aware of our perspectives and biases in order to interrogate ourselves and to take steps within our research process to bring in other perspectives.

Consider Broad Issues of Power

Our initial close readings consider the broad issues within a text before we identify units of analysis and focus on specific passages or visual images. Botelho and Rudman (2009) recommend initial close readings around broad critical issues that allow the researcher to consider the language and visual images in texts and the narrative strategies related to issues of power before moving into close analysis. These broad issues include:

- Focalization—Whose story is told? Who sees? From whose point of view?
- Social processes of characters—Who has power? Who has agency?
- Closure—How is the story resolved? What are the assumptions in the story closure?

Seemi brought these questions into her analysis of the four graphic memoirs, noting the voices of the narrators and how they represented power and agency within themselves and other characters, along with their endings in which the protagonists found safety in a Western country.

Determine the Unit of Analysis

Engaging in these initial close readings also supports decisions about the unit of analysis or smaller chunks of meaning most productive on for close analysis. In a short picturebook, the entire book may be examined closely and so the unit of analysis can be the book itself, or the researcher can select several key illustrations for an in-depth look. In a longer graphic novel or a middle grade novel with illustrations, researchers usually select key illustrations based on the research purpose for close analysis rather than the entire book. The unit could involve identifying visual images that reflect key incidents or selecting images from the beginning, middle and end of the text or at a critical turning point of the text. The unit of analysis will vary with the research purpose and with the characteristics of the text being analyzed.

Angeline selected three key illustrations for her close analysis of a picturebook because she wanted to look at the complex interplay between participants, processes, and circumstances within each visual image rather than patterns across illustrations. Holly selected pages in which characters directly gaze out at readers because of her interest in whether the books treat readers as engaged spectators or distanced observers. Once Desiree, Susan, and Megan realized the extensive use of a dark cloud to signal depression, they focused their close analysis on the illustrations in which the cloud was present.

Most of us engaged with the entire book to look for patterns, because picturebooks allow for that possibility without needing to select smaller units of analysis that would be essential in analyzing a long text such as a novel. In contrast, Seemi was examining graphic novels with many images and panels, so she selected key illustrations that depict the protagonist's response to violence and conflict.

The initial close reading of the text to examine larger issues, such as focalization, social processes, and closure, along with identifying the unit of analysis, provides another important perspective from which to revisit and revise the research questions. Adjustments to the research questions grow out of a strong grounding in the theoretical frame and in the texts themselves.

Organize the Data for Analysis

The complexity of analyzing for patterns across visual data can be difficult when needing to turn pages instead of being able to scan the data from different parts of the text at the same time. Deanna compared a picturebook with a digital app of the same story and found that she first needed to photocopy every page of the picturebook and create a storyboard displayed horizontally on the wall to see patterns across pages. She then added screen shots of the app slides that corresponded with the double-page book spreads to the wall to see visual changes from the book to the app. She also created a two-column document of the written language from the app and the book side by side to look for language changes. Junko and Yoo Kyung describe the multimodal transcript they created as a chart in order to make comparisons across four books. Mary and Tabitha created sets of comparable scenes across two editions of the same book to see verbal and visual changes.

Closely Analyze Selected Images or Words

The next readings involve a close examination of the identified units or visual images within each text, moving between the theoretical frame and the texts, initially making many notes and gradually moving toward identifying significant issues, themes, or categories. This analysis often focuses on broad themes or issues that emerge from the interplay of data and theory in an evolving process as described by Jackson and Mazzei (2012).

Sometimes, we use constant comparative analysis to organize data from these texts into more discrete categories, documenting emerging themes and evidence from the text and gradually developing these into a focused set of categories to report the findings (Corbin & Strauss, 2014). Desiree and Wanda developed open codes and identified emergent patterns that were used to re-analyze the selected visual images and then were re-sorted based on commonality until several categories emerged. Frequently, however, the data examples from the illustrations are organized around broad themes or issues rather than discrete categories, as occurred for Janelle in her analysis of a picturebook highlighting a child's imaginary play.

The research included in these chapters involves closely reading the visual images in picturebooks and graphic novels. To engage in this analysis, we identified a range of visual tools to facilitate critical analysis. Most of these tools were developed by Painter, Martin, and Unsworth (2013) to analyze visual images, and are introduced in Chapter 2 by Clare Painter. Picturebooks and graphic novels are defined as texts in which the illustrations and language are essential to the story. We did not ignore the written language but did give it less emphasis in the analyses shared in these chapters. Because of our focus on visual images, most chapters highlight the use of specific visual tools to analyze visual images, bringing in written language to clarify or expand on a theme.

Hee Young and Kathy provide an example of a study in which both the words and the visual images are viewed as interwoven in the themes identified in the analysis. For each theme, the linguistic features of the text are analyzed through a focus on the meanings of vocabulary within the situations they are used to describe, especially the use of hyponymy and synonymy, to examine how the author is structuring the world. The visual features of illustrations related to each theme are analyzed through the analytical tools of focalization, affect, pathos, ambience, and graduation. The linguistic and visual features together provide a glimpse into a picturebook as a cultural artifact.

Revisit Theory and Texts

The process of analysis remains flexible and recursive with multiple revisits to theory and visual images. Sometimes the need for further reading of theory becomes evident, either within the same theoretical frame or by adding additional theories due to issues arising in the analysis. The illustrations selected for analysis may need to be revisited for further analysis as new themes and issues emerge either from another part of the data or through additional readings. This recursive process of revisiting theory and the data can occur multiple times until the major themes or categories take shape, with strong evidence from visual images to support those themes.

Write Theoretical Memos on the Analysis

We find it useful to write theoretical memos for each major theme or category, providing a description of each one based on the professional literature and on the types of examples found in the illustrations or the written language. This definition or explanation of each theme or category is developed by noting evidence from the texts, citing excerpts and interpretations of those passages or visual images as related to the theme, and interweaving theory into those interpretations. These memos provide the basis from which to write articles and chapters based on the analysis.

Our experiences indicate major differences in how the study is shared based on the type of journal to which we plan to submit a manuscript. Educational research journals typically want a research report format focused around research purpose, theoretical frame and literature review, methodology, findings, discussion and implications, while literary journals begin with a research purpose and then flow into a discussion of the major issues and themes, integrating theory and data throughout the article. Finally, journals that reach out to a broader audience of educators generally focus on sharing key insights from the research and implications for teachers rather than being organized into a research report format.

Given the focus of this book on research methodology, we wrote our chapters using a research report format with an expanded section describing the research methodology within each chapter. The concluding chapter extends the significance of the methodology by discussing the visual tools that we believe have the most potential for classroom inquiry and instruction.

Final Reflections

Although the processes we describe in this chapter may seem logical and step-by-step, the studies we share reflect the many variations of how critical content analysis can play out in actual research. Just as the written curriculum is never the same as the enacted curriculum, our enactment of critical content analysis always differs due to our research purposes, texts, and theoretical lens, as well as our own strengths and experiences as researchers. Readers will notice that some aspects of the processes described in this chapter are not followed or were adapted in each study reported in this book. We see this variation as a strength of critical content analysis. It is also clear to us that other researchers will develop their own processes and analytical tools.

The thread that runs throughout our work is the willingness to take a critical stance as a researcher. This critical stance is woven throughout our research so that every aspect of the research process is based in thinking through a particular theoretical lens. Acknowledging that all research is political, we believe that critical content analysis adds complexity and depth to the discussion of research methodology. As researchers, we are challenged to explicitly identify our stance and take ownership of our responsibility to critique issues of power and oppression in order to take action in our varied contexts.

Overview of the Book

The chapters in this book are organized into five sections. The first section describes critical content analysis as a methodology involving the use of visual tools for analysis. This first chapter represents our current understandings of critical content analysis as a set of flexible processes and procedures that revolve around the use of critical theory as a frame for research. The second chapter by Clare Painter overviews the theoretical framework of systemic-functional semiotics used for image analysis in the chapters in this book.

The next three sections include individual reports of critical content analysis studies in which the researchers use visual analytical tools to analyze either picturebooks or graphic novels. Given our focus on research methodology, the researchers include a fuller description of their analysis processes and their use of visual tools than often found in published studies. Since we are all educators, we locate our studies within educational perspectives, particularly in relation to the purpose and implications of the research. The texts we selected for analysis are ones that reflect a global or multicultural perspective, and our research questions reflect these perspectives as well.

The research studies are divided into three parts. Part II includes studies on picturebooks that resist dominant societal representations to examine how these books provide counter-narratives for readers. Often critical content analysis is associated with critiques of problematic representations of groups marginalized by mainstream society. These studies indicate how this methodology can also be used to analyze how texts work to resist oppressive images. Part III includes studies that highlight how visual images can position readers to interact with a picturebook in a particular way. Part IV includes studies that examine the ideologies in books and how these ideologies construct problematic representations.

Part V is our final chapter in which we reflect on the ways in which we are continuing our inquiry. Our current goal as educators is to consider the implications of our work with critical theory and critical content analysis in our teacher education classrooms and in our work with teachers and students in K-12 classrooms. We share our initial explorations as first steps in each of our settings and in our continued conversations as a community.

References

Albers, P. (2008). Theorizing visual representation in children's literature. *Journal of Literacy Research*, 40(2), 163–200.
Albers, P. & Harste, J. (2007). The arts, new literacies, and multimodality. *English Education*, 40(1), 6–20.

Arizpe, E., Colomer, T., & Martinez-Roldan, C. (2014). *Visual journeys through wordless narratives*. London: Bloomsbury.

Arizpe, E. & Styles, M. (2003). *Children reading pictures: Interpreting visual texts*. London: Routledge.

Arnheim, R. (1974). *Art and visual perception: A psychology of the creative eye*. Berkeley: University of California Press.

Bang, M. (1991/2016). *Picture this: How pictures work*. San Francisco: Chronic.

Bishop, R. (1982). *Shadow and substance: Afro-American experience in contemporary children's fiction*. Urbana, IL: National Council of Teachers of English.

Botelho, M.J. & Rudman, M.K. (2009). *Critical multicultural analysis of children's literature*. New York: Routledge.

Bradford, C. (2016). The critical reading of children's texts. In H. Johnson, J. Mathis, & K. Short, *Critical content analysis of children's and young adult literature* (pp. 16–27). New York: Routledge.

Colomer, T., Kummerling-Merbauer, B., & Silva-Diaz, C. (Eds.) (2010). *New directions in picturebook research*. London: Routledge.

Corbin, J. & Strauss, J. (2014). *Basics of qualitative research*, 4th ed. Thousand Oaks, CA: Sage.

Croce-Zimmerman, C. (2018). Normalizing whiteness on college campuses. *Understanding and Dismantling Privilege*, 8(2).

Duncam, P. (2002). Visual culture art education. *International Journal of Art and Design Education*, 21(1), 15–23.

Evans, J. (Ed.). (2015). *Challenging and controversial picturebooks*. London: Routledge.

Freire, P. (1970). *Pedagogy of the oppressed*. South Hadley, MA: Bergin & Garvey.

Freire, P., & Macedo, D. (1987). *Literacy: Reading the word and the world*. Santa Barbara, CA: Praeger.

Galda, L., Ash, G. & Cullinan, B.E. (2000). Research on children's literature. In M.L. Kamil, P.B. Mosenthal, P.D. Pearson, & R. Barr (Eds.) *Handbook of reading research: Volume III* (pp. 351–381). Mahwah, NJ: Erlbaum.

Gillespie, T. (2010). *Doing literary criticism*. Portland, ME: Stenhouse.

Halliday, M.A.K. (1978). *Language as social semiotic*. London: Arnold.

Hamer, N., Nodelman, P., & Reimer, M. (Eds.) (2017). *More words about pictures: Current research on picture books and visual/verbal texts*. London: Routledge.

Hsieh, H. & Shannon, S. (2005). Three approaches to qualitative content analysis. *Qualitative Health Research*, 15(9): 1277–1288.

Jackson, A. & Mazzei, L. (2012). *Thinking with theory in qualitative research*. New York: Routledge.

Johnson, H., Mathis, J., & Short, K. (2016). *Critical content analysis of children's and adolescent literature*. New York: Routledge.

Kiefer, B. (1995). *The potential of picture books*. New York: Merrill.

Kress, G. & Van Leeuwen, T. (2006). *Reading images: The grammar of visual design* (2nd ed.). London: Routledge.

Krippendorff, K. (2003) *Content analysis: An introduction to its methodology*. Thousand Oaks, CA: Sage.

Luke, A. (2012). Critical literacy: Foundational notes. *Theory into Practice*, 51(1), 4–11.

Malpas, S. & Wake, P. (Eds.) (2013). *The Routledge companion to critical and cultural theory*, 2nd ed. New York: Routledge.

Moebius, W. (1986). Introduction to picture book codes. *Word and Image*, 2, 141–151.

Neuendorf, K.A. (2002). *Content analysis guidebook.* Thousand Oaks, CA: Sage.

Nikolajeva, M. & Scott, C. (2006). *How picturebooks work.* London: Routledge.

Nodelman, P. (1988). *Words about pictures: The narrative art of children's picture books.* Athens, GA: University of Georgia Press.

Norris, S. (2004). *Analyzing multimodal interaction.* London: Routledge.

Painter, C., Martin, J.R., & Unsworth, L. (2013). *Reading visual narratives: Image analysis of children's picture books.* Sheffield, UK: Equinox.

Reynolds, K. (2011). Introduction to research and theory. In M.O. Grenby & K. Reynolds (Eds.) *Children's literature studies: A research handbook* (pp. 123–127). London: Palgrave.

Rogers, R. (2004). *An introduction to critical discourse analysis in education.* Mahwah, NJ: Erlbaum.

Rosenblatt, L. (1938). *Literature as exploration.* Chicago: Modern Language Association.

Satori, A. (2018). Whiteness in development: A critical content analysis of Peace Corps marketing. *Understanding and Dismantling Privilege,* 8(2).

Serafini, F. (2014). *Reading the visual.* New York: Teachers College Press.

Short, K. (Ed.) (1995). *Research and professional resources in children's literature.* Newark, DE: International Reading Association.

Short, K. & Harste, J. (1996). *Creating classrooms for authors and inquirers.* Portsmouth, NH: Heinemann.

Sipe, L. (2008). *Storytime: Young children's literary understanding in the classroom.* New York: Teachers College Press.

Sipe, L. & Pantaleo, S. (Eds.) (2008). *Postmodern picturebooks.* New York: Routledge.

Taxel, J. (1986). The Black experience in children's fiction: Controversies surrounding award winning books. *Curriculum Inquiry,* 16(3): 245–281.

Thomson, P. (Ed.). (2008). *Doing visual research with children and young people.* London: Routledge.

Tyson, L. (2015a). *Critical theory today.* New York: Routledge.

Tyson, L. (2015b). *Using critical theory,* 3rd ed. New York: Routledge.

Utt, J. (2018). Dysconscious policing: A critical content analysis of school resource officer training materials. *Understanding and Dismantling Privilege,* 8(2).

White, M. & Marsh, E. (2006). Content analysis: A flexible methodology. *Library Trends,* 55(1): 22–45.

Willis, A., Montavon, M., Hall, H., Hunter, C., Burke, L., & Herrera, A. (2008). *Critically conscious research.* New York: Teachers College Press.

2

IMAGE ANALYSIS USING SYSTEMIC-FUNCTIONAL SEMIOTICS

Clare Painter

This chapter introduces the theoretical framework used for image analysis in the chapters in this book, beginning with the relation of visual analysis to critical discourse analysis of verbal texts.

Scholars have long been interested in the way readers are positioned by the verbal texts they read, particularly by a text's covert ideological stance and taken-for-granted assumptions about age, gender, ethnicity, social class, and historical, political, or cultural "truths." The field of critical discourse analysis in particular has always had the objective of demonstrating the relationship between language and power by deconstructing written texts to show how they conceal and legitimize certain assumptions and points of view (Fairclough, 1989; Fowler, Hodge, Kress, & Trew,1979; Kress & Hodge, 1979; Martin, 2000). Early work would often focus on media texts, pointing out that different grammatical structures used in "factual" news reports can imply opinion or attitude even where no evaluative language is used. For example, the intransitive clause *Dozens die in protests* assigns no agency to anyone, presenting the event as just something that happened; the transitive clause *Dozens of protesters are killed*, on the other hand implies that there was purposeful action, but its "agentless" passive construction leaves responsibility for it unstated. It can be compared with the active variant, *Police/ soldiers/ vigilantes kill dozens of protesters*, where the cause of the deaths is necessarily stated. Critical analysts use such examples to show that apparently neutral language can still function to convey evaluations and biases.

Much of the original and subsequent work in critical discourse analysis uses the semantically-based grammar of systemic-functional linguistic theory (SFL) developed by M.A.K. Halliday (1978) to reveal how patterns of language across a text play a significant role in positioning readers. SFL is an approach to language that is unreservedly social in its orientation, with Halliday (1978) famously referring to language as a "social semiotic." SFL takes the view that language is shaped by the purposes it serves in our lives and in turn shapes our ways of living and thinking. As well as media discourse, SFL has been used to explore the language of numerous other social domains, including many within the sphere of education, such as classroom discourse (Christie, 2002), shared book reading (Torr, 2004), children's literacy pedagogy (Rose & Martin, 2012; Williams, 2016), and English for Academic Purposes (Coffin & Donohue, 2012), often in association with questions arising in another disciplines, such as the sociology of knowledge (Maton, Martin, & Matruglio, 2016) or socio-cultural theory (Byrnes, 2006). SFL has been particularly useful for such work as it is specifically designed as an "appliable" form of linguistics (Mahboob & Knight 2010) that can be used to explore research questions arising in other fields, including literature, the law, politics, medicine, and advertising, as well as education.

An appliable linguistics has great value in exploring the meanings of verbal texts and showing how these relate to the contexts in which they are embedded. But given the changing nature of discourse in the contemporary world, critical discourse analysis has been expanded to encompass the examination of texts that incorporate non-language modalities, such as visual image, sound, or animation. This has led to the emerging field of critical multimodal discourse analysis (Djonov & Zhao, 2014). As part of this enterprise, key principles of SFL have been used to build descriptive tools for analyzing non-verbal semiotic systems, such as those of body language (Hood, 2011), mathematical symbolism (O'Halloran, 2008), or visual image (Kress & van Leeuwen, 2006; Painter, Martin, & Unsworth, 2013). This inclusion of other communicative modalities within the SFL framework is signaled by the terms multimodal social semiotics or systemic-functional semiotics (SFS) and this work in relation to the visual image is highly pertinent for examining how children's picturebooks work.

It is very clear that a consideration of verbal language alone is inadequate for exploring and assessing picturebooks. To do justice to their complexity, it is most valuable to have available a semantically oriented visual grammar that allows for a systematic analysis of the meanings carried within images. And if such a visual grammar is readily compatible with established ways of examining the verbal component of such books, this has a great advantage—both modalities can then be explored using the same analytical framework. Seminal work in the building of such a visual grammar on SFS principles is provided by Kress and van Leeuwen (2006) in *Reading Images: The Grammar of Visual Design*. Building on their grammar, my work with Martin and Unsworth (Painter et al., 2013) uses picturebook data to apply, extend and develop the earlier work in ways that are particularly relevant for understanding picturebook stories. The remaining chapters in this book draw on this SFS approach in their use of analytical tools to discuss the ways in which visual images contribute to meaning in specific picturebooks. Some key principles of SFS are explored in this chapter, along with a brief overview of analytical tools for visual images. Specific areas of analysis are described in greater detail in the chapters where they are put into service to support the researchers in their critical content analysis.

Key Principles of Systemic-Functional Semiotics (SFS)

A fundamental principle of systemic-functional semiotics (SFS) is that every text, whether verbal or visual (or a combination), expresses three different kinds of meaning at the same time. This is because every text must fulfil three different functions simultaneously. First, and most obviously, every text is about something—it has some content. This kind of meaning is known as the *ideational* function or metafunction of language or image. The content of a story involves the characters, events and settings of the narrative, while that of a sentence relates to "who is doing what to whom; where, when, how and why." The ideational content of an individual image concerns whatever is depicted—any people, objects, actions and settings we can describe when we look at the picture. This is the easiest kind of meaning to recognize and access for an image. It is our commonsense idea of what a picture is about.

In addition, though, every text enters into a communicative relation with those who receive it. In language, for example, the same ideational content can be stated, questioned, exclaimed or commanded, positioning the reader/hearer in different dialogic roles. And in images, as well as verbal text, ideational content can be exaggerated, imbued with feelings, presented more or less impersonally, and so on. In a narrative text, there are also the interactional relations between characters to consider, and the feelings they display, which may be presented both verbally and visually. All these factors involve the *interpersonal* metafunction of language or image.

Finally, every text, whether it be a complete story in words and/or images, or a single sentence or picture, has to organize the ideational and interpersonal meanings into a coherent unity. For example, a story must be organized into stages or phases with links made between them. A single utterance or image will have certain parts made prominent and others backgrounded. Anything that functions to make links and contrasts between different parts of the whole or contributes to bringing elements into and out of prominence is part of the *textual* metafunction.

SFS argues that every image (and every verbal text) makes these three kinds of meaning simultaneously: ideational, interpersonal, and textual. However, to address particular research questions or deconstruct particular texts, it may be that looking through the lens of one metafunction, or even focusing on just one aspect of one metafunction, proves most revealing for the issue at hand.

System and Text

Halliday has always emphasized that language should be thought of as a resource for making meaning, rather than as a set of rules or formal structures. One of the key principles of SFS is therefore that an entire semiotic system, such as language or image, is a resource for meaning, or a meaning potential. This potential can be described as sets of options or possibilities for making meaning.

In looking at a particular instance of a semiotic system, such as a sentence or a picture in a book, we can see which possibilities have been actualized. For example, the meaning potential of language allows for either positive or negative meaning, while the specific sentence *The baby didn't cry* carries the meaning choice of negative. Similarly, from the linguistic potential of past, present or future tense, *The baby didn't cry* actualizes the option of past tense. When we talk of system, we are talking of the potential, the overall set of possibilities. When we refer to text, we are looking at the actual choices that have been made from that potential on a particular occasion. But in talking of choices in this way, there is no implication that the writer or artist is making conscious choices or is consciously thinking about the range of options available—it is simply to say that the overall communicative system allows for certain meaningful possibilities.

SFS represents meaning potential as sets of options and outlines these in diagrams known as system networks, as exemplified in Figure 2.1, which shows how the familiar system of traffic lights could be represented. The network displays all the meaning options available in a square bracket. It also specifies with a sloping arrow how each option is "realized" in some form of expression.

Sometimes one set of options is dependent on a prior option and this is understood by reading the diagram from left to right. Figure 2.2 provides an example in a representation of one small set of choices (one individual system) available for a visual image. As film students are well aware, different effects are obtained by different camera angles. Where the viewer looks up to a person or building on screen, the effect is to make what we are looking at appear powerful and dominant. Conversely, if the camera angle makes us look down on someone, the opposite is the case; that is, when viewed from above a depicted person is likely to come across as more vulnerable.

Figure 2.2, based on Kress and van Leeuwen's (2006) visual grammar, displays these two options, showing that they are available only when power relations between viewer and representation are constructed as unequal. The network states that an image may construct equal or unequal power relations between viewer and representation and, if unequal, either the viewer or the depiction may

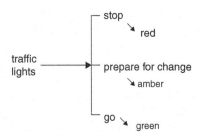

FIGURE 2.1 Traffic Lights Represented as a Simple "System" of Options and Realization

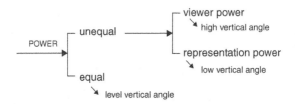

FIGURE 2.2 The Visual System of Power
Source: Adapted from Kress & van Leeuwen, 2006.

be constructed as more powerful. For each final option, the way the meaning is expressed or realized in an image is specified below the sloping arrow.

Once we know how to read it, a system network diagram is an economical way to summarize meaning potential, but it has the weakness of representing meaning options as a matter of either/or with the different possibilities clearly distinct. This is usually appropriate for language—a noun is either singular or plural, a clause is either active or passive, positive or negative, and so on. However, in the realm of the visual, categories are sometimes less clear-cut. For example, how much of a represented person is shown in an image may vary on a continuum from an extreme close-up to an extreme long shot. The shot size chosen puts the viewer in a constructed relation that can vary from apparent close intimacy to great distance.

Kress and van Leewen (2006) represent this meaning potential as a system of social distance with three options: personal, social and public distance, realized by close-up, mid-shot and long shot respectively. It would be more accurate, though, if the network diagram indicated that these options (and their realizations) represent points on a continuum. One way this can be done is by tilting the square bracket to signify that the system is a continuum of choices between extremes (Painter et al., 2013), as shown in Figure 2.3 for the visual system of social distance.

One additional complexity that should be stressed is that there is invariably more than one meaning system in play in any text, even if the text is not a multimodal one. As well as there being three metafunctions, each with its own meaning potential, there are multiple meaning systems available within a single

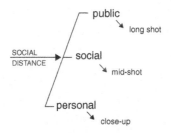

FIGURE 2.3 Visual Power: a System of Options on a Continuum

metafunction. For example, as seen within the interpersonal metafunction of image, there is a system of meaning options for power and another for social distance. While we may be interested in only one of these for our particular analytical purposes, both are independently available at the same time and their realizations will be co-present in an image. If we wish to show this fact in a system network diagram, it is done by means of a curly brace, enclosing simultaneous sets of options, as shown in Figure 2.4. The figure states that an image text will actualize a choice from the set of options for social distance *and* a choice from the set of options referred to as power.

An Overview of Visual Meaning Systems

For each of the three metafunctions, a range of meaning choices is available for the visual semiotic, based on descriptions found in Kress and van Leeuwen (2006) and Painter et al. (2013). This section provides an overview that clarifies the role of each metafunction, suggests its relevance in an educational context, and lists the domains of visual meaning it encompasses. The individual meaning systems taken up in the rest of this book for critical content analysis of an image are described and exemplified in more detail by that researcher.

The Ideational Metafunction

The ideational metafunction essentially concerns what an image is an image of. Because of this, adults generally assume that the ideational meaning of an image is

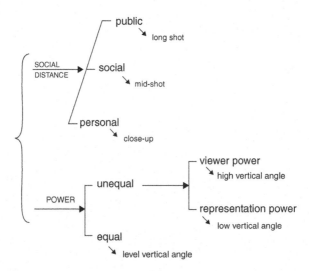

FIGURE 2.4 A System Network Showing "Simultaneous" Systems

completely transparent to a young child. After all, the colors, shapes and forms of the things we encounter in material reality are readily replicated in an image—grass can be represented as green, a ball as round and a road as extending from one point to another. Additionally, an artist can give the illusion of depth and three-dimensionality to an image through perspective, making what is shown replicate more closely what the child sees in life. For this reason, pictures in picturebooks are frequently used to assist children in practicing the corresponding verbal names for things depicted and eventually to help them recognize the written forms of words, which are more abstract and opaque than the images they accompany. These facts should not, however, blind us to the fact that imaged representations are not always transparent to a very young child. For one thing, many images used in books for young children are far from realistic. One only has to think of the cat in Dr. Seuss books or the people and objects in Dick Bruna's famous books to realize that in such cases it may be the adult's accompanying commentary that identifies what is being represented in the first place.

Nonetheless, the depiction of story participants is generally a relatively straightforward matter and can be used to convey non-verbalized details of age, family role, ethnicity, social class, and gender through a human character's size, skin color, clothing, and hairstyle. In this way visual character attribution can clearly be significant in the construction or challenging of social stereotypes. Another way character attribution can add meaning that may not be verbally stated is through symbolic attributes—elements that can be read as conferring a symbolic meaning on the character. For example, the wolf suit that Max wears in *Where the Wild Things Are* (Sendak, 1963) suggests his wildness; the horns of cloud appearing behind the father's head in Browne's (1992) *Zoo* confer on him a satanic quality, at least in the view of the child narrator. Experience with visual symbolic attributes can be an enjoyable way for young children to begin to look beyond the literal meanings in stories to a more literary appreciation of their significance.

As well as the depiction of character in terms of attributes, it may be useful in an educational context to consider whether and at what points a story participant is fully shown. For example, in books designed to assist visual and verbal literacy, only part of a story character might be depicted initially, with the full identity revealed only on a page turn, as in the Ahlbergs' (1978) *Each Peach Pear Plum*. In this rhyming book, different nursery rhyme and fairy tale characters are shown on each spread. A new character is first shown as a small element within a crowded picture—sometimes only a body part being visible. On turning the page, the reader finds the new character revealed in full and in the foreground. Using this strategy, the book encourages very young children to look closely at the pictures, to move through the book appropriately from left to right, page by page, and to gain visual literacy by inferring what is depicted from a partial representation. In general, the amount of inferencing needed on the part of the reader to interpret the ideational meaning is related to the age of the ideal reader. If a character is presented only as a shadow or an arm or without the face visible, or only after its absence in several intervening images, there is more "work" required from the child reader to interpret the meaning. This may be a playful pedagogic strategy in a book for the very young or it may be because the child reader is assumed to be experienced enough to handle less explicitness.

As well as characters, ideational meaning involves the actions or events of the story and the circumstances in which they take place. While spoken language actions may include many interior ones (thinking, deciding, remembering, etc.), the visual semiotic is not so well suited to representing these and naturally favors a focus on physical action. The circumstances surrounding an action can be varied in a verbal text, including the time, place, manner, condition, purpose, or reason for an action, but the visual potential is more limited, almost exclusively related to locations, which can readily be elaborated. How these vary in detail, perspective or kind from image to image can be significant for the narrative—a domain of meaning we can call inter-circumstance.

When considering relations between images within the ideational metafunction, it is important to note another respect in which picturebook images depart from the child's observed experience. This is in the way the passage of time is represented visually. A narrative necessarily involves at least one sequence of events and verbal language has a raft of meaning systems to indicate explicitly the relation between successive actions. For example, there are different tenses available for the verbs and a range of temporal phrases and clauses indicating the ordering of events, as in *after breakfast, before he had gone far, when the post arrived, while she was thinking*, and so on. A story told in pictures does not have comparable resources, so we are left to infer the temporal "and then" relationship from a sequence of images of the same character, usually with a variation in setting. This again is a convention that must be learned. For example, in Helen Cooper's (1996) *The Baby Who Wouldn't Go to Bed*, the left side of the opening double-page spread depicts a toddler driving his toy fire engine in the house, while the right-hand side depicts him driving it out of the doorway into the landscape. The relation between the two is unproblematic to anyone familiar with the conventions of the visual semiotic, but one three-year old looking at this opening spread for the first time remarked to his teacher "Oh, wow, look, he's got two engines," clearly not realizing that an engine in two successive images of a spread represents one engine at different times.

A young child soon learns that successive images of the same person generally represent a single character at different moments in time, either continuing the same action or performing a different one. And the visual semiotic can also pace a narrative, slowing down or speeding up the action over a sequence. It is also particularly well-suited to comparison and contrast relations, even though many other links between events that are available in the verbal meaning potential cannot be visualized, such as purpose (*in order to* …), condition (*if … then* …), and concession (*even though* …).

Visual ideational meaning in a picturebook thus encompasses options related to characters, actions and settings within the story. Rather than presenting each system as a network, ideational meaning systems are listed in Table 2.1 together with an indication of how the options are realized on the page.

The Interpersonal Metafunction

The interpersonal metafunction is both interactive and personal (Halliday & Matthiessen, 2004), and the kinds of meanings it enables are richly deployed in successful picturebooks. The interpersonal metafunction of image is likely to be the most important semiotic resource for initially hooking a child into the reading experience. It is a new experience for an infant to be in a communicative and affective relation with a book—something quite inanimate—rather than in face-to-face interaction with a living, speaking, breathing human being (Rose, 2011).

One way this relation with a book can be established is through the child's engagement with the characters of a story, whose depicted emotions the child can

TABLE 2.1 Visual Meaning Systems within the Ideational Metafunction

Ideational Metafunction	Visual Meaning Systems	Visual Realizations
Character	Character attribution	Depiction of physical attributes of character
	Character manifestation & appearance	Character depiction over a sequence
	Character relations	Adjacent/symmetrical arrangement of different participants
Events	Action:	Depiction of actions, using:
	Physical action	Vectors (diagonals)
	Perception	Gaze vectors
	Cognition	Thought bubbles, face/hand gestures
	Talking	Speech bubbles, face/hand gestures
	Inter-event relations	Juxtaposition of images (+/- change of setting or participant)
Setting	Circumstantiation	Depiction of place, occasionally of time (e.g. clock, moon), manner (e.g. lines indicating speed, trembling)
	Inter-circumstance relations	Shifts, contrasts, continuities in locations

empathize with or perhaps be amused by. Unlike the lived relationships with friends and family members, that between a child and a picturebook character or situation is a purely semiotically constructed one, and the meaning potential of image allows the interaction to be created as more or less intimate (the system of social distance), more or less equal in power (the system of power), and for those depicted to be more or less part of the child's world (the system of involvement).

Different stances towards characters can also be shaped by interpersonal choices realized by drawing style (the system of pathos), while visual as well as verbal options of focalization can place readers in the character's shoes, to take on their point of view or else position them to remain outside the story. Thus, while the depiction of storybook characters as children, adults, animals, or fairies, etc. is a matter of ideational meaning, the depiction of their emotions and the viewer's stance and point of view in relation to the characters belongs within the interpersonal metafunction. Also relevant here is the general emotional tone of a story created for the reader/viewer through color choices, whether these are bright and exciting, dark and somber, or cool and restrained (choices within the system of ambience).

These systems relate to either the personal aspect of interpersonal meaning (emotions depicted on characters or evoked in readers) or to the interpersonal relations between reader/viewer and depiction. However, if we are interested in narrative texts, we must also include within interpersonal meaning the relation between depicted story characters. For example, social distance is relevant not only to the relation between viewer and depicted character but to the relations between different characters within the story. Similarly, power relations between the viewer and depiction (shown in Figure 2.2) are also relevant for how one depicted character is presented visually in relation to another. That is, a character can be shown as looking up to or down on another at any point within the visual story, suggesting the power dynamics involved.

A final and under-researched domain of interpersonal meaning for image is that of visual graduation, which concerns the way meanings may be intensified or minimized. In language we can think of the gradations between *big, very big, huge*, and *gigantic* or *small, very small, tiny*, and *infinitesimal* to get an idea of how an ideational meaning can be upscaled or downscaled. In a visual image, this kind of meaning is a matter of departing from an established norm in some way. This might mean that something is depicted as out of scale in size relative to other things in the image or super-salient in color or noticeably exaggerated in the amount of space it takes up, in the vertical or horizontal angle deployed or in the amount of visual repetition.

Interpersonal meaning in a picturebook therefore includes both feelings and affiliations. Feelings include the emotions depicted for characters and those evoked in the reader/viewer. It also encompasses the way ideational meaning can be graduated to intensify or reduce its force. Affiliations encompass interactive dimensions of various kinds. These include the viewer's stance on the story world, the interpersonal relations between the viewer and the depicted characters and those between character and character within the story world. The various systems involved are summarized in Table 2.2.

The Textual Metafunction

The third metafunction, that of textual meaning—also referred to as compositional meaning for image—has the job of directing the viewer's attention and organizing the ideational and interpersonal meanings within the image, the page, the double spread, and the entire narrative. The two semiotic systems of language and image necessarily use rather different resources to organize text. Those of language are time-based, since language unfolds word by word, phrase by phrase, clause by clause, and paragraph by paragraph. A sequence of images also unfolds sequentially and visual continuities and discontinuities over the sequence can be important to help to create generic staging or phasing. However, with respect to an individual page layout or an individual image, many elements of meaning are made available simultaneously, and it is how they are framed, grouped, and distributed spatially that organizes the text.

TABLE 2.2 Visual Meaning Systems within the Interpersonal Metafunction

Interpersonal Metafunction	Visual Meaning Systems	Visual Realizations
Affiliation	Visual focalization	Direction of gaze of character; reader's gaze aligned or not with character's
	Pathos	Drawing style as minimalist, generic, or naturalistic
	Power	Vertical angle of viewing (high, mid or low) by viewer/reader of book Vertical angle of viewing by a depicted character in relation to another character
	Social distance	Shot size (close-up, mid-range, distance)
	Proximity	Proximity/touch of depicted characters
	Involvement	Horizontal angle of viewer/reader of book
	Orientation	Horizontal angle of character in relation to another +/- mutuality of character gaze
Feeling	Ambience	Color choices in relation to vibrancy, warmth and familiarity
	Visual affect	Emotion depicted in facial features and bodily stance of characters
	Graduation or force	"Exaggerated" size, angle, proportion of frame filled, repetition of elements, etc.

To elaborate on this last point, one important way that oral language creates coherent text is through patterns of intonation, which serve to guide the hearer's attention in relation to a series of units of information. By contrast, a visual text can present multiple units of information simultaneously within the composition. A visual unit of information, referred to as a focus group, consists of whatever is grouped together in the visual composition as some kind of unity to be attended to at a glance. And a key means of bringing visual material together into a focus group, or else keeping visual units separated into different focus groups, is the presence of various kinds of frames and borders. The page edge itself constitutes a kind of frame, as does any border within it such as a white margin surrounding the picture. Within the picture itself, various parts of the ideational content such as doorways, windows or bridges can also serve to demarcate different focus groups.

In other words, everything on the page or double-page spread is visually available to our apprehension at the same time, but by framing-off elements (e.g., words from pictures on the page, or one character and setting from another within the picture), a visual composition can organize the visual material and manage the viewer's attention. In relation to an individual image, many will provide only a single focus group—perhaps a centrally placed character or building, or a single row of characters in a line, or two characters interacting—while others will have a more complex composition with additional focus groups of varying prominence within the major one. In such a case, the viewer may apprehend the major focus group at the first glance and pay attention to others on a longer look or on repeated viewings. Sometimes, too, picturebook artists will include elements of interest that do not have much visual prominence to encourage the child to look closely at the page.

For analysis of a picturebook in terms of the textual metafunction, it is helpful to consider the different facets of three systems of options. We can recognize that the printed words of a picturebook story, regardless of their linguistic meaning, also constitute a visual element within the page layout. This verbiage must be positioned within the composition of the layout and allotted an equal, greater or lesser amount of space vis-à-vis the picture, or the verbiage may be included as a visual element within the picture itself. These matters are choices within the system of intermodal integration, which treats the linguistic element of the story purely in visual terms, regardless of the meanings of the words. Different options in intermodal integration create different relations between the two modes of words and images, and variations over the page sequence may also serve a function in pacing the story.

Then if we narrow our concerns just to the image itself on the single page or double spread, there are a number of choices related to whether and how the image is framed off. This is the system of framing. Perhaps there is no boundary and the unbound image fills the entire page space to the edge of the book, or perhaps there is a margin around one or all sides of the image, or perhaps there is a black line delimiting the image. These different choices all have different effects that need to be considered in relation to the ideational and interpersonal choices made in the image. Often, too, framing choices will vary during the course of the story. A well-known case is Sendak's (1963) *Where the Wild Things Are* in which, over several page turns, an ever-expanding image and a correspondingly ever-shrinking page margin are used to reference the central character's gradually expanding and liberating imagination.

Finally, there is the system of focus. This system specifies the various spatial arrangements that are commonly found in the composition of picturebook layouts and the images within them. Since every focus group has the potential to contain further focus groups within it, each focus group is likely to conform to a relatively limited range of compositional patterns, each of which contributes to meaning in the way it arranges the characters or other elements of ideational meaning.

These systems within the textual metafunction for image are identified in Table 2.3 as the meaning potential for creating prominence. In addition, stability and change in choices of meaning from any system over the course of a narrative sequence will contribute to marking out phases in the story.

Final Reflections

Meanings from all three metafunctions are co-present in every image and in a bi-modal text they are co-present in the accompanying verbal text as well. It is possible therefore to take account of all three metafunctions in both modalities of words and images, examining how they interrelate (Painter et al., 2013). Often, however, it is very revealing to focus on just one of the metafunctions or one particular meaning system within it, in order to address a particular issue or research question. The chapters in this book exemplify how SFS visual analysis can inform a range of explorations of different visual materials.

TABLE 2.3 Visual Meaning Systems within the Textual Metafunction

Textual Metafunction	Visual Meaning Systems	Visual Realization
Prominence	Intermodal integration	Placement of words and images within the layout of the page and book
	Framing	Binding of visual elements into units, and the separation of units via frames, margins, page edges
	Focus	Compositional arrangement
Phasing	(any meaning system)	Visual dis/continuity over a sequence of images

References

Byrnes, H. (Ed.) (2006). *Advanced language learning: The contribution of Halliday and Vygotsky*. London: Continuum.

Christie, F. (2002). *Classroom discourse analysis: A functional perspective*. London: Continuum.

Coffin, C. & Donohue, J.P. (2012). Academic literacies and systemic-functional linguistics: How do they relate? *Science Direct*, 11(1), 64–75.

Djonov, E. and Zhao, S. (2014). *Critical multimodal studies of popular discourse*. London: Routledge.

Fairclough, N. (1989). *Language and power*. London: Longman.

Fowler, R., Hodge, R., Kress, G., & Trew, T. (Eds.) (1979). *Language and control*. London: Routledge & Kegan Paul.

Halliday, M.A.K. (1978). *Language as social semiotic*. London: Arnold.

Halliday, M.A.K. & Matthiessen, C.M.I.M. (2004). *Introduction to functional grammar*. 4th Ed. London: Arnold.

Hood, S. (2011). Body language in face-to-face teaching: A focus on textual and interpersonal meaning. In S. Dreyfus, S. Hood, & M. Stenglin (Eds.), *Semiotic margins: Meaning in multimodalities* (pp. 31–52). London: Continuum.

Kress, G. & Hodge, R. (1979). *Language as ideology*. London: Routledge & Kegan Paul.

Kress, G. & van Leeuwen, T. (2006). *Reading images: The grammar of visual design*. London: Routledge.

Mahboob, A. & Knight, N. (Eds.) (2010). *Appliable linguistics*. London: Continuum.

Martin, J.R. (2000). Close reading: Functional linguistics as a tool for critical discourse analysis. In L. Unsworth (Ed.), *Researching language in classrooms and communities: Functional linguistic perspectives* (pp. 275–302). London: Cassell.

Maton, K., Martin, J.R., & Matruglio, E. (2016). LCT and systemic-functional linguistics: Enacting complementary theories for explanatory power. In K. Maton, S. Hood, & S. Shay (Eds.), *Knowledge-building: Educational studies in legitimation code theory* (pp. 93–113). London: Routledge.

O'Halloran, K. (2008). *Mathematical discourse: Language, symbolism and visual images*. London: Continuum.

Painter, C., Martin, J.R., & Unsworth, L. (2013). *Reading visual narratives: Image analysis of children's picture books*. Sheffield, UK: Equinox.

Rose, D. (2011). Meaning beyond the margins: learning to interact with books. In S. Dreyfus, S. Hood, & M. Stenglin (Eds.), *Semiotic margins: Meaning in multimodalities* (pp. 177–210). London: Continuum.

Rose, D. & Martin, J.R. (2012). *Learning to write, reading to learn: Genre knowledge and pedagogy in the Sydney school*. Sheffield, UK: Equinox.

Torr, J. (2004). Talking about picture books: The influence of maternal education on four-year-old children's talk with mothers and pre-school teachers. *Journal of Early Childhood Literacy*, 4(2): 181–210.

Williams, G. (2016). Reflection literacy in the first years of schooling: Questions of theory and practice. In W. Bowcher & J. Liang (Eds.), *Society in language, language in society: Essays in honour of Ruqaiya Hasan* (pp. 333–356). London: Palgrave Macmillan.

Children's Literature References

Ahlberg, J. & Ahlberg, A. (1989). *Each peach pear plum*. London: Penguin.
Browne, A. (1992). *Zoo*. London: Julia Macrae Books.
Cooper, H. (1996). *The baby who wouldn't go to bed*. London: Doubleday.
Sendak, M. (1963). *Where the wild things are*. New York: Harper & Row.

PART II

Visual Images in Counter-Narratives

3

DRAWING HUMANITY

How Picturebook Illustrations Counter Antiblackness

Desiree Cueto and Wanda M. Brooks

From slavery to the present day, Black American art has been linked to agency and resistance. Brightly colored quilts communicated symbolic messages, directing the enslaved toward freedom. Murals, sculptures, and literature emerged from the Harlem Renaissance to push against social inequality. Photographic imagery documented the implications of segregation and drew worldwide attention to the Civil Rights Movement. Black American artists have continually employed creative processes using wood, fabric, paper, and clay to critique and confront racism. Beyond the power to address complex sociopolitical forces, Black art also serves to define and re-define what it means to be Black in America.

Although less well recognized, picturebook illustrations are included within the tapestry of Black art. Picturebook illustrations created by Black artists commonly challenge societal norms that promulgate antiblackness through portrayals of Black children in previously unseen lights. These future-oriented visions counter racist imagery that is too often perpetuated through mass communication outlets such as television, radio, and the Internet. Yet, as Christopher Myers (2014) points out, there are more books published each year about talking animals than Black children. Black children are, at once, invisible in children's literature and hyper-visible in the broader society. The consequences of this imbalance are devastating. Compared to their peers, Black children are more likely to be adultified and subjected to harsher discipline in schools and the criminal justice system (Epstein, Blake, & González, 2017). They are also far more likely to be innocent victims of deadly police shootings (Tatum, 2015). The ongoing denial of Black children's humanity reveals a need for a reinvigorated and in-depth look at issues of representation—one that examines exactly how picturebook illustrations embody the potential to initiate, support, and promote change.

This chapter offers a critical content analysis of visual images in four picture-books that have garnered praise within the last 20 years: *Crown: An Ode to the Fresh Cut* (2017) written by Derrick Barns and illustrated by Gordon C. James; *I Am Enough* (2018) written by Grace Byers and illustrated by Keturah A. Bobo; *Uptown* (2000) written and illustrated by Bryan Collier; and *I Love My Hair* (1998) written by Natasha Tarpley and illustrated by E. B. Lewis. In this inquiry, analytical tools outlined by Painter, Martin, and Unsworth (2013) and the system of provenance described by Kress and van Leeuwen (2006) help to reveal how the illustrations communicate with viewers on an interpersonal level. At the same time, tenets from Critical Race and BlackCrit theories (Dumas & Ross, 2016; Howard & Navarro, 2016) provide a framework for centering race in the analysis. Bringing together systems of visual communication with critical theory allows for a deep investigation of not only how illustrators portray Black children but also how those portrayals might challenge antiblackness.

Theoretical Frameworks

The Critical Race Theory movement began in the field of law to examine the systematic nature of racism. Over time, Critical Race Theory (CRT) took root in the fields of education, political science, women's studies, and ethnic studies to name a few (Ladson-Billings & Tate, 2016). In education, CRT offers a lens for identifying power structures and theorizing racial inequity in schools. Although much of the scholarship informed by CRT in education addresses broad policy and/or larger scale issues related to school reform (Howard & Navarro, 2016), a growing number of studies have considered CRT within the context of curriculum. Employing CRT's seminal tenet of the permanence of racism (and the rejection of colorblindness), researchers examined the ways in which curriculum can reify or resist the effects of racism on targeted groups (Brown, Souto-Manning, & Laman, 2010; McNair, 2008). In addition, scholars have examined how a counter-story (an analytic tool within CRT that foregrounds experiential knowledge through forms of storytelling) exposes and refutes negative experiences encountered by marginalized racial groups in schools (Martinez, 2017; Solórzano & Yosso, 2002). Likewise, recent studies documented the agentive and potentially liberatory role of counter-stories passed on through the medium of children's and young adult literature (Brooks, 2009; Hughes-Hassell, 2013).

However, while CRT addresses issues of racism's effects and permanence, it does not specify a focus on a particular race or ethnicity. Dumas and Ross (2016) point out that CRT "cannot fully employ the counter-stories of Black experiences … because it does not, on its own, have language to richly capture how antiblackness constructs Black subjects and positions them in and against law, policy and everyday life" (p. 417). They encourage scholars interested in the education of Black children to consider a more deliberate focus on antiblack theorization.

Advancing a BlackCrit theory, Dumas and Ross (2016) contend that it provides a lens for examining the depth and scope of the physical and psychological manifestations of antiblackness in U.S. society. These include actions to sustain Black suffering, violence, and even death (Dumas, 2016). As Dumas and Ross (2016) point out, "antiblackness is not simply racism against Black people, rather, antiblackness refers to a broader antagonistic relationship between blackness and (the possibility of) humanity" (p. 429). The authors envision BlackCrit Theory as a continuation of Critical Race and Black existential thought in that it carries on the work of, "forging refuge from the gaze of White supremacy—where Black children dream weightless, unracialized and human" (Dumas & Ross, 2016, p. 436).

Related Research

A number of scholars have conducted comprehensive studies, analyzing large numbers of Black American picturebooks across a historical trajectory (Martin, 2004; Sims Bishop, 2012). In brief, they argue that viewers who are Black likely see images that reflect and solidify their humanity while other viewers are perhaps compelled to see Black childhood in new ways. Consistent with the rejection of the visual aspects of antiblackness, Sims Bishop (2012) argues in her review of influential Black illustrators of picturebooks that:

> these artists have set out, at least in part, to dignify the images of African Americans in children's books, to challenge old stereotypes and replace them with depictions of African Americans in all their diversity.
>
> *(p. 11)*

Beyond comprehensive reviews, only a few researchers have carried out in depth studies that focus primarily on Black illustrators and their depictions of Black children, adults, and their culture. Thompson's (2001) analysis of three picturebooks about Harriet Tubman (illustrated by Jerry Pinkney, Jacob Lawrence, and Faith Ringgold) stands out in this regard for its detailed visual analysis. Referring to the artists' vastly different depictions of Tubman (through abstract, flat, and naturalistic expressions), Thompson asserts that, "Despite the important variation in their story angles, the three books' most interesting differences lie in how Harriet Tubman has been conceived visually" (p. 101). Another exploration by Millman (2005) focuses on several picturebooks written and illustrated by Faith Ringgold. Millman concludes that a recurring visual theme in Ringgold's books communicates the emphasis, seriousness, and uneasiness of darkness as evidenced through dark illustrations, dark grey figures, and black endpapers. More recent is Garner's (2017) inquiry of children's responses to picturebooks depicting Black people. Although this study primarily focused on exploring children's literary responses to stories, Garner provides vivid descriptions and some analysis of the picturebooks read by the children. More importantly, her work with diverse youth (and their sometimes negative reactions to illustrations evoking Blackness) reveals the continued need to carefully analyze the illustrations found in picture-books against the backdrop of U.S. society's longstanding conflation of Blackness and disapproval. Garner (2017) writes:

> I argue that negative societal scripts about Blackness can influence and limit interpretations of the visual rhetoric in African American picture books. I suggest engaging in critical racial literacy, reading multiple versions of texts, and explicitly teaching children about the semiotic elements, stylistic choices, and representational modes used in ... African American children's literature ...

> *(p. 122)*

Methodology

Extending this line of research, our critical content analysis of visual images was guided by the following research question: How do Black illustrators address antiblackness through their portrayals of Black children? In order to investigate this question, we relied primarily on Painter, et al.'s (2013) analytical tools for interpreting how illustrators create interpersonal meanings. The aim was to determine whether the levels of intimacy, participation and empathy implied within the illustrations might: (1) compel viewers to see other dimensions of Black childhood often unseen through mass media; and (2) solicit deeper under-standings by presenting viewers with representations of Black childhood that are not beholden to normative standards. Drawing on foundational ideas pursued within Critical Race Theory and BlackCrit, we considered the following:

- The importance of countering inaccurate and racist imagery that positions Black people as non-human.
- The need for an intentional focus on the varied lived experiences of Black people, and the creation of spaces where Blackness (particularly Black child-hood) can be (re)imagined.

Text Selection

For this analysis, priority was given to titles that received awards for illustration, starred reviews and/or considerable discussion on websites dedicated to promoting positive messages about Black children. For example, *Crown: An Ode to the Fresh Cut* (Barnes, 2017) received a Coretta Scott King Honor, Newbery Honor, Caldecott Honor, Ezra Jack Keats Honor and was a Society of Illustrators Gold Medal Book and a Charlotte Huck Recommended Book. It was also featured on the Conscious Kid website in partnership with Moms of Black Boys United, and it received five starred reviews. Similarly, *Uptown* (Collier, 2000) received the Coretta Scott King Illustrator Award and multiple starred reviews. *I Am Enough* (Byers, 2018) was named a *New York Times* bestselling book and has received more praise for its illustrations than for its written text. *I Love My Hair!* (Tarpley, 1998) has been purchased and praised by Black women and girls for 20 years. This book has been reviewed on *The Brown Bookshelf, Good Reads, Readers Favorite* and *Publishers Weekly.*

A second consideration was the positionality of each book's creator(s). All of the books in this study were written and illustrated by insiders to the Black American community. In addition, the authors and illustrators reported—through interviews and websites—having a personal desire to create positive change. Not only did they wish to see more varied representations of Black experiences in books; they also wished to see Blackness humanized by their interpretations of Black childhood. For example, on his webpage, Derrick Barnes, author of *Crown: An Ode to the Fresh Cut* referred to the barbershop as, "the only place in the Black community where boys are treated like royalty." His poem was written as a self-affirmation that was brought fully to life by Gordon C. James' majestic oil-based portraits. Similarly, Keturah A. Bobo sought to expertly capture the power, beauty and fortitude of a brown-skinned, afro-wearing Black girl in *I Am Enough*. In an interview with *The Brown Bookshelf*, Bobo (2018) stated that she feels it is her duty to create art that, "inspires, uplifts and advocates for my community." In another interview featured on *The Brown Bookshelf*, Natasha Tarpley (2018) reported that she wrote *I Love My Hair* to capture the nightly "hair-combing" routine she shared with her own mother. This heartening story encourages Black children to celebrate in their heritage and beauty. Likewise, Bryan Collier has said that a significant motivator for his work in children's books was his own experience of not seeing himself or people who looked like him in books. *Uptown* serves as invitation into one Black boy's life, allowing readers to feel his deep connection to his community and to his race.

Crown: An Ode to the Fresh Cut by Derrick D. Barnes and Gordon C. James invites viewers to journey with a young Black boy (about 8 or 9) before, during and after his haircut. Throughout the book, the boy's barber, his friends and random visitors come to the barbershop, providing affirmations and support to the young boy. Describing the protagonist as a "star" and "royalty," the author casts the boy in a majestic light, while at the same time, exposing readers to the processes behind the remarkable haircuts depicted across the pages. Using a fine art, oil painting medium, Gordon James' realistic images capture the importance and necessity of the barber shop to the young boy and his Black community.

I Am Enough by Grace Byers and Keturah A. Bobo grabs readers' attention as a young Black girl (about 7 years old) with a deep brown complexion repeatedly affirms that, "I am here to … " These words are followed by descriptions and illustrations of what the young girl can do and who she might become. Throughout, readers see images of the girl with new acquaintances and old friends who are all visually different in terms of skin tone, facial features, ability, hair styles and relatable yet stylish clothes. Despite their differences, the girl and her friends recognize that understanding, nonjudgment and kindness are important qualities. Although the book's title outwardly asserts, "I am enough," the reader gets the sense that the protagonist already embodies self-love and imagination.

Uptown by Bryan Collier uses the repeated phrase, "Uptown is … " to take readers into the world of a young Black boy (about 8 or 9) as he describes his vibrant Harlem, NY community and the people who reside there. In this picturebook, each page immerses viewers in the heart of Uptown with stunning collage illustrations of food, buildings, transportation, a barbershop, the Apollo theater and more. Readers also gain insights about Harlem through the intimate portrayal of a young boy simply recounting the fullness of his day.

I Love My Hair by Natasha Tarpley and E. B. Lewis highlights the nurturing ritual of a young Black girl (about 6 or 7) getting her hair combed by her mother at the end of a long day. In the opening pages, the dialogue reveals how the mother aims to instill confidence and pride in her daughter by enumerating the benefits and beauty of her type of hair. In pages that follow, this confidence is displayed through naturalistic watercolor illustrations, as the young girl ventures out into the world wearing different hairstyles (an afro, cornrows, and ponytails) and receives largely positive reactions from her community.

Positionality

We are both Black women, mothers, teachers, and scholars. As such, we understand how cruel the world can sometimes be to Black children. Their humanity is too often racialized. They quickly become aware that their skin tone or other phenotypical characteristics might draw suspicion. They learn the delicate balance of celebrating or minimizing their authentic Black selves in order to walk safely through a world, which is "sutured by antiblack solidarity" (Wilderson, 2010, p. 58). Knowing this, we entered the study with a sense of optimism and hope. At the same time, we were careful not to neglect our responsibility to reflect on how we approached the work as researchers. Throughout the process we remained focused in our intent to read data solely through the lens of our selected critical theories and with the analytical tools in the most objective way possible. We regularly engaged in personal reflection by keeping analytical and reflective notes.

Data Analysis

This analysis drew primarily from the interpersonal metafunction outlined by Painter in Chapter 2. To evaluate systems within this metafunction, we first considered how the use of each system might influence the viewer. According to Painter et al. (2013) illustrators encourage intimacy or estrangement with characters through the systems of social distance, proximity, attitude, and orientation.

We evaluated images based on all four systems, giving particular attention to social distance, which determines how closely viewers interact with the characters. Close-up images, for example, require viewers to enter the character's space, creating more intimate relationships. Middle shots create social relationships, and long shots signify impersonal relationships (Painter et al., 2013). In books where close-ups were less frequent, we focused more heavily on the usefulness of: proximity—the closeness or distance between characters; attitude—the viewer's involvement with characters through eye contact or the viewer's positioning on a vertical or horizontal plane that indicates a power dynamic; and orientation—the interactions between characters that reflect the nature of their relationships. Combined with social distance, these systems revealed a level of intimacy.

Other systems within the interpersonal metafunction, such as focalization, pathos and affect, and ambience contribute to the viewer's participation, empathy level, and sense of familiarity with the characters (Painter et al., 2013). Connected to focalization, we evaluated meanings associated with visual positioning and angle of view. For example, we assessed the impact of the viewer's ability to see through the character's eyes versus taking an objective stance. We considered whether the angle of view was representative of equality, domination, or subordination. We also considered pathos and affect, noting that all four illustrators created detailed and naturalistic characters who, despite being works of fiction, appeared life-like and real. Further, we evaluated how choices of color and medium affected the ambience and, connected to this, how "provenance" or meanings based on cultural knowledge of the image shaped the interpersonal connection (Kress & van Leeuwen, 2006).

We read the illustrations alongside scholarship on antiblackness (Dumas, 2016; 2018; Sexton, 2008; Wilderson, 2010). Much of this scholarship grapples with the ways in which Black people have been constructed as "Other" and therefore denied full humanness (Haslam, 2006). Thus, we sought to uncover how each illustrator's choices might highlight the humanity of Black children and also facilitate a deeper understanding of experiences unique to Black culture. Data related to these systems were also concurrently read as potential challenges to the permanence of racism (Ladson-Billings & Tate, 2016).

Coding

After an initial phase of analysis, we sorted and ranked images in hierarchical order based on relevance to the study. In order to select only those images that best met the criteria of addressing antiblackness, we applied a filter to each image. We then created a spreadsheet that included detailed descriptions of the most significant images. We developed open codes, which represented emergent patterns related to the research question. Each image was then re-analyzed based on the open codes and re-sorted based on commonality. From this process, two broad categories emerged. Images that addressed antiblackness by causing the viewer to identify closely with the character (humanizing the character) were linked together under the category of Common Humanity. Those that addressed antiblackness through portrayals of various Black experiences, including references to distinctly Black spaces, culturally specific styles of dress, hair and ways of interacting with family or community were linked together under the category of Imagining the Unimaginable.

Common Humanity—The Use of Social Distance, Proximity, Attitude, and Orientation

The importance of human connection cannot be underscored in the fight against antiblackness. In a recent speech in South Africa, Barack Obama (2018) asked listeners to recognize that we are, "bound together by a common humanity ... that each individual has inherent dignity and worth." Connecting this with our research focus, we describe how the illustrations in our text set exhibit shared characteristics that work to encourage relationships between viewers and characters, thus facilitating the recognition of Black children's humanity. These findings are significant, not only as we consider how illustrations serve to challenge racism, but also as we think about how they help Black children develop a concept of self.

On the covers of each book, the Black child protagonist is introduced at either a close intimate distance—with only the character's head and shoulders visible to the viewer—or through a medium shot that creates a friendly distance. The choice of social distance along with the viewer's ability to look directly into the eyes of the characters helped to facilitate the effectiveness of the images. For example, on the cover of I Love My Hair (Tarpley, 1998), E. B. Lewis uses realistic watercolor to illustrate a young girl with intricately braided hair swirling around her head. The girl is smiling and looking directly at the viewer. The close-up image combined with Lewis' use of direct participation entice the viewer to find out who the girl is and why she is happy. This image resonates with Lewis's (2016) reflection about his art: "I got into the business to talk about the human condition," Lewis said. "We forget how powerful it is just to be human."

Inside the book, Lewis builds on the relationship he created on the cover by inviting the viewer to sit down with the little girl while she goes through her nightly hair combing ritual. From a middle distance, the viewer sees stuffed animals, a teddy bear and a Black baby doll. The little girl sits in the foreground, on her mother's lap. In this image that fills a double-page spread all the way to the edges, she glances off to the right, allowing the viewer to just observe. The sense of detachment generally achieved by an oblique angle is minimized here by Lewis's use of proximity and orientation, which create a sense of involvement with the viewer. In several close-ups that follow, the girl's face holds an expression of wonder, pain, pride and exhaustion as she goes through the nightly routine with her mother (pp. 6–13). These images not only provide direct access to the indescribable sensations evoked by the hair combing ritual, they also convey the little girl's humanity.

Hair serves as a powerful visual metaphor for humanity in several of the books. In *Crown: An Ode to the Fresh Cut*, Gordon James creates nearly all close-up images to portray his protagonist's experience at the Black barbershop. Painted in rich oil colors, the protagonist is introduced on the book's cover from a slightly vertical angle, which gives him more power than the viewer. This technique elicits a sense of respect and adoration for the boy, causing the viewer to want to know more of his story. Inside, images of his experience at the barbershop cover the entire page; several images cover double-page spreads. By reaching to the very edges of the pages with powerfully magnified images, James immerses the viewer in the unique space the boy inhabits. In a particularly poignant image, the boy holds out an honor roll ribbon in one hand and an award for perfect attendance in the other. He stares at the viewer in anticipation of acknowledgement. While making the honor roll is not an uncommon occurrence, it is one not often associated with Black boys in popular culture. In a recent interview, James (2018) pointed to the dehumanizing language and Black boy suffering associated with antiblackness that inspired his illustrations, "You look at Trayvon Martin or Mike Brown, you hear about them having 'superhuman strength and being evil,' and all of these ridiculous statements. It's almost like our boys aren't allowed to be children."

On the adjacent page, James positions the boy at the center of the frame, making him more prominent to viewers. He glances slightly down, causing the viewer not only to look up at him, but to join him in this higher place. Although echoing the text, the star-shaped background extends the significance of the boy's position and what he represents, "You're a star. A brilliant, blazing star." (See Figure 3.1.) Both the author and illustrator counter racist narratives, and this is made explicit through the juxtaposition of these humanizing images.

Like *I Love My Hair* and *Crown: An Ode to the Fresh Cut,* the cover of *I Am Enough* is graced by a striking image of a deep-brown complexioned child (see Figure 3.2). The background is white, which creates a stark contrast, drawing the viewer's attention to the noticeably large afro that frames the girl's tiny face. In this image, her expression is slightly serious, with just a hint of a smile. However, she maintains direct eye contact with the viewer and this, coupled with the frontal angle of the image, fosters emotional involvement.

Once inside the book, Keturah Bobo repositions the viewer to observe the girl and other characters primarily through long shots with full-length depictions. The impact of the physical space between the viewer and the characters, along with the continued use of a white background, erects a temporary barrier, which the viewer must overcome in order to enter the story world. Starting with the first page of the story, attitude, proximity, and orientation become significant systems that Bobo uses to influence the viewer's engagement with the characters. In terms of attitude, Bobo positions viewers at eye-level on a horizontal plane which

FIGURE 3.1 Celebrating the Boy's Position in Humanity (Barnes, 2017)
Source: Reprinted with permission from *Crown: An Ode to the Fresh Cut*, text by Derrick Barnes, illustrations by Gordon C. James, Agate Bolden 2017.

creates a sense of equality and trust. At the same time, she creates permeable boundaries by using oblique angles. With the exception of a few images, all others show the characters looking at each other and not at the viewer. Given the absence of subordination and domination, Bobo's choice to use oblique angles creates a sense of spying on a secret club, rather than detachment. Using orientation, Bobo reveals the relationship between characters and strengthens the relationship between the viewer and the characters. Across mostly double-page spreads, she illustrates the characters' day-to-day lives in the foreground. The girls are depicted in close proximity to one another—either side by side, closely interacting with each other, or embracing one another. The viewer is close enough to see their facial expressions and emotions clearly. As the tone of the story changes from whimsy to uncertainty and disappointment, and finally to encouragement, viewers, invited to look on, see not only what the characters are doing to support one another but also their humanity.

A mid-shot image on the cover of Bryan Collier's *Uptown* features a young boy, wearing a white button-down shirt, a black tie and dress pants (see Figure 3.3). He stares directly at viewers, provoking them to look back at him intently and to fully see a Black boy. In this cover image and one other, the viewer can look into the boy's eyes. He takes pride in himself and his city. Similar to Bobo, Collier uses attitude, proximity, and orientation to maintain a level of involvement with the viewer. In one particularly interesting image, Collier positions the

FIGURE 3.2 Emotional Involvement Achieved through Eye Contact (Byers, 2018)

viewer in a seeming place of power, looking down at the boy through a tight square frame in the ceiling (p. 6). However, given the already established relationship, this glimpse of the boy eating chicken and waffles serves to strengthen his credibility with the viewer. A subsequent image, on the adjacent page, opens a window onto the larger community to which he belongs. Another page turn reveals the exterior of rows of brownstone buildings in a dramatic pan across a double-page spread. Several images that follow alternate between mid-shots of the boy's community and longshots depicting the boy, full-length, within the context of his community. Collier reduces the distance by placing the boy and all

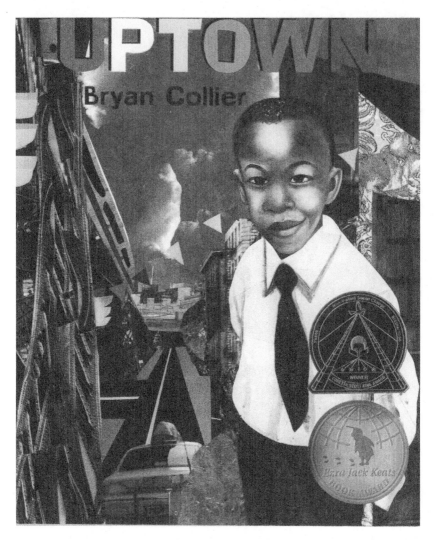

FIGURE 3.3 Human Connection Achieved through Attitude and Proximity (Collier, 2000)

members of his community in the foreground of highly detailed settings. Viewers are invited to experience the images as if they were invited guests or friends. As such, viewers gladly journey with the boy through his city, capturing his unique perspectives of the Apollo Theater, jazz musicians at the Lenox, and a game of pick up ball at the Ruckers. A relationship is created between the reader and the boy—a celebration of their common humanity through this shared experience.

Across the set of picturebooks, the experiences of the hair combing ritual, the Black barbershop, Harlem, and living out typical girlhood experiences reflect the ordinary ways in which Black childhood unfolds. The illustrators use social distance, attitude, and orientation to deepen and evoke varied emotions depending on the viewer and his or her positioning to antiblackness. Viewers who are insiders are likely to see images that reflect and solidify their humanity, while other viewers might be compelled to see Black children's worth and dignity.

Imagining the Unimaginable—The Use of Focalization, Pathos and Affect, and Ambience

Dumas and Nelson (2016) talk about the implausibility of Black childhoods, noting that while, "children in general are materially vulnerable; their perspectives and social worlds seldom acknowledged ... Black children are among the most invisible, most underrepresented and misrepresented" (p. 33). These authors speak to the need for Black boyhood specifically, and Black childhood in general, to be reimagined. They point to the significance of inquiry that asks Black children, "who they are, what they think and what they desire in their lives now" (Dumas & Nelson, 2016, p. 1). Building on these ideas, we consider the capacity of picturebook illustrations to become sites of agency that not only make visible who Black children are, what they think and desire, but also provoke readers to (re)imagine Black childhood in a world that exists beyond the current reality (Bobo, 2018). We center this part of our analysis on systems of focalization, pathos and affect, ambience, and provenance. We provide examples of our analysis by selecting key images from each book.

A common pattern across the text set is the choice to depict characters in a naturalistic style. Style choice influences how real or life-like characters appear to the viewer and how accurately the viewer might interpret the characters' facial expressions and identify or empathize with their circumstances (Painter et al., 2013). A naturalistic visual choice creates the greatest possibility that the viewer will engage deeply with characters, understand the complexities of their lives, and imagine future possibilities.

An example of this is Gordon James's naturalistic oil portraits in *Crown: An Ode to the Fresh Cut*. James establishes strong engagement with the viewer by presenting page after page of strikingly vivid images of his protagonist and the people he encounters inside the Black barbershop. In one of the most powerful and salient images, James' protagonist is positioned in front of his multigenerational community as they cheer and celebrate him (pp. 22–23). The facial expressions of the people are so highly detailed that the viewer, positioned to see through the boy's eyes, experiences validation and acceptance in a very real way. Visiting the barbershop, then, becomes a rite of passage for the boy and for the viewer.

Along with style, medium (the materials used to create the illustration), was a significant part of telling a distinctly Black story. For example, Collier's collage-style in *Uptown* integrates familiar textures, patterns, illustrations, and photographic imagery. This use of elaborate collage art beckons the viewer to spend time on each page. The importance of collage in Collier's representations of Black childhood cannot be understated. In his view, his work allows viewers to imagine themselves and those depicted in his stories as whole:

> A collage is like this wonderful metaphor for life. Now, I have done a book where I painted puzzle pieces in collage … What I try to talk about is if you hold on to that piece—that wonderful puzzle shape—it'll eventually make you whole. If you discard it, then that is your void, and that is where you'll be broken. And that's where collage and life sort of intersect—holding on to that small piece and putting it together to make you whole eventually. And that's what all this is really, really about.
>
> *(Collier, 2010)*

At the same time, Collier's investment in visuality offers viewers an invitation to view Harlem as the center of Black visual culture. As the story progresses, Collier's protagonist serves as a pseudo curator, guiding viewers through scenes of Harlem and his life. There are numerous illustrations depicting traditional African fashion as well as the iconography of Harlem's streets. The boy's pride in his community and the richness of the illustrations signal a shift away from deficit depictions of Black urban neighborhoods.

hooks (1994) speaks to how Blackness has been constructed "one-dimensionally in ways that reinforce and sustain white supremacy" (p. 425). Keturah Bobo's illustrations in *I Am Enough* counter racist ideologies by serving as a reminder of the complex nature of race and identity. Using acrylic paintings, Bobo creates bold images of Black girls in motion, mapped onto familiar childhood scenes like the park and the playground. In the backdrop, she composes digital images that mimic colored pencil or crayon drawings of hearts, trees, birds and rainbows to solicit a playful or exploratory feeling. The contrast in color and style places a high degree of emphasis on the characters, making their day-to-day lives a focal point across the book. In this story world, Black girls define their own identities, rather than conforming to normative views and opinions. Bobo (2018) captures the impetus for reimagining in this way: "So many people have approached me because they want to see representations of themselves in the world. It's such a simple task … something I am fully capable of creating by painting or illustrating."

The concept of self-definition and the portrayal of Black children's lives through their own interpretations resonates across the text set. E. B. Lewis's depiction of afro picks and knocker ball ponytail holders on the endpaper of *I Love My Hair* serves as an excellent example of the system of provenance (Kress & van Leeuwen, 2006). For most Black viewers, these culturally and historically intimate signifiers of Black childhood conjure associative meanings. To extend this, Lewis incorporates an array of symbols—roots, trees, spinning wheels, rows of corn—that are bursting with cultural and historical significance. In key images, Lewis connects his protagonist to the past, present, and future. For example, in one double-page spread, Lewis juxtaposes the text with an image of the little girl, who, instead of an African inspired headdress, dons a globe. The text reads:

> Some days I just let my hair be free to do what it wants, to go any which-way it pleases.Then my hair surrounds my head like a globe.This is my Afro style.

The image matches the text in that it reflects the little girl's point of view (see Figure 3.4). She is depicted from a low angle, which magnifies her prominence in

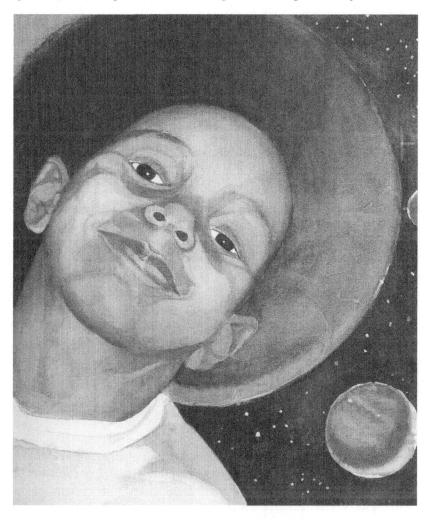

FIGURE 3.4 Girl's Pride in Her Afro Hair (Tarpley, 1998)
Source: From *I Love My Hair* by Natasha Anastasia Tarpley and illustrated by E.B. Lewis, copyright © 1998, 2001, 2003, 2008. Reprinted by permission of Little, Brown and Co., a subsidiary of Hachette Book Group, Inc.

the frame and adds new meaning to who she is— part of a rich continuum. The circular image of world that hovers above her head solidifies this connection. On the next page, the link to the girl's ancestry is confirmed by Tarpley's beautiful writing, "Wearing an Afro was a way for them to stand up for what they believed, to let the world know they were proud of who they were and where they came from." Lewis then ends the book with a glimpse of the future—with an angle that positions the little girl suspended in air. She is in a place, "freed from the gaze of White supremacy—where Black children dream weightless, unracialized and human" (Dumas & Ross, 2016, p. 436).

In this section, we demonstrated how focalization, pathos and affect, ambience, and provenance are used by the illustrators to evoke viewer participation, empathy and familiarity. At the same time, these techniques enable an (re)imagining by viewers. Viewers may either deepen their connection with or perhaps become a little more understanding of Black conditions and experiences as they see the world through each character's eyes.

Implications

A growing body of literature documents the ways in which Black children have been positioned as non-human and denied human protections (Goff, Eberhardt, Williams, & Jackson, 2008). From daily micro-aggressions, to misrepresentations, to violent police shootings, Black children face real ongoing threats to their existence (Dumas & Ross, 2016). This analysis prompts discussion about how Black childhood is portrayed in picturebooks and other spaces as well as how it might be re-imagined. The illustrations examined in the four highly regarded picturebooks in this chapter move one step closer to this goal. Overall, the artistic choices made by the illustrators across this text set not only capture the humanity of the Black child protagonist, but also invite a range of compelling interactions with the viewer. In particular, the future-forward messages embedded within the illustrations provide a gateway for moving beyond the current reality of a world that is systemically racist, to a place in which we reimagine how Black children are seen and understood.

Final Reflections

Black illustrators and the images they produce are not often recognized for their complexity. Our analysis demonstrated the importance of applying analytical tools and critical theory to better understand how these illustrators create images that mitigate against antiblackness. When integrated, scholarship surrounding antiblackness and tools for interpreting visual images reveal the depth, complexity, and possibility these picturebook illustrations hold. On par with the Black artists of previous times, the illustrators in this study are at the fore of social change, creating powerful images that both reflect and inspire the nation.

References

Bishop, R.S. (2012). Reflections on the development of African American children's literature. *Journal of Children's Literature*, 38(2), 5–13.

Bobo, K.A.N. (2016). Keturah Ariel: Artist Spotlight. Retrieved from https://www.naturally curly.com/curlreading/curlykids/curly-illustrator-spotlight-keturah-ariel-bobo-art-by-ariel

Bobo, K.A.N. (2018). Celebrating Our Voices: 28 days later honorees—Feb. 15–Keturah Bobo (Illustrator). Retrieved from https://thebrownbookshelf.com/2018/02/15/da y-15-keturah-a-bobo/

Brooks, W. (2009). An author as a counter-storyteller: Applying critical race theory to a Coretta Scott King Award book. *Children's Literature in Education*, 40, 33–43.

Brown, S., Souto-Manning, M. & Laman, T.T. (2010). Seeing the strange in the familiar: Unpacking racialized practices in early childhood settings. *Race, Ethnicity and Education*, 13, 513–532.

Collier, B. (2010) Interview. Retrieved from www.readingrockets.org/books/interviews/ collier/transcript#collage

Dumas, M. (2016). Against the dark: Antiblackness in education policy and discourse. *Theory into Practice*, 55, 11–19.

Dumas, M.J. & Nelson, J.D. (2016). (Re)Imagining Black boyhood: Toward a critical framework for educational research. *Harvard Educational Review, 86*(1), 27–47. doi:10.17763/0017-8055.86.1.27

Dumas, M. & Ross, K. (2016). "Be real black for me": Imagining BlackCrit in education. *Urban Education*, 51(4), 415–442.

Epstein, R., Blake, J.J., & González, T. (2017, July 18). Girlhood interrupted: The erasure of Black girls' childhood. Retrieved from https://papers.ssrn.com/sol3/papers.cfm?abstra ct_id=3000695

Garner, R.P. (2017). Unforgivable Blackness: Visual rhetoric, reader response and critical racial literacy. *Children's Literature in Education*, 48, 119–133.

Goff, P.A., Eberhardt, J.L., Williams, M.J., & Jackson, M.C. (2008). Not yet human: Implicit knowledge, historical dehumanization, and contemporary consequences. *Journal of Personality and Social Psychology*, 94, 292–306.

Haslam, N. (2006). Dehumanization: An integrative review. *Personality and Social Psychology Review*, 10, 252–264.

hooks, b. (1994). Postmodern Blackness. Retrieved June 13, 2018, from www.africa.up enn.edu/Articles_Gen/Postmodern_Blackness_18270.html

Howard, T.C. & Navarro, O. (2016). Critical race theory 20 years later: Where do we go from here? *Urban Education*, 5, 253–273.

Hughes-Hassell, S. (2013). Multicultural young adult literature as a form of counter-storytelling. *The Library Quarterly*, 83(3), 212–228.

James, G. (2018). Author and illustrator take the crown with book honors. Retrieved from www.thecharlottepost.com/news/2018/02/21/arts-and-entertainment/charlotte-a uthor-and-illustrator-take-the-crown-with-book-honors/

Johnson, D. (1990). *Telling tales: The pedagogy and promise of African American literature for youth.* Westport, CT: Greenwood Press.

Kress, G. & van Leeuwen, T. (2006). *Reading images: The grammar of visual design.* London: Routledge.

Ladson-Billings, G. (2009). Just what is critical race theory and what's it doing in a nice field like education? In E. Taylor, D. Gillborn and G. Ladson-Billings (Eds.), *Foundations of critical race theory in education* (pp. 17–36). New York: Routledge.

Ladson-Billings, G., & Tate IV, W.F. (2016). Toward a critical race theory of education. In A.D. Dixon, C.K.R. Anderson, and J.K. Donner (Eds.), *Critical race theory in education*, 2nd ed. (pp. 21–41). New York: Routledge.

Lewis, E.B. (2016). S.J. Illustrator E.B. Lewis brings the world to children. Retrieved from www.courierpostonline.com/story/life/2016/02/25/eb-lewis/80418848/

Martin, M.H. (2004). *Brown gold: Milestones of African American children's picture books, 1845–2002*. New York: Routledge.

Martínez, R. (2017). "Are you gonna show this to white people?": Chicana/o and Latina/o students' counternarratives on race, place, and representation. *Race Ethnicity and Education*, 20(1), 101–116.

McNair, J.C. (2008, Spring). Innocent though they may seem ... A critical race theory analysis of Fireflyand Seesaw Scholastic book club order forms. *Multicultural Review*, 24–28.

Myers, C. (2014, March 15). The apartheid of children's literature. Retrieved from https://www.nytimes.com/2014/03/16/opinion/sunday/the-apartheid-of-childrens-literature.html

Millman, J. (2005). Faith Ringgolds' quilts and picturebooks: Comparisons and contributions. *Children's Literature in Education*, 36(4), 381–393.

Obama, B. & Langone, A. (2018, July 17). Read full transcript of Barack Obama's South Africa speech. Retrieved from http://time.com/5341180/barack-obama-south-africa-speech-transcript/

Painter, C., Martin, J.R., & Unsworth, L. (2013). *Reading visual narratives: Image analysis of children's picture books*. Sheffield, UK: Equinox.

Roethler, J. (1998). Reading in color: Children's book illustrations and identity formation for Black children in the United States. *African American Review*, 32, 95–105.

Sexton, J. (2008). *Amalgamation schemes: Antiblackness and the critique of multiracialism*. Minneapolis: University of Minnesota Press.

Solórzano, D. & Yosso, T. (2002). Critical race methodology: Counterstorytelling as an analytical framework for education research. *Qualitative Inquiry*, 8(1), 23–44.

Tarpley, N. (2018). Interview. Retrieved from https://thebrownbookshelf.com/28days/natasha-tarpley/

Tatum, E. (2015). Why don't Black lives matter? *New York Amsterdam News*, 106(16), 12.

Thompson, A. (2001). Harriet Tubman in pictures: Cultural consciousness and the art of picturebooks. *The Lion and the Unicorn*, 25(1), 81–114.

Tolson, N. (2008). *Black children's literature got de blues*. New York: Peter Lang.

Wilderson, F.B. (2010). *Red, white & black: Cinema and the structure of U.S. antagonisms*. Durham, NC: Duke University Press.

Children's Literature References

Barnes, D. (2017). *Crown: An ode to the fresh cut*. Illus. by G.C. James. Chicago: Bolden.

Byers, G. (2018). *I am enough*. Illus. by K.A. Bobo. New York: HarperCollins.

Collier, B. (2000). *Uptown*. New York: Henry Holt.

Tarpley, N. (1998). *I love my hair!* Illus. by E.B. Lewis. New York: Little, Brown.

4

EXAMINING THE VISUAL IN LATINX IMMIGRANT JOURNEY PICTUREBOOKS

Janine M. Schall, Julia López-Robertson and Jeanne G. Fain

Today's sociopolitical climate has positioned immigrants as threats to national security and a drain on U.S. resources. As negative views and framing of immigrants as "other" are perpetuated through print and visual media, children's books about immigrant experiences are simultaneously coming to the forefront. While children's books depicting the immigrant experience are not new, interest has increased as classrooms continue to become more global and as authors highlight immigration issues. As educators, we share concerns about the pervasiveness of deficit views of immigrants, Latinx in particular, that make their way into elementary classrooms and educational materials, including children's books. Our experiences, both personal and professional, have made selecting and using immigrant literature in the classroom an important component in our lives.

In this chapter, we use the theoretical frame of Latino Critical Race Theory (LatCrit) to examine ways that Latinx immigrants are positioned in the illustrations of Latinx immigrant journey books. We also examine the ways that immigrant characters show agency. First, we introduce sociohistorical and cultural aspects of immigration. We then discuss LatCrit as a theoretical framework which leads to the research methodology, analysis, and discussion. To be inclusive of intersectional identities, we are using the term "Latinx" as a gender neutral alternative to Latino, Latina, or Latin@.

Sociohistorical and Cultural Aspects of Immigration

Immigrants face real challenges as they move to a new country. Along with leaving their homes, they often find their linguistic and cultural knowledge devalued as they pursue new beginnings due to war, poverty, security, terrorism, and economic opportunity (Lowery, 2001). Immigrants grapple with differences that include language, culture, and ethnicity as they journey into and across the border (Sung, Fahrenbruck, & López-Robertson, 2017). The immigrant experience includes how children and their families are framed as they experience the impact of immigration outrage, challenges with citizenship status, tensions with police, bullying, and labor exploitation (Campano, Ghiso, & Welch, 2016).

Immigration patterns have shifted and changed throughout the years. Since the 1960s there has been a drastic change in immigrant-sending countries from Europe to Latin America and Asia (Bodvarsson & Van Den Berg, 2009). The U.S. foreign-born population increased from 9.7 million to nearly 40 million in 2010, and more than half of immigrants living in the United States came from Central America, South America, Mexico, or Spanish-speaking Caribbean countries. Latin American immigration from countries such as Peru, Ecuador, and Colombia has increased steadily since 1970. States such as California, New York, Florida, and Texas have experienced greater cultural influence of immigrants from these areas. According to the Pew Research Center, future immigrants will account for 88 percent of the U.S. population increase by the year 2065 (López & Bailik, 2017). The influx of Latinx immigration has caused the U.S. economy to consider the influence of the Latinx product demand. Selective enforcement on the part of the United States is a distinctive feature of undocumented immigration since 1960, and, until recently, the United States worked to balance economic, social and humanitarian goals through its admission preferences (Tienda & Sanchez, 2013).

Critical Race Theory and LatCrit as a Theoretical Framework and Tool of Analysis

Our analysis of Latinx immigrant journey picturebooks is guided by Critical Race Theory (CRT) and Latino Critical Race Theory (LatCrit) frameworks. According to Tate (1997), Critical Race Theory is "rooted in the social missions of the 1960s that sought justice, liberation, and economic empowerment; thus, from its inception, it has had both academic and social activist goals" (p. 197). Concerned that advances made during the Civil Rights era had mired or were reversing, legal scholars Derrick Bell, Alan Freeman, and Richard Delgado led the Critical Race Theory movement to "combat the subtler forms of racism that were gaining ground" (Delgado & Stefancic, 2012, p. 4).

Critical Race Theory is a multidisciplinary epistemology originally based in legal studies that places race at the forefront of analysis (Bell, 1995) and seeks to transform the relationship among power, race, and racism. CRT in education is a "set of basic insights, perspectives, methods, and pedagogy that seeks to identify, analyze, and transform those structural and cultural aspects of education that maintain subordinate and dominant racial positions in and out of the classroom" (Solórzano & Yosso, 2002, p. 25).

Solórzano (1997; 1998) argues that there are five significant principles that form the basic viewpoints and pedagogy of CRT in education (Solórzano & Delgado Bernal, 2001; Solórzano & Yosso, 2002):

1. *The centrality and intersectionality of race and racism*: CRT starts from the premise that race and racism are endemic in U.S. society.
2. *The challenge to dominant ideology*: CRT challenges the traditional claims of the educational system and its institutions to objectivity, meritocracy, color and gender blindness, race and gender neutrality, and equal opportunity.
3. *The commitment to social justice*: CRT has an overall commitment to social justice and the elimination of racism and the ability of minoritized groups to empower themselves through praxis, the combination of theory and practice.
4. *The centrality of experiential knowledge*: CRT recognizes that the experiential knowledge of people of color is legitimate, appropriate, and critical to understanding, analyzing, and teaching about racial subordination in the field of education.
5. *The interdisciplinary perspective*: CRT challenges ahistoricism and a unidisciplinary focus of most analyses and insists on analyzing race and racism in education within a historical and contemporary context using interdisciplinary methods. CRT expands a comprehensive literature base in women's studies, ethnic studies, sociology, and history.

CRT and LatCrit share the same beliefs and foundations, but LatCrit is primarily concerned with issues that affect Latinx people: language issues/rights, immigration and citizenship, ethnicity, culture and cultural preservation. LatCrit explicates Latinx multidimensional identities and addresses the intersectionality of classism, sexism, racism, and other forms of oppression (Delgado Bernal, 2002). Davila & Bradley (2010) explain that LatCrit:

> provides a context for the social, historical, and political reception and impact of Latina/os in the U.S. and provides theoretical space to analyze experiences of language and immigration among other lived experiences rooted in the resistance and oppression of Latinas/os.
>
> *(p. 40)*

A noteworthy pedagogical component, storytelling serves important methodological functions and benefits people of color by: (1) allowing people to reflect on their lived experience, (2) allowing the marginalized participant to speak or make public his/her story, (3) subverting the dominant story that is socially constructed by Whites, and (4) using counter-storytelling to empower and transform because sharing one's stories raises a person's awareness of common experiences and "opens the possibilities for social action" (Fernández, 2002, p. 48).

Critical Race methodology in education challenges cultural deficit stories of students of color through counter storytelling. Counter storytelling is a method of telling the stories of those people whose experiences are not often told, including people of color, the poor, and members of the LGBTQ community. Counter stories "counter" deficit storytelling, are grounded in real-life experiences, and are contextualized in social situations that are also grounded in real life (Davila & Bradley, 2010; Delgado Bernal, 2002; Delgado & Stefancic, 2012; Solórzano, 1998). Counter stories are usually shared verbally; one person speaks while others listen, however, similar to Brooks (2017), we "identify counter-stories as they materialize through the pens of writers and the characters personified in novels" (p. 83). Moreover, we extend the content of counter story to include the illustrations in picturebooks. In an effort to identify, name, and address educational issues for Latinx students, CRT and LatCrit were used as frameworks through which we viewed and analyzed the illustrations, with the following tenet emphasized:

- *The centrality of experiential knowledge as shared through counter storytelling.*

Literature Review

There is a dearth of research on Critical Race Theory and/or LatCrit as a theoretical framework or tool of analysis with children's literature. The work that has been done with CRT has focused on African American children's literature, young adult literature, or the availability of multicultural books for students. Franzak (2003) explored two young adult novels, *Tears of a Tiger* (Draper, 1994) and *Whirligig* (Fleischman, 1998), through the lens of CRT. She argues that by reading the novels through this lens, the racial meanings of the text become central to the readers' interpretation and understanding. She concludes that paired together, the books "afford a powerful opportunity for students to explore racial identity and concepts of justice, healing, and hope" (p. 53).

McNair (2008a) conducted a comparative analysis of two sets of African American children's literature: *The Brownies' Book*, a periodical directed primarily at black children created by W.E.B. Du Bois in the 1920s, and contemporary African American children's literature written by Patricia McKissack. McNair's study demonstrated that CRT is a valuable tool for studying children's literature and can be used to help preservice teachers understand children's literature as a social and cultural construct that is not free of cultural phenomena such as racism. In a study that examined Scholastic book clubs order forms, Firefly (preschool) and See Saw (K-1), McNair (2008b; 2008c) sought to determine which authors and illustrators of color were regularly included or excluded. McNair concluded that there is a selective tradition operating within the context of the book clubs and as a result "there are few counter-narratives (stories that challenge dominant ways of seeing and telling) present" (p. 197) in book club forms. Brooks (2009; 2017) framed her analyses of the Coretta Scott King award-winning young adult novel *The Land* (Taylor, 2001) with Critical Race Theory and found that applying CRT allows researchers, teachers, preservice teachers, and students to understand some of racism's lasting effects from the perspective of those impacted.

Hughes-Hassell, Barkley, and Koehler (2009) conducted a content analysis using CRT to determine representation of authors and illustrators of color in books for transitional readers using a leveled book list database containing more than 32,000 leveled books. The findings revealed that "people of color are underrepresented as characters in transitional books, thus suggesting that racism in its most subtle form is present" (p. 13). Finally, Hughes-Hassell's (2013) study suggests that multicultural YA literature "allows teens in the majority culture to see how the world looks from someone else's perspective. It challenges their assumptions, jars their complacency, and invites them to action" (p. 226). As evidenced above, there are few studies of children's literature where CRT was applied as a framework and/or a tool of analysis and no studies drawing upon CRT and LatCrit as a theoretical lens for the critical content analysis of visual images in Latinx children's literature.

Methodology

Stories are "mediated communicative events" (Fernández, 2002, p. 49); the pictures we read for this analysis were mediated by each of us through the cultural lenses with which we view and interact with the world. We are a first generation American Latina scholar and two white scholars, all of whom have worked and respectfully learned with and from Latinx immigrant children in our role as educators and with adults as teacher educators.

As teacher educators who believe in the power of children's literature to help students think critically about the world, we were interested in exploring the ways in which immigrants are depicted. We focused on Latinx immigrants because of our backgrounds working with Latinx immigrant communities. We felt that LatCrit was an appropriate theoretical frame due to its emphasis on "Latinas/Latinos' multidimensional identities that can address the intersectionality of racism, sexism, classism, and other forms of oppression" (Delgado Bernal, 2002, p. 106). We also appreciate its understandings of Latinx students as holders and creators of knowledge.

We considered multiple information sources and reviews for book selection, including Worlds of Words, International Board on Books for Young People, United States Board on Books for Young People, Pura Belpré Award, The Américas Award, and *Language Arts*. We are especially concerned with the framing of immigrants as "others" within picturebooks. In an intentional response to this framing, our book selection process included attention to ethnicity and variation in ages of characters, gender, narrative styles, and female and male authors in sharing the complex stories of journeying to the United States. Our goals were to include Latinx books that would (1) reflect students' cultures and insider knowledge in the immigration narrative, (2) portray positive and sensitive portrayals of the immigrant experience, (3) demonstrate a range of diverse portrayals of immigrant experiences, (4) avoid stereotypical and discriminatory images, and (5) offer in-depth opportunities for thoughtful expansion of understandings within discussion about local immigration issues.

We chose three recent children's picturebooks which feature Latinx immigrant characters making the journey from their home country to the United States. These books were written by insiders to Latinx culture and realistically portray the challenges of crossing the border. We have used these books with students in elementary, undergraduate and graduate classrooms and we have discussed critical issues within these texts. However, we had never formally analyzed the visual elements in them.

My Diary from Here to There/Mi diario de aquí hasta allá, written by Amada Irma Pérez (2002) and illustrated by Maya Christina González, is a colorful bilingual picturebook written as the diary of a young Mexican girl, Amada. Amada learns that her large family will be emigrating to the United States after her father loses his job. On the first stage of their journey, the family moves to the Mexican border to stay with extended family while the father works in the fields in the United States. Because her father is an American citizen, the family applies for green cards and emigrates with legal paperwork. Once their green cards arrive, the family leaves for Los Angeles and begins building a new life. This book is based on the author's own journey from Mexico to the United States as a child.

Pancho Rabbit and the Coyote: A Migrant's Tale by Duncan Tonatiuh (2013) uses anthropomorphized animals in Tonatiuh's characteristic flat style to tell the story of young Pancho Rabbit, who sneaks out of his small Mexican town to find his father who did not return to the family after two years away working in the United States. A coyote offers to help Pancho cross the border so he can find his family but eventually attacks him when Pancho runs out of food. Fortunately, Pancho's father finds him and helps fight off the coyote. Pancho and his father return home, hoping that the crops will be good so they will be able to stay. Author and illustrator Tonatiuh grew up bicultural and transnational, and today splits his time between Mexico and the United States.

In *Two White Rabbits,* originally published in Mexico and written by Jairo Buitrago (2015), illustrated by Rafael Yockteng, and translated by Elisa Amado, a young girl and her father are traveling to an unnamed location, taking a raft across a river, jumping on moving trains, and fleeing from the authorities. They are accompanied by a *chucho*, a slang term, often with negative implications, for a dog in Central America. Author Buitrago is Mexican and illustrator Yockteng is Colombian.

We began our analysis by carefully reviewing the professional literature on LatCrit and building a list of critical LatCrit tenets. From there we developed an initial list of questions for our critical content analysis of visual images in these picturebooks. The questions include: *How are the immigrant characters positioned? In what ways do the depictions of the immigrant characters show agency and what role does the agency play within the story?*

Our analysis occurred in a series of meetings interspersed with time for independent work. First, each person read the picturebooks on her own. Then we came together to refine our questions and research protocol. We then focused our analysis on the visual aspects of interpersonal relations as described by Painter, Martin, & Unsworth (2013). Interpersonal relations is a broad category that includes the various ways the reader/viewer is positioned in relation to the narrative character and the narrative characters are positioned in relation to each other. For example, the visual system of social distance can create a sense of intimacy between viewer and character, while the system of focalization can either invite the viewer to engage with the character or take on the role of observer.

We organized our analysis by major narrative events that commonly describe the immigration journey, such as a beginning, preparing to leave home behind, crossing the border, arriving in a new place, and finally transitioning to a new place and location. Next, we independently analyzed *My Diary from Here to There/Mi diario de aquí hasta allá*, using a chart to organize our thinking (see Table 4.1). Illustrations were analyzed using analytic tools from Painter et al. (2013). In addition, we used picture book codes created by Moebius (1986) and adapted by Serafini (2014). According to Moebius (1986), picture book codes offer a beginning point in analysis and interpretation of illustrations and include codes of position and size, codes of perspective, codes of the frame, codes of line, and codes of color. Codes of position and size describe the location of where characters and objects are placed. Codes of perspective describes how the reader is positioned in regards to the setting

TABLE 4.1 Picturebook Visual Working Analysis Chart

Events	Description of Illustration	Social Relations Techniques (Painter, Martin, & Unsworth, 2013)	Picturebook Codes (Moebius, 1986, Serafini, 2014)
Beginnings: Home Environment Family Community/Neighbors			
Act of preparing to leave home behind			
Crossing the border Traveling to new location:			
Arriving in a New Place			
Transitioning to New Place/Location			

or characters. Codes of line attends to the use of lines in depicting the characters and objects. Codes of color describes how color is used to focus one's attention to the elements situated within a visual image.

We started our analysis using all picturebook codes, but then noticed significant overlap with position and size, codes of perspective, and codes of color with the visual analysis tools from Painter et al. (2013). We discovered that the codes of frame and codes of line from the picturebook codes provided us with new visual perspectives as we analyzed pictures in each book.

We met again to review our independent analyses and to build a set of common understandings and approaches. We then worked independently to analyze the other books before meeting for development of initial themes. Once initial themes were developed, we independently returned to the LatCrit literature and the picturebooks. Finally, we met once again to finalize the themes.

Data Analysis

While our full analysis is too lengthy to include here, in this section we share an extended visual analysis of *My Diary from Here to There/Mi diario de aquí hasta allá* in order to illustrate the way we approached our work.

My Diary from Here to There/Mi diario de aquí hasta allá opens with an illustration depicting an oblique view of young Amada huddled under the covers, wearing a blue nightgown covered in purple butterflies and writing in her diary by the beam of a flashlight (see Figure 4.1). At first, she seems to be alone, but behind the flashlight is the face of a sleeping child next to Amada under the covers. Amada is glancing down at her diary and is positioned on the page with her head and flashlight in the upper left-hand corner of the spread. The colors are primarily cool blues and greens with occasional spots of warmer colors, including the light tan of Amada's face next to the yellowish-white of the flashlight. In the text, Amada writes that she has just learned that the family will be leaving their home in Juárez, Mexico to move to the United States. The overall tone of the illustration is somber, with the viewer's eye first landing on Amada's face, then following the beams of light to her diary. Amada's downward glance at the diary, the oblique view and mid-shot distance of her body all keep the viewer slightly distanced. However, where the relationship between the viewer and the character, Amada, is slightly distant, the relationship between Amada and her family is immediately established as close, with their bodies oriented next to each other. Also, given the position of Amada on the page, the viewer looks at her with a small upward angle; in the relationship between viewer and character, the character has the power.

This first illustration introduces visual aspects that reappear repeatedly: (1) the relationship between viewer and character is usually slightly distant, shown through the mid-shot and long shot, often oblique depictions of Amada; (2) the relationships between characters are usually close as seen in their orientations to each other; and (3) a butterfly is a repeating motif across each page.

FIGURE 4.1 Amada Writing in Her Diary (Pérez, 2002)
Source: My Diary from Here to There. Text Copyright © 2002 by Amada Irma Pérez. Illustrations © 2002 by Maya Christiana Gonzalez. Permission arranged with Children's Book Press, an imprint of Lee and Low Books, Inc., New York, NY 10016.

Painter et al. (2013) note that many picturebooks maintain a sense of social distance, the sense of connection and relationship between viewer and character, influenced by the proximity, gaze, and orientations of the characters to each other, throughout. This is true for *My Diary from Here to There/Mi diario de aquí hasta allá*, with some interesting exceptions. Amada is almost always shown in long shot, with her entire body depicted in the illustration, or mid-shot, with most of her body depicted. Yet, in two illustrations she appears in close up view, which helps create a greater sense of intimacy with the viewer and provides an emotional impact. In the first instance, she is sitting with her father, who is reassuring her about the upcoming move. In the second, she is with her entire family in a huge hug after they have successfully made it across the border and been reunited with her father. Both cases depict an emotional, loving moment between family members. There are also two instances where the viewer is invited to connect directly with Amada. Although she rarely looks directly at the viewer, thus maintaining the status of the viewer as an observer and not a participant in the story, in two cases she looks directly out of the page at the viewer. Again, both are emotional narrative moments. In the first, the family has left Amada's beloved home in Juárez and is driving across the desert to the border. In the second, Amada's father has just left the family behind in Mexicali to wait for their green cards while he crosses the border to work. Amada is surrounded by her family and as she cries, she looks directly out at the viewer, inviting the viewer to connect and empathize with her situation.

Amada is part of a large family, with a mother and father, five younger brothers, and numerous extended family members. The family is consistently depicted as strong and connected through the visual system of orientation, which accounts for how the characters' bodies are positioned in conjunction with each other. Amada and her family are always shown close to each other and usually touching. In illustrations depicting a parent, the parent is almost always above the children, looking down on them. The illustrations convey the sense of a loving, supportive family where the parents are firmly in charge.

Themes across the Immigrant Journey Books

We examined the research questions: How are the immigrant characters positioned? In what ways do visual depictions position the immigrant characters? In what ways do the depictions of the immigrant characters show agency and what role does agency play within the story? The following themes emerged across all three immigration books: Immigrants and agency, immigrants as controlled bodies, immigrants and community, and multiple immigrant stories and journeys.

Immigrants and Agency

In each picturebook, immigrant characters make intelligent decisions and take control of their own lives. The characters in *My Diary from Here to There/Mi diario de aquí hasta allá* (*My Diary*) and *Two White Rabbits* (*Two Rabbits*) make the critical decision to immigrate for economic reasons. In *Pancho Rabbit and Coyote* (*Pancho Rabbit*), Pancho resolves to find his father who has not returned from the North on time. They are resourceful and able to access multiple forms of capital, though not necessarily capital that's valued by mainstream society. The illustrations demonstrate that characters possess experiential and community knowledge of how to immigrate and strategically use their economic knowledge and cultural capital. For example, in *Two Rabbits*, the father knows how to get across the river on a raft and how to hop on the train; in *Pancho Rabbit*, Pancho understands that he needs an expert guide to successfully make it across the border and the desert. Amada's agency in *My Diary* stems from her determination to hold on to her cultural identity and background. This theme shows the second tenet of CRT, which is that characters have agency and challenge the dominant ideology of immigrants. The fourth tenet of CRT represents the experiential knowledge of people of color as legitimate.

Immigrants as Controlled Bodies

Illustrations across all three books depict a range of governmental and/or military authority linked to the act of immigrating. This authority ranges from neutral to aggressive, but in each book, the immigrant's decisions and movements are subject to control by outside forces. This control is most neutral in *My Diary*. The text makes it clear that Amada's father is a U.S. citizen who will easily be able to obtain green cards for the family. However, even with the advantage of parental citizenship, the rest of the family must remain in Mexico for an unknown period of time while the father goes to the U.S. to work and apply for the green cards. Separated from their father, Amada, her mother, and her siblings depend upon their large, loving extended family for shelter. This period of separation is shown visually in several spreads beginning on pages 16–17. In this spread, Amada is on the right page, facing away from her departing father and surrounded by her brothers and uncles who are all oriented towards Amada. The viewer is looking slightly down at Amada and her family. She is crying and looking directly out of the page to make eye contact with the viewer.

On the left page, Amada's mother is comforted by her grandmother as both gaze at a small car, presumably that of her father, driving down a winding road toward a shiny fence topped with razor wire. Whereas the viewer is kept at a slight social distance throughout most of the book, here the viewer is directly invited to connect with Amada as she is facing and making eye contact with the viewer in this highly emotional moment of departure and uncertain future; we feel a "maximum sense of involvement with her as a part of our own world" (Painter et al., 2013, p. 17). Despite the fact that her father is a citizen of the United States, there is no easy trip across the border. Immigration for Amada means family separation, dependence on extended family, and uncertainty. When the green cards finally do arrive, the children and mother make their way across the border. In the illustrations on pages 26–27, the family has been reunited and is shown in close up view in a family hug, with the children looking at their father who is lovingly gazing back at them. This warm and intimate depiction of the family, where Amada, her mother, and siblings have finally completed their immigration journey, is contrasted by a line in the text which states that, "One woman and her children got kicked off the bus when the immigration patrol boarded to check everyone's papers" (p. 27).

While the immigrant characters in *My Diary* are following a legal process for their journey, in the other books the immigrant characters undertake different journeys. Because immigration to the United States is tightly controlled and is often a lengthy, confusing, expensive process, many immigrants—like those in *Pancho Rabbit* and *Two Rabbits*—choose unsanctioned routes. Pancho is guided past the fence that separates the two countries when Coyote helps him bribe the guards and use a tunnel to go underneath the fence. In the illustration, the guards are depicted as rattlesnakes wearing the khaki green caps of the U.S. Border Patrol (p. 17). Their sharp white teeth and angular bodies are in contrast with the softer curves of Pancho's head and ears.

The guards in *Pancho Rabbit* are frightening, but rather easily subverted. In *Two White Rabbits,* however, the controlling authority is both scary and aggressive. As the girl and father travel, it is clear that they must avoid people who are trying to stop them. In one spread about halfway through the book, the train that they have been traveling on has been stopped. The girl and her father flee to the left while on the right angry figures in blue uniforms holding guns are pulling people off the train and putting them in handcuffs (see Figure 4.2). The figures could be soldiers or police; in any case, they are intent on arresting the immigrants on the train.

Towards the end of the book, the girl and her father are traveling in the back of a pickup truck. While her weary father sleeps, the girl stares out at the world and counts things. Although earlier in the book the girl saw sheep and rabbits in the clouds, now she sees soldiers with their caps and guns in the shapes of the nearby mountains. This theme relates to the first tenet of CRT with the themes of centrality and intersectionality of race and racism. Immigrants are judged by figures of authority as they experience the intersectionality of race and racism.

Immigrants and Community

All three books show the immigrant characters as part of strong families and communities. Immigration is not an independent, solo activity; it's an inclusive and community experience. In both *My Diary* and *Pancho Rabbit* the main character comes from a large family that supports the immigrant journey, while in *Two Rabbits* the family unit is smaller, just father and child. All three books visually depict family solidarity, with family members physically oriented toward each other and often touching. The family members rely on each other. For example, in *My Diary* the extended family takes in Amada, her mother, and her rambunctious brothers while they are waiting for their green cards. The family provides comfort as well as shelter. In the illustration discussed earlier a tearful

But we do stop. Because the people who are taking us don't always take us where we are going.

FIGURE 4.2 Immigrants Are Arrested on the Journey North (Buitrago &Yockteng, 2015)

Source: Selection from *Two White Rabbits*. Text copyright 2015 by Jairo Buitrago, Illustrations copyright 2015 by Rafael Yockteng, Translation copyright 2015 by Elisa Amado.

Amada is surrounded by her uncles and brothers who are trying to distract her from her father's departure.

The immigrant journey is also acknowledged and supported by the broader community. In *Pancho Rabbit*, Papá Rabbit leaves for the north in the company of other men from the town. His family and community are ready to welcome him back with a fiesta years later when he has earned enough money to support the family. The community's disappointment is illustrated by a spread showing the musicians and party guests leaving the party when the guest of honor fails to arrive. While *Two Rabbits* doesn't show the same kind of warm community relationships, there is an extended immigrant community depicted throughout the illustrations as shown in one spread where the girl and her father join a large group of people waiting by the train tracks. Later spreads show the top of the train loaded with immigrants, including the girl and her father, all making their way north. This theme clearly demonstrates the fourth principle of CRT in the centrality of experiential knowledge.

Multiple Immigrant Stories and Journeys

There is no single immigrant story or kind of immigrant journey; every immigrant story and journey is unique and varies within each experience. The three picturebooks analyzed in this chapter all show a different kind of journey. In both *My Diary* and *Pancho Rabbit* the movement between countries is explicitly tied to economic reasons; the families need money. In addition, both books illustrate the transnational lives of immigrants. However, Amada and her family experience legal immigration where her father is a citizen—born in the U.S. and moved to Mexico as a child, then moving back to the U.S. with his family as an adult. Amada eventually receives her green card.

Pancho, on the other hand, lacks legal documents and so journeys across the desert and under the border fence with the guidance of an experienced human smuggler (see Figure 4.3). Immigration for Pancho's community also involves movement back and forth between countries. His father has emigrated but hopes to return home to Mexico for good. Welcomed back with a fiesta, the final illustration of the book shows Pancho and his family standing in a circle holding hands while a band plays in the background. The loving depiction of the family in the illustration is tempered by the reality stated in the text—if the rains don't come, Papá Rabbit will need to go north once again, this time, perhaps, accompanied by his family.

In the final book, *Two Rabbits,* it isn't clear if the father and daughter are emigrating for economic reasons or to avoid violence in their home country in Central America. However, like Pancho and his father, they are taking an unsanctioned route and must avoid dangers such as the soldiers. This book has the most ambiguous ending, with a final illustration showing a barren landscape with only two white rabbits and the view to the horizon stopped by a solid fence. The second principle of CRT is prevalent in this theme. The characters have a range of stories which do not fit dominant ideologies and thus challenge them.

Discussion

Prior to the onset of our inquiry we wondered: how are immigrant characters positioned, in what ways do the depictions of the immigrant characters show agency, and what role does their agency play within the story? Critical content analysis of visual images provided us with the time and space to critically examine

FIGURE 4.3 Pancho Rabbit and the Coyote on Their Journey (Tonatiuh, 2013)
Source: Pancho Rabbit and the Coyote by Duncan Tonatiuh. Text and Illustrations
Copyright © 2013 by Duncan Tonatiuh.

and explore these books on immigration. We had read these books several times
but when we used visual tools to stop and analyze illustrations multiple times,
there were many ideas that we missed as readers which were clarified by the
principles of CRT. Although we are competent readers, we missed critical features from the illustrations regarding immigration. In addition, our conversations
with each other assisted us as we formulated new understandings regarding
immigration across these three books. We discovered that our ability to interpret
visual images and construct understandings of the books increased with multiple

reads, numerous attempts with the visual tools, and discussions of our questions regarding the visuals in our digital meetings.

Daily we face a barrage of negative framing and deficit thinking regarding immigrants in the media and within politics. Adichie (2009) believes, "stories have been used to dispossess and to malign. But stories can also be used to empower and to humanize. Stories can break the dignity of a people. But stories can also repair that broken dignity." We believe that together these three books present a counter story to the dominant and majoritarian story of Latinx immigrants. Our critical content analysis of visual images in the picturebooks shows immigrants with knowledge and agency; immigrants making strategic and intelligent decisions; immigrants collaborating with each other and using the resources that they can find as they journey to a new place. Their stories matter. Their lived experiences matter. They matter.

Final Reflections

CRT in education seeks to contest the dominant discourse on racism and race by examining the manner in which educational policy, theory, and practice are used to oppress certain racial and ethnic groups. Counter stories provide access to the experiences of students of color who have been marginalized in our schools and place these stories front and center. These three books provide a counter story to vitriol that has become widespread in the U.S.

During our visual analysis of *My Diary,* we became very aware of the presence of butterflies; they are found on all pages but one. We reached out to the illustrator, Maya Christina Gónzalez, and asked about this. She wrote:

> The butterflies are metaphysical conduits/symbols of spirit that travel beyond time and space to connect hearts. It is the visual/nonverbal vocabulary speaking to the connection between all things and the realm of spirit that we share. This keeps bringing in larger perspectives of being and knowing beyond the Western frame's. This is the embedding of another kind of knowing and communicating that is ours and cannot ultimately be touched by colonization, using the power and the magic available through illustration.
>
> *(Personal communication, January 10, 2018).*

Maya's notion of "embedding another kind of knowing and communicating" is precisely the idea that counter stories "serve as interpretive tools guiding what we listen to in other's stories" (Fernández, 2002, p. 50). Counter stories provide a context for understanding the sociopolitical environment in which Latinx children and families live and present their lived realities as sites of hope, honor, love, and agency. The counter stories guide readers to listen to the voices of those who are exploited and to respect their truth.

References

Adichie, C.N. (2009). The danger of a single story. TED Talk. https://www.ted.com/ta lks/chimamanda_adichie_the_danger_of_a_single_story?language=en

Bell, D.A. (1995) Who's afraid of critical race theory? *University of Illinois Law Review*, 95, 893–910.

Bodvarsson, O.B. & Van den Berg, H. (2009). Hispanic immigration to the United States. *Economics Department Faculty Publications*, 45.

Brooks, W.M. (2017). "Having something of their own": Passing on a counter-story about family bonds, racism, and land ownership. In H. Johnson, J. Mathis, & K.G. Short (Eds.), *Critical content analysis of children's and young adult literature: Reframing perspective.* New York: Routledge, pp. 77–91.

Brooks, W.M. (2009). An author as a counter-storyteller: Applying critical race theory to a Coretta Scott King Award Book. *Children's Literature in Education*, 40(1): 33–45.

Campano, G., Ghiso, M.P., & Welch, B.J. (2016). *Partnering with immigrant communities: action through literacy.* New York: Teachers College Press.

Davila, E.R. & de Bradley, A.A. (2010). Examining education for Latinas/os in Chicago: A CRT/LatCrit approach . *Journal of Educational Foundations*, 24(1/2), 39–58.

Delgado Bernal, D. (2002). Critical race theory, Latino critical theory, and critical raced-gendered epistemologies: Recognizing students of color as holders and creators of knowledge. *Qualitative Inquiry*, 8(1), 105–126.

Delgado, R. & Stefancic, J. (2012). *Critical race theory: An introduction.* New York: New York University Press.

Fernández, L. (2002). Telling stories about school: Using critical race and Latino critical theories to document Latina/Latino education and resistance. *Qualitative Inquiry*, 8(1), 45–65.

Franzak, J. (2003). Hopelessness and healing: Racial identity in young adult literature. *The New Advocate*, 16(1), 43–56.

Hughes-Hassell, S. (2013). Multicultural young adult literature as a form of counter-storytelling. *The Library Quarterly*, 83(3), 212–228.

Hughes-Hassell, S., Barkley, H.A., & Koehler, E. (2009). Promoting equity in children's literacy instruction: Using a Critical Race Theory framework to examine transitional books. *School Library Media Research*, 12.

López, G. & Bialik, K., (2017). Key findings about U.S. immigrants. Retrieved from Pew Research Center website: www.pewresearch.org/fact-tank/2017/05/03/key-findings-a bout-u-s-immigrants/http://pewrsr.ch/2qz2zvx

Lowery, R. (2001). Literature: Teaching children about diversity. *Children's Book and Media Review*, 22(5), 2.

McNair, J.C. (2008a). A comparative analysis of The Brownies' Book and contemporary African American children's literature written by Patricia C. McKissack. In W. Brooks and J. McNair (Eds.), *Embracing, evaluating and examining African American children's literature.* Lanham, MD: Scarecrow, 3–29.

McNair, J.C. (2008b). The representation of authors and illustrators of color in school-based book clubs. *Language Arts*, 65(3), 193–201.

McNair, J.C. (2008c). Innocent though they may seem … A critical race theory analysis of Firefly and Seesaw Scholastic book club order forms. *Multicultural Review*, 17(1), 24–29.

Moebius, W. (1986). Introduction to picture book codes. *Word and Image*, 2(2), 141–158.

Painter, C., Martin, J.R., & Unsworth, L. (2013). *Reading visual narratives: Image analysis of children's picturebooks.* Sheffield, UK: Equinox.

Serafini, F. (2014). *Reading the visual: An introduction to teaching multimodal literacy.* New York: Teachers College Press.

Solórzano, D.G. (1998). Critical race theory, race and gender microaggressions, and the experience of Chicana and Chicano scholars. *International Journal of Qualitative Studies in Education,* 11(1), 121–136.

Solórzano, D.G. (1997). Images and words that wound: Critical race theory, racial stereotyping, and teacher education. *Teacher Education Quarterly,* 24(3), 5–19.

Solórzano, D.G. & Yosso, T.J. (2002). Critical race methodology: Counter-storytelling as an analytical framework for education research. *Qualitative inquiry,* 8(1), 23–44.

Solórzano, D.G. & Delgado Bernal, D. (2001). Examining transformational resistance through a critical race and LatCrit theory framework: Chicana and Chicano students in an urban context. *Urban Education,* 36(3), 308–342.

Sung, Y.K., Fahrenbruck, M.L., & López-Robertson, J. (2017). Using intertextuality to unpack representations of immigration in children's literature. In H. Johnson, J. Mathis, & K. Short (Eds.), *Critical content analysis of children's and young adult literature: Reframing perspective.* New York: Routledge.

Tate IV, W.F. (1997). Critical race theory and education: History, theory, and implications. *Review of Research in Education,* 22(1), 195–247.

Tienda, M. & Sanchez, S. (2013). Latin American immigration to the United States. *Daedalus,* 142(3), 48–64.

Children's Literature References

Buitrago, J. & Yockteng, R. (2015). *Two White Rabbits.* Trans. by E. Amado. Toronto: Groundwood Books.

Draper, S. (1994). *Tears of tiger.* New York: Atheneum.

Fleischman, P. (1998). *Whirligig.* New York: H. Holt.

Pérez, A.I. (2002). *My diary from here to there: Mi diario de aquí hasta allá.* Illus. by M.C. González. New York: Lee and Low Books.

Taylor, M. (2001). *The land.* New York: Scholastic.

Tonatiuh, D. (2013). *Pancho Rabbit and the coyote.* New York: Abrams Books.

5

A VISUAL ANALYSIS THROUGH THE EYES OF AN APACHE

Angeline P. Hoffman

We talk to the Universe. The Universe speaks to us and taught us a language. We know it comes from a very special entity … from a sacred place. Language is a pathway into our Native Culture. It is that unique sound of our voice which identifies us and is particular to our own culture. Our words are beautiful. They convey our knowledge and messages to the future generations.

Angeline Hoffman (2011, p. 54)

Oral literature is integral to Indigenous culture; only in the last 30 years has literature written by Apaches for local people on the Fort Apache Reservation been available. Since the text and illustrations in books by Apache author/illustrators reflect cultural symbolism embedded in a deep knowledge of story, researchers need to draw from a rich knowledge base of experiences within Apache culture to thoughtfully interpret the books. Some of these books are Apache folktales, which are especially important in teaching about traditional dynamics of meaning-making within Apache life, including the significance of mythology, ecological awareness, family kinship, relationship, love, the need to honor family and all life, and visionary dimensions and spirituality. These teachings of cultural epistemology engage young children in taking part in the legacy and influences within their Indigenous communities.

In this chapter, my focus is on the illustrations in a picturebook by an Apache author/illustrator. I want to examine the cultural knowledge and symbolism embedded in the illustrations and the ways in which these images position readers relative to the characters. *Antelope Woman* (1992) was written and illustrated by Michael Lacapa, an author/illustrator who gained his inspiration from traditional storytellers, using his cultural roots and artistic training to develop imaginative stories filled with unique designs and patterns found in the basketry and pottery indigenous to the Southwest. I am interested in how the images in this Apache folktale position readers in relation to the characters, particularly through Indigenous symbols and their relation to teachings within Apache culture.

The Sociocultural Context of Oral Traditions

Oral literature can be defined as a body of literary works, with relatively standard features, which a people have disseminated and preserved for many generations through oral performance (Silko, 1981; Katanki, 2005). Myths, legends and ritual dramas, prayers, chants, and songs are all considered forms of oral literature. When a story is told by an Indigenous speaker to an Indigenous audience, Deloria (1970) says that the story comes to life through the shared history of audience and storyteller. Fitzgerald (2007) argues that these oral stories include the shared knowledge of tribal customs and are based in a geographical region as well as family and personal history (Basso, 1996). Cajete (1999) further states that the language of the storyteller adds dimensions to a story that writing cannot capture.

Shared history is the structure that builds understanding for hearers of these stories and directs them towards awareness of their own cultural perspectives. In Indigenous culture, the term "oral literature" did not originally exist. Only when European societies arrived with their emphasis on writing on paper did Indigenous stories come to be regarded as oral literature and later to become a written literature. Scholars support the cultural relevance of this literature, with Champagne (2001) noting that major themes include place-centered tribal worldviews and reverence for the power of the word. Cajete (2000) asserts that Words are sacred to a child as are kinship ties (to living and dead relatives, to supernatural beings, to celestial bodies, to animals and other spirits in nature) and belief in the importance of renewal.

In contemporary Indigenous settings and communities, storytelling plays an essential role in the revitalization and preservation of culture (Reese, 2007; Cajete, 2000; Smith, 1999; Deloria & Wildcat, 2001; Basso, 1970). To understand the place of oral tradition within Indigenous literature, oral literature must be recognized as playing a continuous role in people's lives. The weaving together of oral traditions with writing reveals the unique features and values of cultures across time and the significance of the narrative language as well as the language of the visible world. In particular, folktales are the cornerstone of Indigenous worldviews. Champagne (2001) notes that myth is sacred story, and even though the content of myth is fantastic—that is, beyond the realm of facts as we know it—people who hold their sacred stories see a deep, holistic truth.

It is important that cultural literature be studied because it educates the imagination and promotes cultural consciousness. Reese (2007) notes that we need to provide children with literature that expands their knowledge and authentically portrays Indigenous beliefs (p. 217).

Related Research

This study is informed by my previous research (Hoffman, 2011) on evaluating the authenticity of Indigenous literature and examining the responses of Apache children to Indigenous literature as well as to international Indigenous literature. Over several years I developed an evaluation tool to evaluate the authenticity of Indigenous children's literature based on two main resources (McCluskey, 1993; Slapin & Seale, 1998).

Only a few Indigenous researchers work in the field to examine Indigenous children's literature, and their studies are significant in informing this study (Reese & Caldwell-Wood, 1997; Mendoza & Reese, 2001; McCarty & Dick, 2003; Demmert & Towner, 2002; Costantino & Hurtado, 2002). In addition, AfricanAmerican researchers, such as Brooks (2006) and Sims Bishop (1992) have engaged in research that informs this study. as does the work of AsianAmerican researchers, such as Cai (1994) and Ching (2001). These studies involve researchers from a specific cultural community examining books from their culture. Researchers outside the culture being studied see through the window of literature into the culture but can only glimpse the life of a people and by no means see deeply into that culture.

Theoretical Frame of Decolonization

For thousands of years, millions of Indigenous people flourished in beautiful forests and Mother Earth provided food, clothing, shelter, and water. It was a world of paradise without pollution. The way of life of Indigenous cultures is complex and often misunderstood. Indigenous cultures are attuned to the natural universe rather than the artificial world of concrete cities, factories, highways, locks and keys, prisons, and insane asylums. Indigenous cultures lived in harmony with nature and all living things. They carry a deep knowledge of Mother Earth, the sky and water.

About 500 years ago, foreigners came and altered our way of life. Land was taken by force, the bountiful food sources were decimated and tragically many people were eradicated and enslaved. Supremacist colonial ideology and its ethnic cleansing of Indigenous people led to a dehumanized, devastated, and traumatized people (Smith, 1999). The cellular memory of trauma carries to succeeding generations, leading to detrimental social and physical problems such as mental illness, suicide, deviancy, and civilization diseases (poverty, diabetes, high blood pressure, heart disease, and alcoholism).

Linda Tuhiwai Smith (1999) writes from a Māori perspective about the catastrophic effects of colonialism. She reframes research on social problems resulting from colonialism through decolonization as a theoretical frame, arguing that Indigenous people need to develop their own effective initiatives for action to resolve these social issues. She argues that colonization and postcolonialism are terms that allow power to remain with imperialist oppressors who brutalized, terminated, and exploited other human beings for land and wealth. Their continuing lineage-based ways are untrustworthy in their research because they are the colonizers who belittled Indigenous ways of knowing. Smith argues that mainstream institutions are programmed along those precepts. Theoretically reframing critical theory around decolonization rather than postcolonialism is a deterrent for mainstream assimilation programs. Smith (2012) argues that decolonization is a process that challenges imperialism and colonialism at multiple levels as Indigenous people engage in their own projects and research to solve the problems of colonization. Postcolonial discourses have been defined in ways that leave out "Indigenous peoples, our ways of knowing, and our current concerns" (p. 24).

Smith (1999) believes that becoming aware of Western ideological research and attitudes toward colonized people leads Indigenous people to question the biases in research from Western perspectives. She argues that Indigenous people need to retrieve the stories of their cultures, languages, and social practices to develop their own approaches to research. This kind of reframing can thwart Western biases in solutions to Indigenous social issues. Indigenous people need to take control of the issues by defining and resolving problems through their vision and community involvement.

Michael Lacapa, the author/illustrator of the book examined in this research, was aware of the prevailing system's imposition of biased views. Although he faced many challenges, he took initiative and created unique stories about his Indigenous culture. He knew it was important for Indigenous people to carry on traditional deep knowledge of earth wisdom and the people. Certainly, the stories of children's lives are also part of this theory. His work fits with Smith's (1999) argument that Indigenous peoples need to be involved in "rewriting and righting our position in history" (p. 28). Lacapa is an example of her belief that Indigenous people want to "tell our own stories, write our own versions in our own ways, for our own purposes" (p. 28). He "wrote back" as a counter-narrative to the many versions of traditional tales written by white mainstream authors, while also writing for and to ourselves.

Research Methodology

My study is guided by the question: What are the ways in which Apache culture influences the visual symbolism of *Antelope Woman*? I address this question by analyzing the story content, tracking and comparing the descriptive attributions and relationships of characters/symbols, and by examining how readers of the story are positioned by the book's text and visual strategies relative to the characters/symbols.

Author and Text Selection

Michael Lacapa, an Indigenous Apache, lived on the Fort Apache Reservation through his childhood, graduating from Alchesay High School. He attended

Arizona State University, majoring in Art Education, and furthered his education by attending Northern Arizona University, getting his master's degree in Fine Arts. Michael had an interest in sketching Indigenous subjects as a youth and moved from sketching to painting. His paintings focused on ancient Indigenous symbols and concepts, and later moved to contemporary themes. Talented and creative, he combined traditional cultural art with modern Indigenous art in style and themes.

Gradually, Michael's passion moved from visual arts to storytelling. He was a people person, and storytelling drew people to his art work and books. Michael produced several children's picturebooks and received an international reputation as an artist, illustrator and storyteller.

Antelope Woman was one of the books he produced. He also produced picturebooks that included Western Apache folktales, Hopi folktales and other Indigenous traditional tales. He was an Apache, with Hopi and Tewa lineage, and was committed to research and affirmation of Indigenous epistemologies. He passed away due to injuries suffered in a car accident and so his work was cut short. Michael believed a good story moved the heart, and made the mind grow. He stated,

> All of us have one great story and it's up to us to share or do something with it. Stories may be a huge chronology. That's why when we read it, it makes such a great connection and awakens a story in us.

Antelope Woman is a beautifully illustrated Apache traditional story featuring a mysterious young man who comes to a village speaking of reverence for all things. A young Apache woman is mesmerized by his teaching and follows him one day as he leaves the village. She sees him go through four sacred wooden hoops and transform into an antelope. He beckons her to follow, and she does, spending time with his family in his world of the antelope. They return to the young woman's village and marry, but when she gives birth to twins, the people will not accept them because they consider twins to be a bad omen. The young family goes through the hoops to return to the young man's family because they will be accepted and their family honored. The story ends with the reminder that the Apache learned to honor all things great and small and to never hunt antelope but honor them because Antelope Woman and her children are among the herds and are part of Apaches.

My Positionality as a Researcher and Apache

My interest in understanding representations of Indigenous, particularly Apache, peoples in children's literature comes out of my experiences as an Indigenous Apache and my own epistemological positions. During my quest for books to meet the needs of children in schools on my reservation, I met with Michael Lacapa, a talented local artist also born on the Fort Apache Reservation in Whiteriver, Arizona, and read his books. He created authentic representations of Western

Apache in his children's books. Michael was an educator as well, working with school-age children on the reservation, and so I often interacted with him. The information included in this chapter about Michael is written from my personal knowledge of him.

I learned about storytelling from an Apache perspective and became aware of the complexities of cultural authenticity in my academic studies and research on Indigenous children's literature. Being an Apache, raised and schooled on the Fort Apache Indian Reservation, and through my awakening interest in my culture, I decided to pursue academic study. Reading Indigenous children's literature and analyzing representation of cultural authenticity, critical responses to literature, and reader response theories heightened my awareness of difficult issues. My studies prompted me to look at my role as an Indigenous researcher, educator and learner to seek more practical knowledge and identify challenges. Many issues of cultural misrepresentation, accuracy and authenticity are raised by Indigenous researchers and educators because so many of the children's books on Indigenous peoples are created by non-Indigenous authors and illustrators.

Storytelling is important. It is our own way of life and survival of that way of life for ourselves and future generations. Stories influence the way children think about themselves and their place in the world as well as the way in which they think about other cultural perspectives and learn to treat people with respect. This affirmation matters in the lives of Indigenous and non-Indigenous educators, children and adolescents.

The point of retelling our traditional stories is to teach about cultural identity, our origin, and the deep knowledge of our beliefs to formulate thoughts and determine their importance. Oral traditional teachings convey across generations all that we are and hope to be. The Apache people use oral narratives to teach children, particularly how our children should conduct themselves as Apache people, with dignity and respect for all things, especially their elders. In our culture, the elders are our teachers and professors; the knowledge they have gained throughout the course of lifetimes is important to pass on to the next generation.

Certainly, stories in children's literature featuring Indigenous books written by Indigenous authors are a powerful voice for equality. Lakota Sioux anthropologist Bea Medicine (1971) suggests that mainstream culture pays deference to the printed word and when Indigenous authors present their own history, there are sometimes allegations of bias or ethnocentrism. For many centuries our voices have not been heard. Now, our perception and voices are being expressed on paper through word and image to share stories about Indigenous people in ways that are significant, philosophical and practical. Story has kept us alive for thousands of years.

Data Analysis

My analysis is based on the visual analysis tools developed by Painter, Martin, and Unsworth (2013) from systemic-functional semiotics. The visual tools I used in this analysis were drawn from the metafunction of ideational meaning with a focus on three categories of meaning: participants, process and circumstances.

Picturebooks are accessible to young children because they offer visual representations along with linguistic signs. Children gradually learn to recognize the visual images of characters and environments in books because even realistic illustrations differ from the actual objects and many depictions in books bear little resemblance to the real world children know. Only as they engage in many experiences of connecting spoken words with visual images are they able to construct meaning from these images through interpreting the interplay of participants, actions, and circumstances (Painter et al., 2013).

The illustrated depiction of participants, settings, process of movement and their interplay between participants together create the ideational meaning in an illustration. For example, on page 38 of *Antelope Woman*, the faint image of the young woman is seen in the wavy lines of a multi-colored sky, while a herd of antelopes runs on the yellow plains below. The scene weaves together the young woman with the antelopes within a setting that combines a mystical background in the wavy blue/green lines of the sky with the solid yellow on which the antelopes run. The setting also continues a red jagged line from the previous page to indicate the pathway that the young family is following to return to the antelope family. The most visible movement on the page is the running of the antelope herd but further action is evident once the reader's eyes move to the faint image in the sky to make a connection to the act of transformation. The reader must put together all three categories of visual meaning to create an interpretation for the page. The meaning of a story is not found in the actual series of events but is illustrated in their symbolic value in constructing the narrative.

Ideational meaning has three categories of meaning according to Painter et al. (2013):

- *Participants* refers to the identities and attributes of the characters as portrayed in visual images. Children sometimes have difficulty understanding the meaning of illustrations, so many variables are used to help children figure out what is significant in an image. Visual images depict characters' emotions, appearances, and reappearances and the relations between them through spatial orientations in a scene to help readers recognize where to pay attention and what is important. Readers also need to track participants and their actions across multiple pages, including pages where they disappear and later reappear.

  a   In *Antelope Woman*, the age, gender and ethnicity of the participants as well as their role and place in the family are evident in the visual images. There are also transformations of participants as people become antelope and vice versa.

- *Process* refers to the portrayal of characters as engaged in specific actions. Characters usually are depicted within activities or narrative processes that move the story forward and keep readers engaged. Often this action is portrayed through diagonal lines in an image to indicate movement in a certain direction or through a series of successive images that unfold over time and pages. The action can be a single participant or one participant interacting with another or the thinking of a participant.

  a   In *Antelope Woman*, the characters often extend an arm or lean their bodies in a diagonal line to indicate action or to direct the readers' eyes to go in a certain direction. The primary strategy for relating one event to another across pages in this book are the zigzag lines and lines consisting of a series of triangular shapes across the bottoms of the pages. Many of the characters are depicted in stable, unmoving positions so these lines are what move the eyes forward, with the meanings of the lines embedded in Apache cultural traditions.

- *Circumstance* refers to the physical environment in which the participants interact. The background or setting of the scenery is used to explain the characters' interplay within a specific spatial environment. This background can be detailed so that the fictional world is accessible to the reader, or it can be white space when the focus is on the character, rather than the character's interactions in a setting.

  a   In *Antelope Woman*, the background context is not a detailed realistic depiction of the desert, but a symbolic depiction based in geometric shapes and colors whose meaning is deeply embedded in Apache culture. These shapes and colors depict a low dry desert terrain containing dry-hardy plants (yucca, agave, dry grass, cactus). This is Apache land.

Tracking Key Participants and Processes in the Illustrations

The four main characters are the elderly Apache man and his son and the young Apache woman and man. The first illustration shows an elderly Apache man telling a story to his son. The book then moves to long ago as his story begins. In this story, the second illustration shows a young Apache woman picking berries, followed by an illustration where she gathers firewood as young men try to get her attention. Then a mysterious young Apache man appears alone in an illustration. In the following three scenes, he teaches the village people while the young woman observes. When he leaves, the illustration shows her following him. The next scene is an antelope jumping through four hoops, followed by a later scene of a lone antelope after his shapeshifting, motioning for her to follow him. The next scene shows her transformation as the woman leaps with half of her lower human body in the big circular hoop and the other half of her emerging as an antelope. The next five antelope scenes depict both the young Apache man and woman in the shapeshift form of antelopes as they engage in activities such as a coyote chase and running with the herd, before they return through the hoops to transform as humans. Then three scenes show the mother greeting them as they seek permission to marry; the young woman's pregnancy; and the young couple's new twins; followed by the mystical scenery of antelopes running as a group with an image of the young Apache woman in the sky. The last scene is the elderly man (after finishing his story) walking away and the son kneeling, holding a feather to bless the hunting ground.

Symbolism through Culture

The significance of Indigenous culture is specific to each Indigenous nation. Littlebear (2000) argues that the way culture is viewed is significant for children's knowing and living within their Indigenous ways of life and knowledge. Aspects of this knowledge may be shared in relation to culture, practice and images (Hoffman, 2011) but are also as diverse as the location and the people. Furthermore, Smith (1999) argues that storytelling provides a focus for dialogue and conversation among Indigenous peoples—to ourselves and for ourselves. Such approaches fit with the oral traditions which are still a reality in day-to-day Indigenous lives.

Bradford (2007) discusses aesthetics and sociocultural values, arguing that a text operates as a site where meaning is negotiated by readers who bring their culture and language to the act of reading. In this analysis, I bring my cultural knowledge as an Apache woman to a visual analysis of *Antelope Woman*. I have selected three key illustrations from the book to examine the ways in which participants, process, and circumstances are portrayed in relation to Apache culture.

Storytelling as Knowledge

The first illustration of the book depicts an elderly father speaking to his son. Their relationship is made evident in the words, "Listen, my son."

Although the man and the son are not the only principal characters in the story, I selected this image to look at ideation because they represent contemporary Apache characters and so are more likely to resemble someone in the young reader's life. They serve the function of encouraging readers to make a connection and become interested in the book. The clothing and colorful setting is modern, with the close-up view of an Apache man sitting on a rock and the son kneeling on one knee, holding a rifle, listening (Figure 5.1). They are flanked by a tall yellow grass which has the appearance of an explosion of the rays of the sun. At their feet is a small blue jagged line that depicts a stream.

The participants set up a compare/contrast configuration as the father, wearing a cowboy hat, explains to the young son (before the hunt) about strange

FIGURE 5.1 Illustration of the Father as Storyteller to His Son (Lacapa, 1992)
Source: Antelope Woman, illustrated and authored by Michael Lacapa. Copyright ©
1995 Northland Publishing Company.

happenings long ago. The father and son are similar in size and shape and both
are at ground level, embedded in the landscape. The two characters are at eye
level and have no difficulty conversing with each other. At first glance, from a
non-Indigenous view, the son may appear to be ignoring the father; however
even though the son is looking the other way, he is listening. In the Apache Way
it is considered disrespectful to look at each other when conversing. There are no
physical barriers blocking the visual gaze to each other; they have chosen to not
engage in eye contact. They are connected to each other by the father's finger
pointing to the son and the son's careful turning of his face so that his ear connects to his father.

In terms of process, the illustration sets up the act of storytelling. The participants are not moving, they are stationary and stable in a resting stance as the son
listens to the father. Storytelling is an act in which the knowledge of the ancient
people is transferred by the father through an oral story. The knowledge he narrates is passed on to the son about the need to "honor all things great and small."
When the old man's story ends, the last scene in the book shows the elderly man
walking away from his son. The son is kneeling and blessing the ground with a
feather. This page conveys the father's message, the teaching from the story, and

so ends the storytelling process. In between these two illustrations, the rest of the book consists of the words and illustrations of the traditional story.

The circumstance/setting of the book depicts the dimensional perception as viewed by the illustrator. The writer visualizes and projects the environmental background—the scenic colors of the background of nature and its activity of life with the tall yellow grass and ambient elements swaying and expressing spiritual and ancient memories—through carefully selected colors to express the emotions of the moment. The setting is a symbolic representation, not a realistic representation as typically found in non-Indigenous books; for example, the stream is a zig-zag of turquoise. The color selection is purposeful with yellow, green and turquoise to reflect the desert setting.

This first page establishes the context for the story as an invitation for readers to enter along with the son. The father opens mystical dimensions of strange happenings of the days of old to his young son and reveals through storytelling the ancient characters who are the main characters for that story.

The Process of Transformation

The second illustration (pages 20–21) I selected is a double-page spread of the Antelope Woman changing into an antelope as she goes through four sacred hoops when she decides to follow the young man after watching him change into an antelope (Figure 5.2).

The ideational meaning of this illustration is the mysterious visual transformation of the human Apache woman into an antelope. The visual image shows the Apache woman diving into a single circular hoop, but the written story makes clear that she goes through four hoops. In the Apache world, four signifies the

FIGURE 5.2 Illustration of the Young Apache Woman Transforming into an Antelope (Lacapa, 1992)
Source: Antelope Woman, illustrated and authored by Michael Lacapa. Copyright © 1995 Northland Publishing Company.

four cardinal directions of the cosmos, starting at the center of the universe where life began. In traveling through the four hoops she shapeshifts into an animal. Hoops are circular rims about two or three feet in diameter that are used in ritual ceremonies.

This illustration depicts one moment in the process of transformation for the young woman. The illustration shows the lower half of her as a human and the top half as an antelope. Readers must follow the process in the illustration to realize that it is the same character emerging as an antelope from the fourth hoop. The transition from human being to an antelope is a dimensional change. The setting shifts over the two images, shifting from an outside view as she jumps into the hoops to the view at the other end as she exits as an antelope.

Another ideational meaning utilizing a semiotic device as a perspective is to represent dimensionality, which allows images to be viewed in a way that imitates the physical material reality it depicts. The ambient surrounding is evoked by the color choices of the yellowish background with speckles of multicolored small triangles, squares, and circles. The design of the hoop is circular with the inner part of the design colored yellow with turquoise designs in triangle patterns formed into a circle. Inside the circular hoop is a bolt of lightning that touches the woman as she jumps through the hoop. The four white eagle feathers on the hoop represent the four cardinal directions from the center point of the black vortex where creation began, where invisible power exists. Within Apache beliefs, that power is given to individuals for strength and endurance to overcome anything by moving lightly and swiftly like an eagle. The symbol of the lightning is the power element which creates life, and where the speed of transformation into an antelope is established. In Apache ways, there are four colors of lightning (black–east, blue/green–south, yellow/red–south, and white–north) symbolizing the four corners of the universe.

This visual image thus contains knowledge deeply contained within Apache teachings. Each element is not present just for aesthetic purposes as might be true in non-Indigenous books, but instead Lacapa's images reflect his deep knowledge of Apache traditions. The transformation of the Apache woman into an antelope occurs within images that reflect deep knowledge of the four sacred hoops and establishes the cause of that change within that knowledge. Apache women are brave. With courage, change becomes a reality.

Making a Decision to Honor Family

The third illustration (pages 36–37) that I selected is of the young woman with her husband and twin babies as they reflect on Apache people's rejection of their family and consider whether to return to his family (Figure 5.3). Within Apache culture at that time, twin births were unusual and considered a sign that the woman had in some way spiritually disconnected from the tribe.

FIGURE 5.3 Illustration of the Young Apache Family with Their Twins (Lacapa, 1992) *Source: Antelope Woman*, illustrated and authored by Michael Lacapa. Copyright © 1995 Northland Publishing Company.

In this image, the couple are in human form and have married, living in the village and eventually having twins, a boy and a girl of whom they are both proud. The village people do not accept the twins and so the couple must decide what to do, with the father suggesting they return to his people. The image shows the young mother and father with the babies in cradleboards. The couple appear to be sad. The man is patting the woman on the shoulder, as if consoling her. The woman is looking down and thinking about her relatives in comparison to her husband, children, and his family. Since Apaches are matrilocal, meaning that a new family resides with the wife's family or tribe, this decision is a difficult one that goes against tradition.

The visual representation of the young woman's thinking is displayed through the emotional red, including her red dress color and the red vertical arrowhead triangular design daggered into the ground to the left of her, which connects to the red horizontal lightning bolt below her and to the yellow color of the sunshine in the zig-zag design next to the man. The red color also represents the blood of her ancestors, the red clan of family, and the color direction of the west. The father is also thinking of the decision they must make. The image shows a sign for the decision through the rays of sunlight; the sun's breath provided a visual response with a red zig-zag pathway as a way home to the antelope family.

The green triangles below the family represent the pine trees on Apache land which are considered holy and represent life for the young couples and the babies. The Apache believe the sun and the pine tree are sacred. Both live in the world of the antelope which honors the family and all things, while the world of people rejects them.

The participants in the image are a complete family, connected as a family unit by the father's arm as they discuss their decision as a family. In the depiction, the family is in a setting of green and yellow plants. Some of the plants (tall grass) form into an unusual design motif that is culturally significant as the shape of the sun's rays. Underneath them, the ground is a red color design leading outward (a sign to leave) in a jagged design almost like lightning. This is a symbol of a path they must follow to return to the husband's family, who honors the family. Again, all of the colors and shapes are not decoration but significant in carrying meanings from an Apache perspective.

The cradleboards are an Apache design used for carrying and keeping a baby secure, with the bowed wooden cover slats over the baby's head to protect the baby should the cradleboard be dropped. The cradleboard is significant for mobility, but also symbolizes the need to protect future generations. This symbol of protection is then extended to the antelope at the end of the book. Since they were once our people, we do not hunt them. "We must honor them; all things great and small" are the instructions given by the father before his son goes on his hunt. This statement about honoring all around us refers not only to the antelope but to the twin babies.

Cultural Visual Style Increases Understandings of the Characters

The story is a folktale told through generation after generation of the people. Since Michael Lacapa is Apache, he visually positions the characters in the story relative to their circumstances and creates visual context that narrates important cultural aspects of the story. The book has visual elements in the illustration that are appropriate to the story being narrated.

The visual representations of the book's characters include accurate facial and body proportions, as seen from the three illustrations provided. The artist accurately represents Apache people through their clothing; men wearing cloth head bandanas, the calico camp dress of the woman, the men wearing breech cloth, the Apache moccasins, the wicki-up (dwelling), and the semi-arid terrestrial desert environment.

The combined visual elements, such as cultural symbols throughout each illustration, the colorful array of shapes around the characters, and the richness of the emotion in the characters, reinforce the story's deep knowledge of the ways in which Apache people are to act in the world. They also indicate the Apache/Antelope woman's special position within our culture and thinking. The transformation is not just that of the Apache woman into an antelope but the transformation of our

Apache Way of Life through how we learned that we must honor all things, no matter how small or how large.

In *Antelope Woman*, the content of each image shows key ideational choices by the illustrator. The story is full of images that portray characters and their appearances, the process of storytelling and transformation, and circumstances that create a culturally symbolic rather than realistic setting. The young Apache woman is a participant along with the young man, the men and women of the village, the young woman's mother, the twins, and the family of antelopes. In the story, the young woman engages in many actions that range from being an energetic worker who gathers wood and berries, to making strong baskets, to being a courageous explorer beyond her village life, and a co-creator of children. She is always the focus of each illustration. The dynamism in the images comes from the geometric motifs of the plants, mountains, rivers, the clothing, and the sky. In this way the natural world appears more beautiful, possessing the spirits of ancient memories and the invisible energy that exists in these memories that promote the learning of all things.

Final Reflections

In this research, I applied the decolonization theory of Linda Smith (1999) to argue that instead of using postcolonialism, Indigenous peoples are better served by reframing their thinking through decolonization. Decolonization gives agency to Indigenous people to take initiative to solve issues of oppression and colonization. In this case, I believe that Michael Lacapa is an example of an Indigenous author/illustrator asserting the right of Indigenous people to tell their own stories and to create visual images deeply embedded in the culture. This analysis provides a positive critique of how Lacapa offers a counter-narrative from white mainstream narratives of Indigenous peoples. My analysis reveals how this Indigenous author/illustrator was able to embed both deep and surface cultural knowledge throughout the illustrations.

Stories do matter in the lives of Indigenous peoples when they gather together to hear narratives told by the elders of the tribe. These stories convey information about the specific Indigenous culture of that community and about the origin and history of the people. They are also usually transmitted through that people's Indigenous language, which supports the maintenance of Indigenous identity. Embedded in these stories is the important knowledge that we, as Indigenous peoples from specific tribal cultures, must acquire to survive and conduct ourselves appropriately.

This deep knowledge explains knowledge through the eyes of an Apache and so allows for a different understanding of the embedded cultural meanings than would be evident to other researchers. This research brings the eyes of an Apache to this book to reveal the visual ideational meanings in this story. As an Indigenous researcher, this analysis reflects the significant values that were revealed through a close look at the illustrations as informed both by my cultural knowledge and visual analysis tools. Learning the ways of the Indigenous through visual ideational meaning is deep knowledge.

Reading is important in my life because it takes me on adventurous imaginary journeys into reality and creativity. The Apache picturebook *Antelope Woman* is brought to life by readers who attend to visual ideation to spark their attention and imagination and bring the text and illustration to life. This statement by one of our Indigenous elders tells why this kind of teaching must continue for our people:

> Let us boldly implement what our ancestors practiced and take the time to bring forth the knowledge, values and ceremonies, social and political institutions that is the spirit of every human child, no matter what child.
>
> *(Wilkins, 2010)*

In conclusion, the narrative content of story should be retold in every Indigenous classroom to stir old memories, discover traditional values, bring back to life the ancient past to reconnect with the power to live, restore passion for the earth, human beings, and other life forms, and provide understandings of life. Story thus encourages Indigenous perspectives and knowledge of cultural traditions and past stories. Linda Smith (1999) states that, for many Indigenous writers, stories are ways of passing down the beliefs and values of the culture in the hope that the new generation will treasure them and pass the story down further. The story and the storyteller both serve to connect the past with the future, one generation with the other, and the land with the people and the people with their own story. My hope is that my analysis encourages educators to provide authentic cultural stories from all cultural communities, told by authors, illustrators, and publishers from those communities.

References

Basso, K. (1996). *Wisdom sits in places: Landscape and language among the Western Apache* Albuquerque, NM: University of New Mexico Press.

Basso, K. (1970). *The Cibecue Apache*. Tucson: University of Arizona Press.

Bishop, R. (1996). *Collaborative research stories*, Palmerston, NC: Dunamore.

Bishop, R.S. (1992). Multicultural literature for children. In V.J. Harris (Ed.), *Teaching multicultural literature in grades K- 8* (pp. 203–241). Norwood, MA: Christopher Gordon.

Bradford, C. (2007). *Unsettling narratives: Postcolonial readings of children's literature*. Ontario: Wilfred Laurier University Press.

Brooks, W. (2006). Reading representations of themselves: Urban youth use culture and African American textual features to develop literary understanding. *Reading Research Quarterly*, 41(4), 374–393.

Bruchac, J. (1997). *Tell me a tale*. San Diego, CA: Harcourt.

Cai, M. & Bishop, R.S. (1994) Multicultural literature for children. In A.H. Dyson & C. Genshi (Eds.), *The need for story: Cultural diversity in classroom and community* (pp. 57–71). Urbana, IL: National Council of Teachers of English.

Cajete, G. (1994). *Look to the mountain: An ecology of Indigenous education.* Skyland, NC: Kivaki' Press.

Cajete, G. (1999). *Igniting the spark: An Indigenous science education model.* Skyland, NC: Kivaki' Press.

Cajete, G. (2000). *Native science.* Santa Fe, NM: Clear Light.

Champagne, D. (2001). *The Native North American Almanac.* Farmington Hills, MI: Gale.

Ching, S. (2005) Multicultural children's literature as an instrument of power. *Language Art,* 83(2), 128–136.

Costantino, M. & Hurtado, D. (2002). *Reading and the Native American Learner: Research report.* Seattle, WA: Evergreen State College.

Deloria, V. (1970), *We talk, you listen: New tribes, new turf.* Lincoln: University of Nebraska Press.

Deloria, V. (1997). *Indians and anthropologists: Vine Deloria Jr. and the critique of Anthropology.* Tucson: University of Arizona Press.

Deloria, V. (1999). *Spirit and reason.* Golden, CO: Fulcrum.

Deloria, V. & Wildcat, D.R. (2002). *Power and place: Indian education in America.* Golden, CO: Fulcrum.

Demmert, Jr., W.G. & Towner, J.C. (2003). *A review of the research literature on the influence of Culturally Based Education on the academic performance of Native American students.* Portland, OR: Northwest Regional Educational Laboratory.

Eagle Man, E.M. (1995). *Native wisdom: Perceptions of the natural way.* Minneapolis: Four Directions Publishing.

Farrer, C. (1991). *Living life's circle: Mescalero Apache cosmovision.* Albuquerque: University of New Mexico Press.

Fitzgerald, M. (2007). *The essential Charles Eastman (Ohiyesa): Light on the Indian world.* Bloomington, IN: World Wisdom.

Hoffman, A. (2011). *Stories that matter: Native American fifth graders' responses to culturally authentic text.* Tucson: University of Arizona Press.

Katanki, A. (2005). *Learning to write "Indian": The boarding-school experience and American Indian literature.* Norman: University of Oklahoma Press.

Littlebear, R. (2000). To save our languages, we must change our teaching methods. *Tribal College Journal of American Higher Education,* 11(3), 18–20.

McCarty, T.L. & Dick, G.S. (2003) Telling the people's stories: Literacy practices and processes in Navajo Community School. In A. Willis (Ed.), *Multicultural issues in literacy research and practice* (pp. 105–122). Mahwah, NJ: Erlbaum.

McCluskey, M. (1993). *Evaluating Native American textbooks and other materials for the classroom.* Helena: Montana Office of Public Instruction.

Medicine, B. (1971). The anthropologist as the Indian's image-maker. *The American reader in anthropology.* San Francisco: Indian Historian Press.

Mendoza, J. & Reese, D. (2001) *Examining multicultural picture books for the early childhood classroom. ECRP* 3(2). Urbana, IL: University of Illinois.

Nikolajeva, M. (2005). *Aesthetic approaches to children's literature.* Lanham, MD: Scarecrow.

Painter, C., Martin, J.R., & Unsworth, L. (2013). *Reading visual narratives: Image analysis of children's picture books.* Sheffield, UK: Equinox.

Peat, F.D. (2002). *Blackfoot physics: A journey into the Native American universe*. Grand Rapids, MI: Phanes Press.

Reese, D. (2007). Proceed with caution: Using Native American folktales in the classroom. *Language Arts*, 84(3), 245–256.

Reese, D. (2008). Native voices. *School Library Journal*, 54(11), 61–62.

Reese, D. & Caldwell-Wood, N. (1997) Native Americans in children's literature. In V. Harris (Ed.), *Using multiethnic literature in the K-8 classroom* (pp.155–193). Norwood, MA: Christopher-Gordon.

Silko, L.M. (1981). *Storyteller*. New York: Arcade Books.

Slapin, B. & Seale, Doris (1998). *Through Indian eyes: The Native experience in books for children*. Los Angeles: University of California Press.

Smith, L.T. (1999). *Decolonizing methodologies: Research and indigenous peoples*. New York: Zed Books.

Smith, L.T. (2012). *Decolonizing methodologies: Research and Indigenous people*. London: Zed Books.

Stockel, H. (1991). *Women of Apache nation: Voices of truth*. Reno: University of Nevada Press.

Wilkins, D. (2010). www.Finestquotes.com

Woodson, J. (2003). Who can tell my story? In D.L. Fox & K.G. Short (Eds.), *Stories matter: The complexity of cultural authenticity in children's literature* (pp. 41–45). Urbana, IL: National Council of Teachers of English.

Children's Literature References

Lacapa, M. (1992) *Antelope Woman*. Taylor, AZ: Storyteller Publishing House.

6

DEVELOPING AGENCY AND SOCIALIZATION THROUGH INTERPRETIVE PLAY

Janelle Mathis

Perceptions and expectations of childhood have varied over generations and eras. Earlier centuries found young individuals, who would today be considered children, in positions of work, marriage, and raising families. Childhood as defined today is socially constructed and conceptualized, and the role children play in society is most often considered a less important role than that of the adults around them. Recently educators have acknowledged that children need to develop the ability to take a critical stance and become contributors to their local, national and global communities.

As one who strives to teach to a critical stance and promote agency in learners of all ages, I question conceptions of childhood in light of issues of who has power, whose voice matters, and whose perspectives are considered. I believe perceptions of the needs of today's child affect how educators and parents support the development of a strong identity as reflected in a sense of agency. As adults realize the potential of children to interact and take part in social situations, they develop attitudes that value and place significance on this period of life. In particular, my own focus on the role of play in childhood has opened new venues for my thinking about setting the contexts for play in keeping with Vygotsky (1987). Vygotsky's theories are key to building understandings of child play as purposeful, identity building, and aligned with the sociocultural context in which the child lives.

Closely aligned with purposeful play is the role of story and ultimately children's literature. Hearing, seeing, adapting and enacting story is often a response to literature children share with supportive parents, teachers, and care givers. The role of story, especially seen in the imagination and creativity of interpretive play, has the potential to inform the development of identity and agency in young children. For the purposes here, I consider agency as "the strategic making and remaking of selves, identities, relationships, activities, cultural tools and resources and history as embedded within relations of power" (Lewis, Enciso, & Moje, 2007, p. 5). Added to this, Sanchez-Eppler (2005) describes children as "participants in the making of social meaning" (xv). My own focus on agency as demonstrated in children's literature (Mathis, 2016) points to the significance of literature in providing demonstrations of agency development and, thus, propelled me to seek other such demonstrations of agency in literature especially created for young children—literature where the emphasis is on illustration to tell the story.

Evidence of agency can be difficult to locate, however, often because it is challenging to interpret. One source of this challenge is the ongoing dialogue among scholars of children's literature and childhood studies regarding agency. The notion that children function solely as passive recipients of culture is challenged by scholars such as Sanchez-Eppler (2005) who regards "children not merely as objects of socialization but also as 'individuals inhabiting and negotiating' societal conceptions of what it means to be a child" (p. xv). Gubar (2016) brings to the forefront that children are not independent actors since they are dependent on adults for early survival and care but are capable of defining their own terms and grounds of power and meaning. Thus, Gubar argues for a middle course in considering agency through a kinship model. Nodelman (2008) discusses children as colonized in an effort to explain how children are often regarded as lesser citizens in society. This notion is questioned by some in that children do come into society in a state of dependency and adults are ethically required to provide guidance and parameters (Gubar, 2016).

Children's literature offers images of children in a variety of realistic and imaginary situations. In looking at literature through the metaphor of mirrors and windows (Bishop, 1990), the images mirrored are hopefully ones that enhance the potential for children to develop their identity and agency through a variety of means. Such images are those that demonstrate a sense of value for the role of children in everyday life and acknowledge the potential of children's actions to enhance their sense of self. Children's literature offers young children numerous opportunities to interpret, improvise, and pretend. Their involvement in story includes creating their own stories as well as engaging in dramatic play that reveals their use of themes, characters, and ideas from literature. Imagination becomes a way for children to develop their own reality and take a critical stance on the world around them. Therefore, books that portray children engaging in play at the intersection of imagination, culture, and reality offer to all readers a powerful perspective on the significance of play.

In seeking books for young readers that reflect agentic children engaged in imaginative situations, I identified *Niño Wrestles the World* by Yuyi Morales (2013) in which illustration is the predominant method of storytelling. This analysis focuses on the visual telling of the story of a young boy who is playing a *luchador* in *lucha libre*. In Mexico, these wrestlers dress "in character" to represent well-known folklore figures, and the match that ensues is as full of story as strength. The young boy in Morales's story is engaged in wrestling imaginary supernatural opponents, and Niño wins each contest, not with physical strength but with child-created tactics, only to discover he has yet to face the most difficult challenge of all—his younger twin sisters. Of course, being quite creative, he decides the best way to do this is to get them on his side in his role of *luchador*. Sparse text, consisting of many onomatopoetic expressions, relies on the vivid images of Morales to reveal a child negotiating his identity at the intersection of imagination and reality within his cultural context. Interpretive reproduction, a child's reproduction of the adult culture, involves the negotiation of the ideologies and realities of Niño's world with that of his imaginary world as he also reveals an awareness of socialization.

Luche Libre

Yuyi Morales offers information about the tradition of *luche libre* at the conclusion of *Niño Wrestles the World*. She describes it as theatrical, an action-packed form of wrestling that consists of bright masks reflecting heroes, villains, animals, and other traditional characters. Further insight into its history goes back to the 1900s when Mexico was in a revolution and people sought diversions from the conflict. Two Italian businessmen began endorsing fights to entertain called *Lucha Libre*, "free fights" more violent than organized wrestling today. In 1929 Salvador Lutteroth González became interested in the sport of wrestling as he worked in the US and took the sport back to Mexico. In the 1940s the first wrestler used a mask to develop his unique personality and afterwards masks became popular and added to the mystery and identities of those involved. Today Mexico City is home to the 16,000 seat arena that houses the Consejo Mundial de Lucha Libre, the longest running active professional wrestling promotion company in the world (Cocking, 2016). Lucha Libre's popularity is not without opposition, however, as some believe the gambling accompanying it creates financial problems for individuals and families.

Theoretical Frame

> Texts and theory are performative: they do something, and therefore incur important ethical responsibilities. These ethical responsibilities are not narrowly conceived in terms of moral content and values (or lack of them) advanced by texts. Rather, they are concerned with larger issues of truth, representation, and being (selfhood, identity, subjectivity).
>
> *(Mallen and Bradford, 2011, p. 9)*

In agreement with these scholars, I examine the potential of children's literature, in particular *Niño Wrestles the World*, to demonstrate the development of child agency through interpretive reproduction that draws from culture, social constructs, and imagination. Interpretive reproduction is the belief that childhood socialization is not linear but reproductive in that children contribute to the reproduction of the adult culture through both the children's interactions with adults and their creation of cultures with other children (Corsaro, 1993). The focus draws from Vygotskian sociocultural theory as it applies to identity and play. "Play is also the medium of mastery, indeed of creation, of ourselves as human actors. Without the capacity to formulate other social scenes in imagination, there can be little force to a sense of self, little agency" (Holland et al., 1998, p. 236).

The varied perspectives on the agency of children lead naturally to considering the critical lens of childism as a way of identifying and disrupting the stereotypes of childhood. Pierce and Allen (1975) say that childism is the automatic presumption of superiority of any adult over any child; it results in the adult's needs, desires, hopes, and fears taking unquestioned precedence over those of the child. In more recent times, it is most often associated with micro-aggressions that lower a child's "self-esteem, dignity, and worthiness by means of subtle, cumulative, and unceasing adult deprecation" (p. 18). Such attitudes diminish adult perspectives of the significance of play. In 2012, Young-Bruehl brought attention to childism in seeking a term to incite scholars and researchers to focus their studies on how "prejudice is built into the very way children are imagined" (p. 5). In using this frame for critical analysis, Short (2017) states that a theoretical frame of childism "provides insights into the ways in which children are discriminated against by adults, particularly in assumptions about children's reasoning abilities and rights and their development of agency" (p. 138).

Although it is important to acknowledge the source of "anti-child prejudice and oppression," there is also value in identifying what nurtures agency in children (Wall, 2013, p. 71). By considering the theoretical frame of childism, I explore the potential of literature to present a counter model of childhood that promotes and values children's contributions. Such a model represents an antithesis of, and resistance to, childism. Thus, the counter tenets of power and agency, disruption of childhood stereotypes, and child decision making are key lenses in this analysis along with the Vygotskian notion of the embodiment of imagination through play.

Also, as with any reader/text response, I conduct this inquiry in keeping with Rosenblatt's (1938) transactional theory. This visual analysis is based on the transaction between myself as the researcher and the text. The meaning resides within the multiple reading events throughout the analysis, and the transactions experienced by other readers may produce different responses. Not all readers will experience *Niño Wrestles the World* in a similar way, such as those with negative perceptions regarding the sport of *lucha libre*.

Methodology

As a university educator focused on the role of children's literature to inform and transform, I took on the challenge of addressing critical literacy, multimodality as a valid and significant way to communicate, and the development of agency as seen within characters and contexts of literature (Mathis, 2016). As I became more involved with global literature and those who create it, I realized the many ways that agency was portrayed and enacted across the global community and how this can inform readers about the strength and complexity of their global neighbors—insights far beyond media portrayal. Thus, books such as *Niño Wrestles the World* came to the forefront of my attention in my own reading and instruction. Not only did this book offer much in terms of the agency of this young boy, but it also invited me to explore the cultural and social aspects of the story. In this story, as Niño imaginatively becomes a *luchedor*, he reveals his awareness of this cultural sport and the characters who could possibly be opponents. He draws upon his knowledge of these characters to create appropriate ways to defeat them. Each approach, while child-like in its nature, gives him control of the challenge in non-violent or non-threatening ways, including his approach to the challenge his young sisters bring to Niño, *el luchedor*. My choice of this book was also determined by the similarity of family dynamics and interpretive play I had observed with younger members of my own family—both in response to the illustrations of this book and to other titles (Mathis, 2015).

My research question became: How does interpretive play influence agency and cultural representations in *Niño Wrestles the World*? With very limited text, the illustrations of Morales are key in answering this question. Therefore, critical content analysis of visual images is the key methodological framework used in this inquiry. Albers, Vasquez, and Harste (2011) say that "visual analysts are concerned with studying the systems of meaning that underpin the visual marks." To examine these particular structures, I turn to the work of Painter, Martin, and Unsworth (2013), who remind readers that the visual images are significant in creating the relationships established between a child and a book and to support the child as s/he negotiates meaning from the printed text. This insight can be extended to include the role of the visual images to also distinguish the "voice" of the characters within the book as part of this relationship.

Of the three meaning-making functions found in systemic-functional semiotics that Painter et al. (2013) state exist simultaneously in all texts, the interpersonal metafunction provides insight into my identified critical stance of children. This metafunction considers the relationships between the reader and writer, as well as between reader and character or between characters, and attitudes and stances created through the illustrations. From this metafunction I chose the analytical tools of focalization, affect, pathos, and ambiance. These tools are described further within the examples of analysis findings. Additionally, social semiotics serves as a tool to support the visual analysis. Social semiotics is a form of semiotics that studies how we use music, art, language, and dance among other systems to communicate and represent. It focuses on how people use sign systems within particular historical and cultural social settings (van Leeuwen, 2005).

My analysis began with reading and rereading both the sparse text and vivid images with attention to sociocultural notions of play and its significance in identity development. With simple intuitive codes of identity, agency, power, culture, tradition, imaginary play, enactment/embodiment, and family, I repeatedly examined the images. Then, using the various tools of the metafunction system, each image was described in terms of what the tools of focalization, affect, pathos, and ambiance offered in light of these codes. Some descriptions were repetitive as Niño was consistently portrayed throughout; however, different contexts that related a complexity of his personality offered instances of identity building and agency development.

Findings from Visual Analysis

At the intersections of culture, imagination and play, insights emerged that point to identity and agency and that inform both adult and child readers. As depicted in Figure 6.1, the elements of interpretive play (imagination, story, and creativity) interact reciprocally and continuously with the realities of Niño's young life (family, traditions, social ideologies, and physical toys), to reveal insights to Niño's identity. Agency development is put into motion and manifested through power,

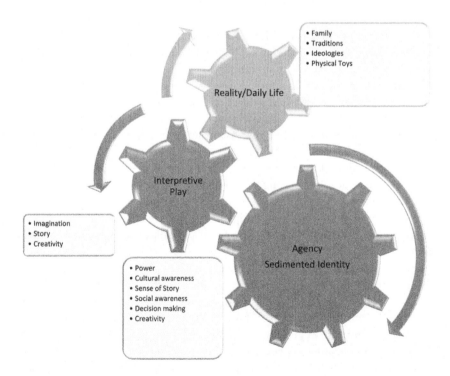

FIGURE 6.1 Identity/Agency Gear

cultural awareness, social awareness, decision making, creativity, and the power of story. This ongoing transmission of force and motion is evident in the illustrations and in a critical content analysis through the theoretical lens of a counter-narrative to childism. The analysis is based in elements of agency as Niño creates and recreates his identity through strategic and empowering relationships using cultural resources. Added to this is Sanchez-Eppler's (2005) notion of children participating in making social meaning (xv). This discussion of findings of the critical content analysis is organized around the strategies and tools of interpretive play that contribute to Niño's agency as revealed in the illustrations.

Self Perceptions of Power

A reader's first view of Niño is on the book's cover where he is strategically placed upon a winner's ribbon, encircled by stars, with rays extending from behind him in yellow and gold (see Figure 6.2). Positioned boldly with outstretched arms, he is wearing his *luchedor* mask, underwear, and shoes. His gaze at the reader/viewer is pleasant with a slight smile that indicates his personal pleasure, but it also demands the viewer's respect for the empowered child. The focalization is that of mediated direct contact that situates Niño looking directly at the reader as if presenting himself to viewers as a self-confident boy who is ready to demonstrate his abilities in his role of *luchedor*. The use of a generic style of character provides an effect that Painter et al. (2013) say resembles an "every man" and invites the child reader to stand in the character's shoes. Such pathos, they say, "expects the child reader to see themselves in the protagonist's role" (p. 33) and in the case of Niño, this role is one of empowerment as he faces the world.

The cover reflects the book's ambiance through full saturation in the use of colors. The vibrancy of this color choice supports the energy and excitement that occurs throughout the story, indicative of the empowering activities of Niño. The use of warm colors throughout begins with a focus on gold and orange hues, indicative of less familiarity as might be true of the make-believe world of play. However, as the story proceeds and Niño brings the make-believe into his reality, more warm colors appear, increasing a sense of the familiar.

The story begins with a child playing alone amidst a floor of toys, one of which is a toy stage for *lucha libre*. He glances aside as he hears his mother calling him but his attention is drawn to a mask on his floor. He appears to purposefully make the choice to be a *luchedor* at this time, despite the continuous calls of "Niño" from outside the room where he is playing. The next page finds him donning the mask, removing his clothes except his underwear while shouts of "Niño! Niño!" scatter the page. The next page reveals a full-length image of Niño, similar to the cover. He sets the stage in these first pages for a mediated relationship between reader and character, thus implying power over the reader. As the story continues, the focalization moves to an unmediated scenario, since Niño is exerting power over the various contestants while the reader is observing

FIGURE 6.2 Cover of *Niño Wrestles the World*
Source: From *Niño Wrestles the World* © 2013 by Yuyi Morales. Reprinted by permission of Roaring Brook Press, a division of Holtzbrinck Publishing Holdings Limited Partnership. All Rights Reserved.

the conflict and relationship between Niño and the various characters. He returns to a mediated focalization, looking directly at the reader again, indicative of his continuing power after he has conquered his rivals.

Cultural Awareness as a Strategy

Niño's knowledge of *lucha libra* is the first evidence the reader has that this child is aware of traditional cultural events. In this case it is one typically based on traditional folk characters and legends. Both his specific awareness of the *lucha libra* event and his insight into the stories behind the characters who participate are evident through the imaginary characters he tackles. Figure 6.3 is organized with successive images of Niño and one of the contests Niño has with a folklore character, the Guanajuato Mummy. Niño's extensive knowledge of these cultural figures is obvious as he realizes the story behind each and uses this in devising a plan to defeat the character.

Within *Niño Wrestles the World*, Niño makes evident the interactions he has experienced around cultural events, even having his own mask for play. Holland et al. (1998) suggest the significance of play as they describe how play creates social boundaries that are passed on to others in the process of learning about the cultural world. "The mastery we gain over our play is mastery over our imagination" (p. 236).

Story as a Tool for Thinking

The significance of story cuts across all ages beginning with very young children.

> Our views of the world are a web of interconnected stories, a distillation of all the stories we have shared. We connect to these interconnected past stories in order to understand new experiences (Rosen, 1986). This web of stories becomes our interpretive lens for new experiences so that story is our means of constructing the world—of world making.
>
> *(Short, 2012, p. 10)*

Niño defeats the Guanajuato Mummy with the Tickle Tackle!

FIGURE 6.3 Niño Tackling the Guanajuato Mummy (Morales, 2013)
Source: From *Niño Wrestles the World* © 2013 by Yuyi Morales. Reprinted by permission of Roaring Brook Press, a division of Holtzbrinck Publishing Holdings Limited Partnership. All Rights Reserved.

The visual aspects of this book provide evidence of Niño's developing sense of cultural story through the interpersonal systems revealed in the illustrations. As Niño creates his personal story of being a *lucha libre*, the illustrations reveal his awareness of the stories of each character that he brings to his own narrative. He can imagine these creatures as contestants, indicating his awareness that they exist in the world of oral stories. As he approaches each challenge before him, his actions are shown across the pages in a narrative format, indicative of an episodic story that he is creating as he plays. The stories found in the various cultures and retold become the fabric within which strands of identity and agency—personal, social, and cultural—become interwoven as the child not only enters the story but uses these stories to tell others of his own making. In a like manner, books like *Niño Wrestles the World* can potentially add to the weave of identity for young readers.

Decision Making as Empowerment

The folk-based opponents are introduced on the end pages of the book and as each new figure appears within the story, Niño makes decisions as to how to conquer him or her. As a decision maker, Niño shows autonomy and creativity in his choice of strategies, such as the Tickle Tackle, the Puzzle Muzzle move, Doll Decoy, Marble Mash, and the Popsicle Slick. His well-considered approaches reflect the use of brain over brawn, and in each case his decision is made and implemented without hesitation as the images reveal Niño taking immediate intentional action. And, of course, Niño is the victor in each contest, although not without physical dexterity, as shown in the images as he combats each challenger.

Awareness of Social Expectations

The connections to cultural ideologies through traditional stories and cultural social expectations are shared events that become internalized as the child tries on these cultural notions. Within the images that reflect Niño's knowledge of the cultural world, viewers also see evidence of his awareness of the social world of his existence. Each confrontation reveals a non-violent plan to maintain power and each image reveals Niño accepting the challengers in a positive way. Additionally, Niño is seen grouped with the various previous contestants when the most significant opposition approaches—his twin sisters. An image prior to the appearance of the sisters shows Niño staring at the clock as it strikes the end of nap time—the "dreadful" hour. This two-page spread gives a whole page to the striking clock on the left and Niño is positioned staring at it on the facing page with an expression of alarm. This is the only time he reveals this expression, but it is at a point when his social reality interrupts the imaginary world where he is in control. This static image of Niño gives readers a chance to pause and realize the significance of this particular time of day for the boy.

When the sisters appear, the illustration reflects his awe of these challengers as he stands aligned with the previously conquered creatures and looks upward at the twins. He never appears disrespectful of them due to their age or size; he realizes they bring significant impact to the context he has created. As he enters into this most difficult challenge, the series of images depicting the various stages of their struggle reflect his acceptance of this challenge. Through moves and holds visually depicted with bodily contact, hints of smiles, and evidence of a quick wit to decide the next strategy, Niño retains his agency during this struggle (see Figure 6.4).

"If you can't defeat them, join them!" is the text accompanying a picture of Niño in his signature confident pose, this time with a sister at each hand and a glance at the reader that reveals direct eye contact in this mediated focalization. Niño's social awareness includes a sense of the power of collaboration, and the reader just might be drawn in by the pathos that seemingly aligns these siblings as they hurry away and leave the text on a scooter. The reader is reassured that Niño is in control as the reigning *luchador*.

Creativity in Negotiating the World

New Literacy Studies redefine play as a set of imaginative practices that change the meanings of ordinary artifacts and alter opportunities for social participation. Wohlwend (2013) states that critical sociocultural perspectives on literacy interpret creativity as a collaborative cultural production. Such acts of creative play are

FIGURE 6.4 Niño and Las Hermanitas (Morales, 2013)
Source: From *Niño Wrestles the World* © 2013 by Yuyi Morales. Reprinted by permission of Roaring Brook Press, a division of Holtzbrinck Publishing Holdings Limited Partnership. All Rights Reserved.

the beginnings of adapting and adopting culture as they invite imagining with others to create and agree on what it means to be and belong to a particular group. Each image reveals Niño confidently engaging in energetic encounters depicted on unbound pages that indicate the endless possibilities of his imagination. As Niño wrestles the world, he creatively negotiates the complexity of his imaginary world, his cultural world, and his reality. Readers are invited through illustrative techniques to enter his "figured cultural world" (Holland et al., 1998) and cheer for Niño.

Final Reflections

I believe in the role of art to invite and encourage learners to see differently, aesthetically, emotionally, parsimoniously (Harste, 2014). This belief is supported by the often cited definition of a picturebook by Bader (1976) that speaks of its total design of text and images, its importance as a social and cultural document, and an experience for children. She extols its limitless possibilities as an art form that depends on both pictures and words and "the drama of the turning page" (p. 1). Add to this rich description the unique, unpredictable response of a child through interpretive play and the possibilities are limitless for engagements that enrich identity and position children as agents of their own imagination and learning. Books such as *Niño Wrestles the World* offer unique opportunities to negotiate meaning through the energy on each page and the illustrative techniques. The multimodal experience with Niño, so well described through illustration, affords children the opportunity to live through Niño's growing identity and agency. Experiencing Niño's world through multimodal means invites children to access books, experience narrative, and explore their own imaginative interpretations. Yuyi Morales skillfully employs artistic signs to engage readers in experiencing Niño's sense of identity and agency. Such invitations value the role of interpretive play in both Niño's world and the actual world of the child.

In closing, I am left with high expectations of the potential of literature for young readers, as well as questions that point to considerations about how such literature is used to best demonstrate the agency of Niño and nurture agency in young children. Obviously, agency, this empowering sense of self, comes from a complexity of sociocultural aspects of the world that together render each person's perceptions about self and role in society. So, while story or literature can play a strategic role for young learners, how its reading is contextualized is a determinant as to whether such agency is realized or enhanced, particularly whether children have an opportunity to enact, interact, and improvise around the stories they hear and see around them. Also, availability of resources for engagements that inform as well as extend a child's imagination is important in providing opportunities to entertain differently constructed worlds.

These opportunities and resources are dependent on adult perceptions of interpretive play as highly regarded or, as seen from a childism stance, inferior actions that do not respect children's reasoning abilities and agency. Such stories as *Niño Wrestles the World* reflect universal traits of childhood and can add significance to the role of interpretive play in agency development. Identity is contextualized within many sociocultural factors. Story is a powerful resource in creating individuals who can imaginatively meet life's challenges with a strong sense of their place in our global community.

References

Albers, P. (2014). Visual discourse analysis. In P. Albers, T. Holbrook, & A.S. Flint (Eds.), *New methods of literacy research* (pp. 85–97). New York: Routledge.

Albers, P., Vasquez, V., & Harste, J.C. (2011). Making visual analysis critical. In D. Lapp and D. Fisher (Eds.), *Handbook of research on teaching the English language arts*. 3rd ed. Retrieved from https://search.credoreference.com/content/title/routengart?institutio nId=4982&tab=contents

Bader, B. (1976). *American picturebooks from Noah's ark to the beast within*. New York: Macmillan.

Bishop, R.S. (1990). Mirrors, windows, and sliding glass doors. *Perspectives: Choosing and Using Books for the Classroom*, 6(3), ix–xi.

Cocking, L. (2016). The Lucha Libre: A brief history of Mexican wrestling. Retrieved from https://theculturetrip.com/north-america/mexico/articles/the-lucha-libre-a-brief-history-of-mexican-wrestling/

Corsaro, W. (1993). Interpretive reproduction in children's role play. *Childhood*, 1(2), 64–74.

Gubar, M. (2016). The hermeneutics of recuperation: What a kinship-model approach to children's agency could do for children's literature and childhood studies. *Jeunesse: Young People, Texts, Cultures*, 8(1), 291–310.

Harste, J. (2014). The art of learning to be critically literate. *Language Arts*, 92(2), 90–102.

Holland, D., Lachicotte, W., Jr., Skinner, D., & Cain, C. (1998). *Identity and agency in cultural worlds*. Cambridge, MA: Harvard University Press.

Lewis, C., Enciso, P., & Moje, E., (2007). *Reframing sociocultural research on literacy: Identity, agency, and power*. Mahwah, NJ: Lawrence Erlbaum.

Mallen, K. & Bradford, C. (2011). Introduction: Bringing back theory. In K. Mallen and C. Bradford (Eds.), *Contemporary children's literature and film* (pp. 1–11). New York: Palgrave Macmillan.

Mathis, J. (2015). Demonstrations of agency in contemporary international children's literature: A critical content analysis across personal, social, and cultural dimensions. *Literacy Research and Instruction*, 54(3), 206–230.

Mathis, J. (2016). Literature and the young child: Engagement, enactment, and agency from a sociocultural perspective. *Journal of Research in Childhood Education*, 30(4), 618–629.

Nodleman, P. (2008). *The hidden adult: Defining children's literature*. Baltimore, MD: Johns Hopkins University Press.

Painter, C., Martin, J., and Unsworth, L. (2013). *Reading visual narratives*. London: Equinox.

Pierce, C.M. & Allen, G.B. (1975). Childism. *Psychiatric Annals*, 5(7), 15–24.

Rosenblatt, L. (1938/1995). *Literature as exploration* (5th ed.). Chicago: Modern Language Association.

Sanchez-Eppler, K. (2005). *Dependent states: The child's part in nineteenth-century American culture*. Chicago: University of Chicago Press.

Short, K. (2012). Story as world making. *Language Arts*, 90(1), 9–17.

Short, K. (2017). The right to participate: Children as activists in picturebooks. In H. Johnson, J. Mathis, & K. Short (Eds.), *Critical content analysis of children's and young adult literature: Reframing perspective* (pp. 137–154). New York: Routledge.

Van Leeuwen, T. (2005). *Introducing social semiotics*. New York: Routledge.

Vygotsky, L. (1987). Imagination and its development in childhood. In *The collected works of L. S. Vygotsky, vol. 1: Problems of general psychology*. Trans. Norris Minick (pp. 339–349). New York: Plenum.

Wall, J. (2013). Childism: The challenge of childhood to ethics and the humanities. In A. M. Duane (Ed.), *The children's table* (pp. 68–84). Athens, GA: University of Georgia Press.

Wohlwend, K. (2013). *Literacy playshop: New literacies, popular media, and play in the early childhood classroom*. New York: Teachers College Press.

Young-Bruehl, E. (2012). *Childism: Confronting prejudice against children*. New Haven, CT: Yale University Press.

Children's Literature References

Morales, Y. (2013). *Niño wrestles the world*. New York: Roaring Brook Press.

PART III

Visual Images and Positioning

7

THE POWER OF A GAZE

Inviting Entrée into the World of a Picturebook while Positioning a Lived Reality

Holly Johnson

Young people learn about the world through direct observation, sociocultural acquisition and lived experience, along with picturebooks. It is through illustrations that readers encounter codifications (Freire, 1993) of the world, both real and imaginary, thus facilitating understandings of both verbal/narrative language as well as the language of the material world. Studying picturebook illustrations allows readers to recognize the power of images and how those images may position them as readers, as emotional beings, and as consumers of the word and the world (Freire & Macedo, 1987).

In this chapter, I discuss the power of illustrations, particularly the power of a character's direct gaze, to position readers emotionally and cognitively. I utilize three years of USBBY's Outstanding International Books. This list was created in response to U.S. publishers bringing so few books from other countries to the U.S. and USBBY's intention to establish an award list to encourage more interest and market for these books. As a member of the OIB Committee during 2015–2017, I was especially interested in the books selected during those years for consumption by American readers. What were we inviting U.S. readers to know and feel? And what actions had we afforded our targeted readership by our selections?

Purpose of the Research

Painter, Martin, and Unsworth (2013) assert that a character's gaze has the power to "invite" readers into the world of the text. I selected USBBY's Outstanding International Books specifically because of my own indirect complicity in compiling a corpus of books for American readers that represent "knowing" from around the world. The question that guided my research was:

- In what ways are readers positioned through character gaze in picturebook illustrations?

With this question, I was able to determine the types of situations or experiences that contain a character gaze, and those that do not, and examine the ways a character's gaze or lack thereof invites or distances readers from the situations or experiences.

Theoretical Frames

To address my question, I selected several theories with a focus on a critical lens. Reading across theories, I discovered four theories that pertained to my work and selected tenets from these lenses: (1) the concept of codification, (2) positioning theory from marketing studies, (3) critical discourse analysis, and (4) gaze theory.

Paulo Freire (1993) proposed the concept of codification as a way for the oppressed to objectify their life circumstances so as to make sense of the situations that limit their "practices of freedom," a concept aligned with Foucault's (1990) critical analysis of the world. Codifications can be oral tellings, sketches, or even photographs of objects that serve as mediating devices for critical analysis. In this study, illustrations served as codifications through which reader-viewers transact when learning about the author's and/or illustrator's concepts of the world. May (1995) asserts that "all authors consider the sort of impact they hope to have on their audiences and pick the appropriate voice" (p. 64). In this study, I suggest that illustrators may have similar intentions, and thus the focal points of my analysis (with written text for context). The tenet utilized in respect to codification was:

- Authors and illustrators position consumers of picturebooks in ways similar to an ideal reader, who is positioned as the type of reader-viewer with whom the author primarily communicates.

Illustrations codify particular ways of knowing, being, or acting in the world. It is the codification and context of a character's "gaze" that served as my primary focus of analysis. Through the codified gaze, readers are positioned.

Positioning theory states that the dynamic between two identities/people in relation to each other is a social interaction (Davies & Harré, 1990). It has also been used to explain the strategic use of communication to position products for consumption (Krolökke, 2009). When applied in tandem, positioning theory includes both products and consumers. Van Langenhove and Harré (1994) assert, "one can position oneself or be positioned as ... powerful or powerless, confident or apologetic, dominant or submissive, definite or tentative and so on" (p. 363). I applied the following tenet from positioning theory for my research:

- Reader-viewers, as consumers, are positioned by what they view/consume.

In respect to my study, reader positioning relates to film studies, particularly the concepts of audience, viewer, and spectatorship (Sturken & Cartwright, 2009). With picturebooks, authors and illustrators conceive of an ideal reader-viewer for their work (Nikolajeva, 2005). In film studies, "lookers" fall within the audience–viewer–spectator continuum depending on who has been idealized in respect to the work presented. According to Sturken and Cartwright, audiences are a collection of lookers, while a viewer is an individual. Spectatorship addresses *the envelopment* of a hypothetical viewer. When considering picturebook production, audiences are the mass market that may purchase books, while viewers are individual readers, and spectators are those who get lost in the world of the text. Both viewers and spectators are relationally positioned by what they view. Spectatorship is the *created discursive relationship* of what is viewed, by whom, and how presented for consumption and response. It is distinguished from an observer stance by the distance created between the viewed and the viewer. Observers are not enveloped within the illustration, but stand outside it. Picturebook illustrations of lived experiences or metaphors of human activity serve as "the viewed" in this study.

To better elucidate this difference, I think of those who attend a baseball game. There are those who are deeply engaged with the play-by-play action, participating fully with what they are viewing and perhaps even with what they see and hear from other fans. Then there are those who attend games or view them on the television, but remain distanced from the actions on the field. Those who are enveloped in the action are spectators, while those remaining distant still watch the game, but are positioned as observers.

To specifically address a character's gaze, I consulted gaze theory. Gaze theory applies to the concept and power of a subjective and/or objective gaze, and is often present at the intersection of feminism, film studies, and postcolonialism. The gaze, which means to look intently or deliberately at something, has come to mean an intention, a dynamic bridging of at least two entities. I used the image of the direct gaze, which involves a character looking out of the frame at readers. Foucault (1963) asserted that within a gaze not only is the object of knowledge constructed but also the knower. Direct gaze applies not only to the illustrated gaze of what is seen/examined and interpreted, but also the reader-viewer who is simultaneously positioned by that illustrated gaze. In essence, a relationship is built between the reader-viewer and the illustration. It is important to understand that a gaze is not something someone has or owns, but is a relationship between the subject and the object of the gaze, thus its connection to positioning theory.

Addressing the use of the direct gaze as proposed by Painter et al. (2013), a character's direct gaze has the power to invite a reader into the situation presented in a picturebook. As such, a reader is positioned as both subject who reads/gazes as well as object positioned into a particular role. Foucault (1990) conceptualized that even within a gaze, the object of the gaze still has "practices of freedom" to resist the position in which one may find oneself. The tenets of gaze theory I utilized were:

- A gaze, regardless of origin (i.e. a person, a painting, a film character, a picturebook illustration) positions both that which is seen as well as the one viewing.
- Power created by the gaze can be accepted or resisted within practices of freedom.

As to methodology, I utilized critical visual discourse analysis, particularly the works of Lacan (1991) and Foucault (1963), which intersect at the concept of reading as a social practice involving language, power, and multimodal literacies. Aspects of discourse as theorized by Jacques Lacan (1991) explore forms of discursive power. Lacan theorized four discourses in which people or institutions engage. I was especially interested in his "master" discourse and the "university" discourse, both of which address issues of power. Master discourse addresses the dialectic between "the master" and "the subject." Since my study focused on the element of a gaze, I was intrigued by how a gaze establishes a relationship of power between the reader-viewer and an object. When a character gazes back at a reader-viewer, where does power reside? Who is the master and who is the subject if the gaze has the power to position a reader-viewer?

The "university" discourse addresses the concept of knowledge as neutral rather than constructed. Frequently, a text is considered neutral and the reader is expected to acquire knowledge without addressing how the text may be positioning the reader. The gaze has power to position, and knowledge is never neutral, which aligns with Foucault's (1963) concept of how discourse, which is replete with power, works as a positioning agent. Power is a central tenet of any critical discourse analysis, and thus I utilized the following tenet:

- Power is an element between subject and object within a discursive positioning relationship.

While I employed these theories and tenets, reader response theory (Rosenblatt, 1995) fits strongly within any negotiation of meaning in a text, regardless of its format, and aligns with the practices of freedoms theorized by Foucault (1990). Thus, viewers of illustrations can oppose their positioning by those visuals and "read/gaze" in alternative ways. I further acknowledge that while I have analyzed the books within this study, it is with a reflexivity that embraces the limitations of that analysis and meaning-making due to my own political positioning and sociocultural values.

Connecting to Relevant Literature

As a way to embed this study, I found several studies that addressed the analysis of visuals, but note there is a dearth of analysis of picturebook illustration through a critical lens. Other disciplines, however, have conducted analysis of visuals, including film studies (Andrew, 1984; Stam, 2000), marketing studies (Adeyanju, 2016), and art studies with the beginning of the study of the painting *Olympia* by Édouard Manet. It is from the work in film and art studies that the element of the gaze became a visual device to study and interrogate, which has been done extensively (Mulvey, 1975; hooks, 2010; Said, 1978) and remains a contested aspect of critical studies across disciplines.

In literacy studies, visual analysis has been conducted with digital texts, reader-viewers, and materials production (Pahl & Rowsell, 2006; Rowsell & Kendrick; 2013; Siegel & Panofsky, 2009). Studies have also been conducted about reader-viewers interpreting illustrations (Arizpe & Styles, 2003; Kachorsky, Moses, Serafini, & Hoelting, 2017; Panteleo, 2017). Many theories, including social semiotics, have been utilized in these studies; however, the use of gaze theory has not as yet been conducted in respect to reader-viewer response or the analysis of picturebooks.

As for positioning readers emotionally, Nikolajeva (2013–14) asserts that even as an illustration presents no physical danger to a viewer, "the brain still responds to the image as if it were real" (p. 250). She further noted that facial expression is the most salient way of representing emotions, which ties to my interest in the use of a gaze to position reader-viewers. Painter et al. (2013) have done extensive analysis of picturebook illustrations, and I closely consulted their work.

Methodology

To address the role of the character gaze within picturebooks, I employed the theoretical tenets along with a critical content analysis of visual images within 59 picturebooks included in the USBBY's Outstanding International Books lists between 2015 and 2017. A critical methodology woven from Lacan's (1991) and Foucault's concepts of power, knowledge, and discourse fits the study of picturebook illustrations and how reader-viewers could or would be positioned by the power of a character's gaze. It is the social modality of a picturebook illustration—an image—that is interrogated for its strategies of persuasion. Similar to how verbal language and word selection is used to position a reader, illustrations and particular facial expressions in a picturebook can be scrutinized for their effects on reader-viewers.

As a member of the USBBY OIB Committees from 2015 to 2017, I was part of a nine-person group made up of an equal number of librarians and educators with a chairperson from either group. Typically, the group is represented in respect to race/ethnicity and gender. I am a teacher-educator, who identifies as European American and female. For the last year of my participation I served as chair of the committee.

Book Selection and Criteria

Of the 125 books on the USBBY 2015–2017 honor lists (comprised of books published between 2014 and 2016), 82 books contained illustrations spanning media from drawings to collage. The first criterion I used to determine the sample for my study, however, was that *illustrations were equal or more dominant than verbal text*. I thus removed books that had illustrations, but in which the verbal text was the dominant form of communication. I also removed books that employed photography as an illustration style as they were not discussed as an illustration style within the Painter et al. (2013) guidelines I utilized. The second criterion addressed *a narrative or storyline*. I subsequently removed several books that were more conceptual than narrative. I also removed poetry books that contained several poems, but kept poetry books that contained a sense of narrative. The third criterion addressed the *size of the illustrations*. I wanted renderings large enough to analyze a character's gaze, and thus removed texts with illustrations too small for clear analysis. Twenty-three books were deselected; totaling 59 books for analysis.

Process of Analysis

I closely scrutinized the 59 books for a "direct gaze." Twenty-six books did not contain a gaze while 33 books contained at least one character's direct gaze. I then worked with each of these two text sets separately so as to address my question about the types of situations or experiences into which readers are invited (positioned as Spectators) or held in abeyance (positioned as Observers).

Each of the text sets contained at least two books from each of the three illustration types as identified by Painter et al. (2013) because of the facial characteristics described within each type that connects to the concept of a gaze's invitation. Illustration types fall within a *continuum* between minimalistic to generic to naturalistic. Minimalistic renderings lack the individuation of more detailed illustration types, and are considered more social commentary with a written narrative often told in third person. Generic illustrations move into more detailed expression in the face, especially around the mouth. This allows for more behavioral interpretation while also positioning readers to "see themselves" in the characters through a commonality stance—an "every person" sensibility with the injunction to behave in similar ways to the characters. Finally, naturalistic illustrations are the most nuanced and detailed, with elements that produce the most realistic portraiture, and readers are able to make greater inferences in respect to character emotion. Readers are positioned to engage with characters on a more individual and sympathetic level.

I addressed the set of books with no character gaze and then worked with the books that contained a gaze. (See References for the books that are included under each category.) I then divided each set by the three illustration types, and explored the content of books that fell under illustration type. Sturken and Cartwright (2009) note that context is necessary in the produced meaning of images. Spitz (2000) asserts that no single illustration can be interpreted outside the entire text and its illustrations. Thus, the verbal contents of those texts cannot be ignored, and it is within the context of the whole text that I was able to make meaning from individual gazes as well as discuss topics that are "distanced" from readers due to a lack of a gaze. This is where my own subjectivity in the analysis came into play. While I utilized the summaries of each of the books as determined by the USBBY committee and printed in articles about each year's honor list (Dales, 2015; Hong, 2016; Johnson, 2017), I still re-read each book to determine a theme/topic for each book.

Once I determined a theme/topic for each book, I did a cross-analysis of the books within each illustration type to construct common themes of narrative content. I then conducted a final check to ensure the books fit the theme/topic where I placed them. Several books overlapped across several themes, but by adjusting the title of each theme, I felt that the categories constructed appropriately reflected the themes of the narratives as well as the theoretical tenets that guided my study. I tentatively selected an overriding topic for each illustration type, and most have several themes under that topic. The results are in Table 7.1.

Because of the length of my analysis, I have included only a brief discussion of the Observer Text Set, concentrating on the Spectator Text Set for this chapter. I utilize the concept of "Spectator" for the text set containing a direct gaze because of the discursive positioning relationship created between reader-viewer and character by the gaze. As noted earlier, spectators are enveloped within a film (similar to the concept of being lost in a book).

TABLE 7.1 Overall Categories and Topics

Text Set One: Observer (No Gaze)	*Text Set Two: Spectator (Direct Gaze)*
Minimalistic: Imparting Cultural Mores (17 books)	**Minimalistic**: Developing Agency (16 books)
• Connection to the natural world is expected (5 books). • Perseverance reaps rewarding experiences (4 books). • Deception or oppression is eventually overcome (3 books) • Appreciation of our support networks is customary (5 books).	• Agency requires action (4 books). • Agency requires speaking out (3 books). • Agency requires knowledge (9 books).
	Generic: Acquiring Relationship (10 books)
Generic: Sharing Common Experiences (7 books)	• Remembering creates relationship (3 books). • Relationship involves giving back (4 books). • Relationships make life easier (3 books).
• Violence is something all experience (2 books). • Compassion bridges differences (2 books). • Information connects people (3 books).	**Naturalistic**: Acknowledging (In) Humanity (7 books)
Naturalistic: Addressing Apprehension (2 books)	• The Holocaust erased reciprocal humanity (2 books). • Questioning the unknown increases humanity's development (2 books). • Cooperation escalates humanity (3 books).
• Fear grows in our imaginings.	

As my research question did not directly address gender or number of gazes, while interesting, these aspects of analysis are not primary to this chapter. When relevant, however, I address placement of gaze within the text. I list the books in their particular text set at the end of this chapter, thus do not include author or year when discussing each of the books.

Themes of the Gaze or Lack Thereof

Both text sets—Observer and Spectator—have points of interest in respect to how they might position a reader. According to Painter et al. (2013), readers are positioned as "invited" or "distanced" by a character's gaze or lack thereof. Spectators are enveloped within the viewing of a picturebook by a character's gaze. With the lack of a character gaze there is no invitation, and thus, reader-viewers are held in abeyance from the world within the text. They remain Observers. In essence, Observers are an audience, but not positioned with the agency or the sense of engagement of an enveloped Spectator.

The Lack of a Gaze Produces Distance

Twenty-six picturebooks lacking a gaze fell under eight themes/topics. Four of the themes involved minimalistic illustrations, three categories generic, and one naturalistic. Due to copyright restrictions, I do not use any illustration examples in my discussion of books that contain no gaze because my central focus was on illustrations portraying a gaze.

Minimalistic Illustrations Impart Cultural Mores

Minimalistic illustrations function as social commentary or as a device for learning literary devices, and the world. The 17 picturebooks with minimal illustrations I labeled with the umbrella term, "Imparting Cultural Mores." Since the books contained no direct gaze, the four themes primarily address ways the narratives position readers to observe the illustrated situations and relationships as learning devices.

Connection to the Natural World Is Expected

Five books showcase a relationship between a human and animal character. *I Am a Bear* directly utilizes symbolism, a tenet of minimalistic illustrations. High-lighting the plight of a homeless bear with illustrations containing no gaze from the bear or any other character within the book invites readers to distance themselves from homelessness. Yet, through the character of a young girl who ignores her father's admonishment to "stay away" from the bear, humans should not fear those who are homeless. The lack of a gaze, however, positions readers to understand that homelessness is an aspect of the world to be acknowledged, but when thinking critically about how discourse works, readers do not need to "interfere" with the roots of homelessness.

Perseverance Reaps Rewarding Experiences

Three books have human characters that position readers to learn about the rewards of moving beyond the known. All inspire readers to persevere, which is a common human activity that allows individuals and the community to progress. And while readers are inspired to persevere, they are not compelled to act, but rather are shown how people do so.

Deception or Oppression Is Eventually Overcome

As with many minimalist illustrations, all three of these books use humor as a way to teach or position readers to learn about cultural ways of knowing. Each allows readers to observe the silly situations within the narratives in which valuable "lessons" play out. Readers can laugh at the stories, but the underlying theme positions readers, though distanced from political activity, to consider how deception is never long lasting.

Appreciation of Our Support Networks Is Customary

When considered as a text set, these six books all portray characters that appreciate others, language difference, friends, those who help alleviate problems, and even material goods and the history of those materials. *Why Dogs Have Wet Noses* falls into the tradition of a pourquoi tale that delights readers, but also points out the loyalty of dogs and their patience with humans. This social commentary, when viewed critically, suggests animals are there for human commodity or disposal. Readers are positioned to rethink what they are (or should be) thankful for, as well as in what ways humans "use" animals and material goods.

Generic Illustrations Sharing Common Experiences

Seven books contain generic illustrations that position readers as common participants in the realm of human experience who often share the same types of experiences as those portrayed in picturebooks. Yet, without a gaze, readers remain detached observers.

Violence Is Something All Experience

Two books portray the violence of bullying or outcome of violence from war. *Once a Shepherd* and *Red* present illustrations that position readers as members of the universal experience of violence albeit on different levels. On the surface, and because they lack a character gaze, these might be considered just sad situations, but if viewed with a critical lens, they position readers to consider how people continue to harm one another, reminding them that they are not so distant from violence and its outcome.

Compassion Bridges Differences

Two books, *Hurry Up, Henry* and *Two White Rabbits*, present situations that could position the "every person" reader to consider the characters through a more compassionate, "that-could-be-me" manner. Because no gaze or eye contact invites readers to experience vicariously the discomfort of the situations in these books, readers are positioned to observe, and perhaps dismiss, the real world phenomena within the narratives.

Information Connects People

The three informational texts include ways of gardening, the biography of a famous writer, and the story of a rambunctious little dog. They position readers as distance learners who connect to the observed protagonists by noting the connection to either everyday activities or stories that connect people to others in the world.

Naturalistic Illustrations Addressing Apprehension

Two books address apprehension with a sense that fear grows as a result of our imaginings. *Mr. Squirrel and the Moon* and *Night Guard* contain narratives where the protagonists are apprehensive or fearful because of the situation in which they find themselves. The discursive positioning in *Mr. Squirrel* may seem like a silly tale about a squirrel who believes a round of cheese that fell onto his tree branch is the moon, yet it is the fear of jail that makes this book so interesting. From an observer's position, the concept of punishment underlies the plotline and drives the squirrel's actions. Readers are not "invited" into the situation, but the potential of punishment lingers.

The Gaze Invites and Empowers

According to Painter et al. (2013), a character's gaze invites readers to a much different positioning than the lack of a gaze. Invited into the narrative or situation, readers move from the role of indistinct audience to that of spectators, who are enveloped into the visual encounters. As with the text set containing no gaze, the text set of 33 books with a direct gaze were separated by illustration type and then themes within them.

Minimalistic Illustrations to Develop Agency (16 Books)

Minimalistic illustrations affording a sense of agency through the gaze invite readers to consume the social commentary depicted in the narratives, and to engage in agentic behaviors as a result of that consumption.

Agency Requires Action

Three books invite readers to act. *Sidewalk Flowers, Like a Wolf*, and *The Girl with a Parrot on Her Head* address acts of kindness requiring characters to move outside what is expected. The gaze, however, while direct, may involve the character from whom kindness is sought. In *Like a Wolf*, the wolf gazes directly at the reader. Left in a shelter, a dog that looks "just like a wolf" is not dangerous, but is perceived as such. When a young shepherd sees beyond the wolf's exterior and adopts the dog, readers discover the dog is a gentle and wonderful shepherding dog. Through the gaze, readers are invited to act in similar ways: to see beyond, to act kindly, and to make a difference in the world. In essence, the gaze suggests, "you, too, can see and act."

Agency Requires Speaking Out

Three books invite readers to discuss, speak out, to let their voices, and different ways of being and thinking, be heard. The direct gaze of a character brings readers into the narrative, the situation that positions readers to feel the emotions and acknowledge that difference should be embraced. In *The Pros and Cons of Being a Frog*, two children become friends in spite of their differences and the way they know and understand the world (see Figure 7.1). The embrace between the friends at the end of the book is an invitation to know that one will be "embraced" for being just who they are. When read critically, it is interesting that there is no direct gaze until the final illustration. Readers are positioned to observe and think about the social implications of differences, and that it is through choice that we embrace those differences. All three books position readers as thoughtful judges who have the agency to ponder and then acknowledge that differences are acceptable and appreciated.

Agency Is Motivated by Knowledge

A large number of books invite readers to develop knowledge, as agency first requires a knowledge base. In essence, people with knowledge can act. The nine books include informational texts as well as humorous texts, with several that include both elements. Five humorous books position readers to observe the action, and then join in the thinking about how to treat others or recognize the concept of "self" that involves both the physical and the philosophical. In *I Am*

FIGURE 7.1 *The Pros and Cons of Being a Frog* (deGennaro, 2016)

Henry Finch, one bird among all the other birds comes to recognize his own sense of self and that he has agency. The illustrations of finch bodies, appropriately consisting of human fingerprints, speak to the individual self and what one finch (sic) can do. By knowing their limits, abilities, and need for others, readers are challenged to consider these possibilities for themselves. By using humorous illustrations, young people are encouraged to consider serious issues without fear.

The other four books address more serious issues and do not utilize humor to tell their stories. Readers, who are assumed to be young people from the United States (by the committee who selected the books for U.S. consumption), are positioned to learn about/invited into situations of other young people who are more overtly from situations outside their knowledge-base. Situations that involve family separation, either by choice or political circumstance, or movement across wide cultural divides, are topics covered. They are informational texts, either true stories or real circumstances, such as *The Journey* that "others" experience in "other" places. When read critically, these books position readers to acknowledge the invitation to know the characters/people, but the minimalistic renderings disrupt further empathizing. There is a strong sense of "othering" in these books that may position readers through the gaze to feel superior rather than empathetic. While these books involve universal experiences, the gaze positions readers to indulge the young characters (and perhaps themselves) in a type of superiority when read critically.

Generic Illustrations on Acquiring Relationship (10 Books)

Generic illustrations give readers a sense of an "every person," thus allowing characters and readers to see each other as connected by their humanity as well as having the ability to behave, ponder, and respond in similar ways given similar circumstances.

Remembering Creates Relationship

Three books address the importance of remembering in connection to knowing. Two of the books involve family relationships, while the third, *Imagine a City*, highlights the importance of connecting to a literary heritage. The gaze in each places readers into the narrative with differing results. Generic illustrations suggest an "every person" connection, and while this works with *Imagine a City* when read critically, the heritage is only Western and typically white. The gaze in *Not My Girl* is about the pain experienced by the young Inuit protagonist who left the reservation to go to boarding school and, upon return, is initially not "recognized" by her mother. This recognition is cultural, not physical, and thus when read critically, the pain may or may not be recognized by the reader-spectator.

Relationship Involves Giving Back

Four narratives address the concept of reciprocity. Two books are based on true stories out of Africa, the others fictional. All utilize a direct gaze in instances that produce anxiety. While readers are invited to think about ways they, too, might give back, when read critically, there is no "labor of love" in giving back, but rather suffering, anxiety, and punishment. This is especially noticeable in *Gon, the Fox*, a Japanese tale about a mischievous fox that steals fish from a villager and then discovers that the villager's mother died. Gon feels terrible for stealing and attempts to make amends for his wrongdoing by stealing from other villagers to help the first victim. Through the direct gaze, readers are invited into Gon's shame for stealing and his vow to make amends. Ironically, Gon is shot while making amends. The gaze invites action while the result of that action ends in tragedy. When thinking critically about this narrative, the difference in cultures needs to be addressed to fully engage the narrative.

Relationships Make Life Easier

Three books address a variety of emotions and life situations often difficult for young people. Two involve disruptions in life situations when the characters move across geographical distances, while *Rules of Summer* presents the relationship of brothers. All three books, while ultimately containing positive themes and endings, include points of pain. It is at these points that readers are invited by a direct gaze to feel the pain, anger, or alienation the characters are experiencing. The gaze disrupts the reader's position as bystander. Figure 7.2 is an example of an illustrated emotion from *Arto's Big Move*.

Naturalistic Illustrations for Acknowledging (In)Humanity (7 Books)

Naturalistic illustrations give readers a sense of the characters represented as individuals, and in many ways, the singular. There is no person uniquely like another person, and that singularity presents the character or the character's situation as one to recognize, to acknowledge, and often, to empathize and embrace.

The Holocaust Erased Reciprocal Humanity

Two books address the inhumanity that took place during the European Holocaust of World War II. Both contain multiple instances of a direct gaze at times that are especially dangerous or alienating. Readers are invited to witness the inhumanity within a particular situation. In *Lindbergh: The Tale of a Flying Mouse*, the illustrations authentically create a metaphor of the Holocaust while the written text could be read as just a "cat and mouse" story. The dark images give voice to the terror of the Jews who did not make it out of Germany before the Nazis began their "cat and mouse" searches and eventual persecution of those who had hoped to remain in their homeland. Readers are positioned as the mouse and the gazes in the images represent the source of the mouse's terror (see Figure 7.3). The discourse of terror is visited upon readers who go beyond witnessing to experiencing.

Questioning the Unknown Increases Humanity's Development

Two books address the concept of the unknown and the human need to explore it. Both forefront individual quests into the unknown. At the beginning of each narrative, readers are invited to join the journey and accept the reasons for the

FIGURE 7.2 Arto's Emotion (Arnaldo, 2014)

Source: From *Arto's Big Move*, used by permission of Owlkids Books, Toronto. Text and illustration © 2014 Monica Arnaldo.

quest. *Anna's Heaven* is about the death of a parent, and Anna gazes out to the reader while on a swing, positioning her upside down. Readers are thus invited to a world that is not-right-side-up, and the confusion, questioning, and emotional displacement that accompanies such a positioning.

Cooperation Escalates Humanity

Three books address ways in which people interact in connection with nature or with each other. Connection requires a sense of working together for the

FIGURE 7.3 Hunting Gaze in *Lindbergh* (Kuhlmann, 2014)
Source: From *Lindbergh: The Tale of a Flying Mouse* by Torben Kuhlmann. © NordSüd.
Used with permission.

best of humanity and perhaps for the natural world to be created. In *Greenling*, the harvest is represented by a green baby who is found by a farmer and his wife. While the greenling is present, the harvest blooms and there is enough for everyone. Once the greenling leaves, the harvest is over. Through the gaze of the greenling itself, readers are invited to recognize that through taking care of nature, nature will take care of them. The other two books address how working together—to harvest a last apple before winter, and to understand how migrants make their way across borders—might afford sharing in the good life.

Discussion of Power in a Character's Gaze

As Spitz (2000) notes, "Even when they are not intended to do so, picture books provide children with some of their earliest takes on morality, taste, and basic cultural knowledge, including messages about gender, race, and class" (p. 14). And as bell hooks (2010) notes, "there is power in looking" (p. 94). When considering the potential of a character's gaze to invite or envelop a reader, exploring reader positioning becomes essential. Juxtaposing the distancing that can occur when there is no gaze is equally important to examine. Visual knowledge presented or represented is never neutral (Lacan,1991), and like all visuals, picture-books position readers in particular ways.

Minimalistic Illustrations: Observation vs. Agency

Of the 59 books analyzed, 33 contained minimalistic illustrations, suggesting a social commentary or a position of learning. The largest number of books in each text set positioned reader-viewers through minimalistic illustrations.

Comparing themes within the two text sets, a sense of agency is afforded spectators that is not apparent when reader-viewers are positioned as observers. A gaze not only invites agency, but positions readers to develop their agency. Readers positioned as observers are taught *about* particular cultural mores, but not necessarily invited to apply their knowledge. Subsequently, the lack of a gaze in minimalistic illustrations assumes a "banking" or filling-an-empty-vessel stance of learning rather than a constructivist approach to learning afforded by the Spectator Text Set (Freire, 1993). Given the large number of books with minimalistic illustrations in comparison to the other illustration types within the text sets, the positioning of readers is not only startling, but disconcerting. The books within the Observer Text Set contain admirable themes worthy of addressing directly with readers: connection to and care of the natural world, personal attributes that would create better citizenship, and ways in which community could be built. Yet, it seems they are relegated to commentary rather than action.

Generic Illustrations: Connection and Humanity

Generic illustrations naturally invite a common stance among people with situations all may experience. Themes within the ten books in the Spectator Text Set address acquiring relationship through processes of remembering and giving back, which ultimately benefit people's interconnected lives. Again, a sense of agency is directly invited by the use of a character gaze. One must do something to gain a relationship, and by extension, this process creates a common good.

In juxtaposition to a sense of relationship, the Observer Text Set presents common experiences shared by people such as violence, knowing, and compassion. Each of these practices require doing or actively being something, but readers are not afforded that potential in their own lives. What is disconcerting about the theme of violence is the lack of an invitation due to an observer stance. It limits readers to believing that what others might be able to do in respect to intervention, the everyday person is powerless to replicate. In *Red*, readers observe how the characters directly—and collectively—address bullying. This could be read as how such individual and collective action *might* work, but perhaps is not possible in the reader's real world.

Naturalistic Illustrations: Apprehension and (In)Humanity

These text sets contained the fewest number of naturalistic illustrations, which is intriguing given that naturalistic illustrations present nuanced representations of individuals and emotions. It is ironic that USBBY's OIB List functions to invite U.S. readers to be more globally literate. Read critically, this lack of representation can be interpreted as a lack of adult belief that children would be interested in specifics, or that instances of a dangerous world are not appropriate for children (a form of childism), or more likely, that a wider purchasing audience is a greater possibility with less individualistic portrayals. The theme of fear/apprehension was apparent in the Observer books; specifically fear that grows within our imaginings or assumptions about the world and how it works. Because there is no gaze, readers are positioned to adopt an amused stance in respect to the squirrel's fear in *Mr. Squirrel and the Moon*, while *Night Guard* positions readers to contemplate the character's anxiety, but not participate or have empathy for that anxiety.

In contrast to the observer stance, the Spectator Text Set challenges readers to respond, question, and cooperate with others in addressing humanity, or in the case of the Holocaust, inhumanity. The two books about the Holocaust envelop readers through the strength of the naturalistic portrayals of those victimized by the inhumanity of the Nazis. Readers are compelled to feel the emotions of the characters. In the two books that ponder the unknown and a world turned upside down, readers are compelled to question or wonder with the characters. Questioning is active thinking, and wondering requires active imaginings. Finally, the remaining books include themes of cooperation, which requires action, and readers are invited into that action.

In reviewing the two text sets (Observer and Spectator) regardless of illustration type, the inclusion of the gaze as agentive is distinguishable. Through the invitation—the envelopment—from a character's gaze, readers are participants and positioned as actors who are afforded the potential of changing the world. Yet, there are other considerations to ponder when comparing these narratives. There are times when distancing allows for reflection, and pondering ideas within a picturebook may be necessary before action can be considered. And regardless of an observational or agentic positioning, discussion of what is read is always a way of creating pathways for actions that lead to agency. Thus, I am not advocating that picturebooks that contain no gaze should not be honored or used, but rather that discussion should be encouraged as a way of moving learning from a banking process to a constructive activity.

In addition, while I discuss these texts and the meaning I made from them, I need to address the importance of exploring the values portrayed in the books, and how those values often reflect the culture from which they originated. Furthermore, books that have been translated from another language could diffuse the deeper cultural understandings. Thus, understanding how translations can re-interpret the original text should be discussed during a reading event. Furthermore, when engaging with a book, the location of where the gaze exists is important to note. Many times, books utilized the gaze at the beginning of the narrative as a way of introducing the character to the reader. Thus, readers are invited to become spectators of the entire situation as it progresses. Other times, the gaze is presented at the end of a narrative, as in *The Pros and Cons of Being a Frog*. This ending gaze invites readers to the shared message of the narrative, and by extension, the lesson that can be learned through the reading. Other times, the gaze is in the midst of the action, which serves as a touchstone to the reader-spectator, an "empathize with me" device as in *Mr. Frank*. Noteworthy, however, is the variable ways to read the gaze, which makes transaction theory and reader-response an important consideration when working with illustrations (Rosenblatt, 1995).

Finally, considering the "voice" of illustrations is important during analysis. May (1995) asserts that "all authors consider the sort of impact they hope to have on their audiences and pick the appropriate voice" (p. 64). Illustrators are selected because of their specific illustration styles, and understanding relationships between author/illustrator and publishing house is necessary. Who makes the decision to publish a particular text and who decides which illustrator or translator to use? Decisions such as these need to be discussed in the contextualization of any picturebook. Discussions about who decides what values will be presented and in what ways can be especially inviting to readers and fall squarely into a critically theoretical framework. Furthermore, the power of a gaze, texts from countries that may not share a Western cultural location, and how reader-spectators interpret both their own positioning as well as the positioning of the Other through character representation should be considered.

The dialectic subject–object relationship is complex, and who "looks" and how reader-viewers accept or oppose their positioning based on cultural considerations (as well as gender, class, race) may become more apparent with cross-cultural texts. Interrogation of reader (observer or spectator) response and the positioning of a gaze or no gaze complicates the typical view of gaze theory. Historically, representations of persons without a gaze objectified them and allowed a sense of domination or ownership by the viewer over the viewed. A direct gaze within a representation creates an oppositional stance, claiming a more equitable relationship of power. Utilizing both Foucault's (1963) and Lacan's (1991) concepts of power and gaze creates a dialectic in positioning. There is subjectivity and objectivity in the positioning of both the illustrated character and reader-viewer. In this sense the character's gaze empowers both the character in the situation viewed and invites the reader to spectatorship, and thus to action and agency.

Final Reflections

As John Berger (1972) noted almost a half-century ago, "seeing comes before words. The child looks and recognizes before it can speak" (p. 7). Through the systematic study of picturebooks and specifically their illustrations, readers have a better sense of what they are seeing and how that seeing may position them. In this study, I wanted to better understand theory about the gaze and the potential of the gaze to position readers. I realize, however, that even this potential has its affordances and limitations. For as Berger further asserts, "although every image embodies a way of seeing, our perception or appreciation of an image depends also upon our own way of seeing" (p. 10), thus allowing agency through practices of freedom (Foucault, 1990) to oppose the positioning of a gaze or to interpret the gaze according to what readers bring to that image. In the twenty-first century, readers are more and more positioned by the images around them, but if given the tools to investigate how they are positioned by those visuals they are better equipped to read the word and the world (Freire & Macedo, 1987).

As educators continue to explore the way illustrations work, we might also investigate how those materials are positioned in our lives. Any cultural institution's responsibility of presenting the world to young people might better understand the ways in which visual images work so as to expand our understandings of the world, ourselves, and the relationship between the two. In this study, the use of USBBY's Outstanding International Book List allowed me to address both the content of the narratives selected for children and the ways in which those works afford or limit readers' relationships to the world.

References

Adeyanju, A. (2016). Symbols and not manifestoes are the selling point here: A multi-modal critical discourse analysis of two contemporary Nigerian political parties' images and slogans. In D. Owenjo, D. Oketch, & A. Tunde (Eds.), *Political discourse in emergent, fragile, and failed democracies* (pp. 265–285). Hershey, PA: IGI Global.

Andrew, D. (1984). *Concepts in film theory.* Oxford: Oxford University Press.

Arizpe, E. & Styles, M. (2003). *Children reading pictures: Interpreting visual texts.* London: Routledge.

Berger, J. (1972). *Ways of seeing.* New York: Penguin.

Dales, B. (2015, February). Now we are ten: USBBY presents its annual outstanding international book list. *School Library Journal.*

Davies, B. & Harré, R. (1990). Positioning: The discursive production of selves. *Journal for the Theory of Social Behaviour*, 20, 43–63.

Foucault, M. (1963). *The birth of the clinic: An archeology of medical perception.* New York: Vintage Books.

Foucault, M. (1990). *The history of sexuality, volume 1: An introduction.* Visalia, CA: Vintage.

Freire, P. (1993). *Pedagogy of the oppressed.* New York: Continuum Publishing.

Freire, P. & Macedo, D. (1987). *Literacy: Reading the word and the world.* Santa Barbara, CA: Praeger.

Hong, T. (2016, February). Presenting the 2016 USBBY outstanding book list: Welcome disruptions. *School Library Journal.*

hooks, b. (2010). The oppositional gaze: Black female spectator. In A. Jones (Ed.), *The feminism and visual cultural reader.* New York: Routledge.

Johnson, H. (2017, January). Outstanding international books: Presenting the 2017 USBBY selections. *School Library Journal.* https://www.slj.com/?detailStory=outstandin g-international-books-presenting-the-2017-usbby-selections

Kachorsky, D., Moses, L., Serafini, F., & Hoelting, M. (2017). Meaning making with picturebooks: Young children's use of semiotic resources. *Literacy Research and Instruction,* 56(3), 231–249. doi:10-1080/19388071.2017.1304595

Krølkke, C. (2009). *Encyclopedia of communication theory.* Thousand Oaks, CA: Sage.

Lacan, J. (1991). *The seminar of Jacques Lacan: The four fundamental concepts of psychoanalysis (Vol. Book XI).* New York: Norton.

Mackey, M. & Shane, M. (2013). Critical multimodal literacies: Synergistic options and opportunities. In K. Hall, T. Cremin, B. Comber, & L. Moll (Eds.), *International handbook of research on children's literacy, learning, and culture* (pp. 15–27). New York: John Wiley.

May, J. (1995). *Children's literature and critical theory.* Oxford: Oxford University Press.

Mulvey, L. (1975). Visual pleasure and narrative cinema. *Screen,* 16(3), 6–18.

Nikolejeva, M. (2005). *Aesthetic approaches to children's literature: An introduction.* Lanham, MD: Scarecrow Press.

Nikolejeva, M. (2013–14). Picturebooks and emotional literacy. *The Reading Teacher,* 67 (4), 249–254.

Pahl, K. & Rowsell, J. (2006). *Travel notes from the new literacy studies: Instances of practice.* Clevedon, UK: Multilingual Matters.

Painter, C., Martin, J.R., & Unsworth, L. (2013). *Reading visual narratives: Image analysis of children's picture books.* Sheffield, UK: Equinox.

Panteleo, S. (2017). Critical thinking and children's exploration of picturebook artwork. *Language and Education,* 31(2), 152–168.

Rosenblatt, L. (1995). *Literature as exploration.* New York: Modern Languages Association.

Rowsell, J. & Kendrick, K. (2013). Boys' hidden literacies: The critical need for the visual. *Journal of Adolescent & Adult Literacy,* 56(7), 587–599.

Said, E. (1978). *Orientalism.* Visalia, CA: Vintage.

Siegel, M. & Panofsky, C.P. (2009). Designs for multimodality in literacy studies: Explorations in analysis. In K. Leander, D.W. Rowe, D. Dickinson, R. Jimenez, M. Hundley, & V. Risko (Eds.), *58th National Reading Conference Yearbook* (pp. 99–111). Oak Creak, WI: National Reading Conference.

Spitz, E. (2000). *Inside picture books.* New Haven, CT: Yale University Press.

Stam, R. (2000). *An introduction to film theory.* Oxford: Blackwell.

Sturken, M. & Cartwright, L. (2009). *Practices of looking: An introduction to visual culture.* Oxford: Oxford University Press.

Van Langenhove, L.V. & Harré, R. (1994). Cultural stereotypes and positioning theory. *Journal for the Theory of Social Behaviour*, 24, 359–372.

Children's Literature References (Arranged by Text Sets)

Spectator Text Set

Minimalistic: Overall Topic: Developing Agency

Agency Requires Action.

Elschner, G. (2015). *Like a wolf.* Illus. by A. Guilloppé. Chicago: Minedition.
Hirst, D. (2016). *The girl with a parrot on her head.* Somerville, MA: Candlewick.
Lawson, J. (2015). *Sidewalk flowers.* Illus. by S. Smith. Toronto: Groundwood.

Agency Requires Speaking Out

deGennaro, S. (2016). *The pros and cons of being a frog.* New York: Simon & Schuster.
O'Leary, S. (2016). *A family is a family is a family.* Illus. by Q. Leng. Toronto: Groundwood.
Robertson, F. (2015). *A tale of two beasts.* La Jolla, CA: Kane Miller.

Agency Is Motivated by Knowledge

Cole, T. (2014.) *Wall.* Somerville, MA: Candlewick.
Deacon, A. (2015). *I am Henry Finch.* Illus. by V. Schwarz. Somerville, MA: Candlewick.
Dubuc, M. (2015). *The bus ride.* Toronto: Kids Can Press.
Dubuc, M. (2016). *The animals' ark.* Toronto: Kids Can Press.
Haughton, C. (2014). *Shhh! We have a plan.* Somerville, MA: Candlewick.
Isabella, J. (2015). *The red bicycle: The extraordinary story of one ordinary bicycle.* Illus. by S. Shin. Toronto: Kids Can Press.
Kuhn, C. (2016). *Samira and the skeletons.* Grand Rapids, MI: Eerdmans.
Rocha, R. (2016). *Lines, squiggles, letters, words.* Illus. by M. Matoso. New York: Enchanted Lion.
Sanna, F. (2016). *The journey.* London: Flying Eye Books/Nobrow.
Shyam, B. (2015). *The London jungle book.* Chennai, India: Tara.

Generic: Overall Topic: Acquiring Relationship

Remembering Creates Relationship

Hurst, E. (2016). *Imagine a city.* New York: Doubleday.
Jordan-Fenton, C. & Pokiak-Fenton, M. (2014). *Not my girl.* Illus. by G. Grimard. Toronto: Annick.
Luxbacher, I. (2014). *Mr. Frank.* Toronto: Groundwood.

Relationship Involves Giving Back

Davies, N. (2014). *The promise*. Illus. by L. Carlin. Somerville, MA: Candlewick.
Niimi, N. (2015). *Gon, the fox*. Illus. by G. Mita. London: Museyon.
Prévot, F. (2015). *Wangari Maathai: The woman who planted millions of trees*. Illus. by A. Fronty. Watertown, MA: Charlesbridge.
Walters, E. (2015). *Hope springs*. Illus. by E. Fernandes. Toronto: Tundra.

Relationships Make Life Easier

Arnaldo, M. (2014). *Arto's big move*. Toronto: Owlkids.
Hohn, N. (2016). *Malaika's costume*. Illus. by I. Luxbacher. Toronto: Groundwood.
Tan, S. (2014). *Rules of summer*. New York: Scholastic.

Naturalistic: Overall Topic: Acknowledging (In)Humanity

The Holocaust Erased Reciprocal Humanity

Kuhlmann, T. (2014). *Lindbergh: The tale of a flying mouse*. New York: NorthSouth.
Cohen-Janca, I. (2014). *Mister Doctor: Janusz Korczak and the orphans of the Warsaw ghetto*. Illus. by M. Quarello. Toronto: Annick.

Questioning the Unknown Increases Humanity's Development

Hole, S. (2014). *Anna's heaven*. Grand Rapids, MI: Eerdmans.
Kuhlmann, T. (2016). *Armstrong: The adventurous journey of a mouse to the moon*. New York: NorthSouth.

Cooperation Escalates Humanity

Argueta, J. (2016). *Somos como las nubes/We are like the clouds*. Illus. by A. Ruano. Toronto: Groundwood.
Oral, F. (2015). *The red apple*. Chicago: Minedition.
Pinfold, L. (2016). *Greenling*. Somerville, MA: Candlewick.

Observer Text Set

Minimalistic: Overall Topic: Imparting Cultural Mores

Connection to the Natural World Is Expected

Adderson, C. (2014). *Norman, speak!* Illus. by Q. Leng. Toronto: Groundwood.
Bogart, J. (2016). *The white cat and the monk: A retelling of the poem "Pangur Bán."* Illus. by S. Smith. Toronto: Groundwood.
CamCam, P. (2014). *Fox's garden*. New York: Enchanted Lion.
Dumont, J. (2015). *I am a bear*. Grand Rapids, MI: Eerdmans.

Kalluk, C. (2014). *Sweetest Kulu*. Illus. by A. Neonakis. Toronto: Inhabit Media.

Perseverance Reaps Rewarding Experiences

Das, A. (2015). *Hope is a girl selling fruit*. Chennai, India: Tara.
Lee, J. (2015). *Pool*. San Francisco: Chronicle.
Uegaki, C. (2014). *Hana Hashimoto, sixth violin*. Illus. by Q. Leng. Toronto: Kids Can Press.

Deception or Oppression Is Eventually Overcome

Leroy, J. (2016). *A well-mannered young wolf*. Illus. by M. Maudet. Grand Rapids, MI: Eerdmans.
Martins, I.M. (2016). *Don't cross the line*. Illus. by B. Carvalho. Wellington, New Zealand: Gecko Press.
Viswanath, S. (2016). *The blue jackal*. Illus. by D. Joshi. Grand Rapids, MI: Eerdmans.

Appreciation of Our Support Networks Is Customary

Daly, N. (2015). *Thank you, Jackson: How one little boy makes a big difference*. London: Frances Lincoln.
Dubuc, M. (2014). *The lion and the bird*. Somerville, MA: Candlewick.
Kobald, I. (2015). *My two blankets*. Illus. by F. Blackwood. New York: Houghton Mifflin Harcourt.
Sanabria, J. (2016). *As time went by*. New York: NorthSouth.
Steven, K. (2015). *Why dogs have wet noses*. Illus. by ⊠. Torseter. New York: Enchanted Lion.
Vallat, C. (2014). *Celia*. Illus. by S. Augusseau. New York: Peter Pauper.

Generic: Overall Topic: Sharing Common Experiences

Violence Is Something All Experience

deKinder, J. (2015). *Red*. Grand Rapids, MI: Eerdmans.
Millard, G. (2014). *Once a shepherd*. Somerville, MA: Candlewick.

Compassion Bridges Differences

Buitrago, J. (2015). *Two white rabbits*. Illus. by R. Yockteng. Toronto: Groundwood.
Lanthier, J. (2016). *Hurry up, Henry*. Illus. by I. Malenfant. New York: Penguin.

Information Connects People

Fenton, C. (2016). *Bob, the railway dog: The true story of an adventurous dog*. Illus. by A. McLean. Somerville, MA: Candlewick.

Landmann, B. (2014). *In search of the little prince: The story of Antoine de Saint-Exupéry*. Grand Rapids, MI: Eerdmans.

Muller, G. (2016). *A year in our new garden*. Edinburgh: Floris.

Naturalistic: Overall Topic: Addressing Apprehension

Lea, S. (2016). *Night guard*. Illus. by S. Hole. Grand Rapids, MI: Eerdmans.

Meschenmoser, S. (2015). *Mr. Squirrel and the moon*. New York: NorthSouth.

8

DE(MIST)IFYING DEPRESSION

Dark Clouds and the Construction of Disability

Desiree Cueto, Susan Corapi and Megan McCaffrey

In the original *Winnie the Pooh* series (Milne, 1926), Pooh's friend Eeyore is sketched with slumped shoulders and drooping ears. His gloomy comments hint at the diagnostic possibility of depression. In 1966, when the Walt Disney Corporation acquired the rights to the Pooh series, a dark cloud was drawn above the grey stuffed donkey. It is not clear why Disney opted to add this detail, but what is evident is that the metaphor endured. Generations of children have come to associate depression—one of the most disabling psychosocial conditions, worldwide—with dark clouds (World Health Organization, 2017).

One interpretation of the pervasive dark cloud is that it can be conceptualized through ableist ideologies as misfortune, calling forth pity, or worse, social isolation. With an increase in the number of individuals who suffer from stress, anxiety, and depression (Pratt, Brody, & Gu, 2017; World Health Organization, 2017), children are likely to encounter psychosocial conditions, either personally, through family members, or friends. Examining how visual images perpetuate stigma and misunderstanding around these conditions is, thus, critical.

Our chapter begins at the intersection of visual literacy and disability studies. We offer a critical visual analysis of four books: *Willy and the Cloud* (2017) by Anthony Brown, *Meh* (2015) by Deborah Malcolm, *The Princess and the Fog* (2015) by Lloyd Jones, and *Sadly the Owl* (2015) by Linnie Von Sky and illustrated by Ashley O'Mara. Each book deals with depression and was published recently in a Western country. Throughout our analysis, we explore illustrations through the metaphor of the dark cloud. This metaphor appears consistently, albeit in different forms, across our text set. In *Willy and the Cloud* and *Sadly the Owl*, a traditional raincloud hangs above the character's head, whereas, a cloud of black fog encircles the main character in *The Princess and Fog*, and a grey smoke cloud consumes the central character in *Meh*. We contextualize dark clouds within different compositions to better demonstrate how elements work together to help readers construct meaning. We find that, while static images add to the stigmatization of people living with psychosocial conditions, illustrators who are aware of this possibility can disrupt stereotypes by offering more complex depictions that produce revisionist possibilities.

Theoretical Frame of Critical Disability Studies

The field of disability studies emerged as a corrective to individualist and medicalized thinking (Corker & Shakespeare, 2002; Shakespeare, 2008, Campbell, 2008). British scholars coined the term "social model," which serves as the core paradigm that challenges Western medicine's location of disability as a biological defect to be fixed or cured (Barnes, 1996; 2007). In contrast to the medical model, the social model maintains that disability is a product of social oppression.

Scholars in the field locate disability "in a political, social, and cultural context, that theorizes and historicizes [it] in similarly complex ways to the way race, class, and gender have been theorized" (Davis, 2010, p. xvi). Common underpinnings of disability studies are that disability is socially constructed and must be viewed in terms of historic attitudes and political structures, and that valid research should advance an understanding of disability oppression that highlights disabling social structures, rather than individual impairments (Brown, 2001; Barnes, 2007).

Within the last decade, the term "critical disability" has been increasingly employed by scholars to indicate a shift toward a more radical perspective (Meekosha & Shuttleworth, 2009; Goodley 2013; Hosking 2008; Campbell 2008). According to Meekosha and Shuttleworth (2009), critical disability studies (CDS) signifies that, "the struggle for social justice and diversity continues, but on another plane—one that is not simply social, economic and political, but is also psychological, cultural, and discursive" (p. 50). CDS also represents "a distancing away from those who have co-opted disability studies for normalizing ends" (p. 51). Concepts deriving from CDS push attention toward what Lennard Davis (2014; 2010) has long referred to as "the hegemony of normalcy" to critical examinations of the ways in which ableism is constructed and maintained in society.

Davis (2010) argues that the power of the need to feel normal is part of "the very heart of cultural production" (p. 17). He further suggests that part of fostering an awareness of disability issues must include other ways of considering the abnormal. Vital to this work is an understanding of the ways the concept of the norm is perpetuated, and how it intersects and fuels stigmatization, marginalization, and ableism.

Tanya Titchkosky (2009) builds on Davis's scholarship and argues that because disability is theorized based on the norms of a culture, it begins and ends in the imagination of the people who create that culture. Titchkosky (2009) explains that images help people theorize normalcy and disability at a subconscious level. She points to how the universal access sign (a wheelchair) demarcates the inaccessibility of any site not marked with this symbol. Essentially, the image helps to create a world appearing accessible to those constructed as abled—a world that is, in actuality, almost entirely inaccessible. Titchkosky's observation of subtle signs that manipulate and reinforce access borders in the imagination provides a unique site of analysis. She concludes that "we might now heed the call of the art of theorizing" in order to imagine a livelier, more provocative construction of disability (p. 83).

Related Research

Most research on depictions of mental illness for children centers on film and media. Outside the confines of traditional children's literature, Otto Wahl (2003) is the most prominent scholar to examine illustrations in popular culture of mental illness. In his analysis of comic strips and cartoons, Wahl identifies several common graphic elements used in the characterization of the mentally ill, such as eccentric features and distorted appearance. Wahl argues the illustrations set the mentally ill apart as others.

Our search for scholarship on depictions of depression and mental illness in picturebooks led to one article by Imogen Church (2018) in which she examines the visual depiction of female mental illness in four picturebooks published in the twenty-first century. Two titles deal with a depressive episode (*The Red Tree* by Shaun Tan, 2001; *Misery Moo* by Jeanne Willis, illustrated by Tony Ross, 2003) and use a common image (a dark cloud) to represent the character's depression. Church finds that in appealing to a younger audience the texts avoid a direct mentioning of depression. Beyond Church's specific research on books that address female mental illness, a dearth of scholarship surrounds this subject. Our study fills a gap in research by exploring the ways illustrations of depression position readers either toward or against ableist ideologies.

Methodology

The following research question guided our study: How is ableism visually constructed or deconstructed in Western, Global North, picturebooks about depression? We used critical content analysis of visual images as a method of inquiry and based our analysis on key concepts within critical disability studies. We analyzed the illustrations in four picturebooks, with the aim of examining ableist ideologies. Because of the overt focus of critical disability studies on dominant/subordinate systems of power, several concepts within this field were particularly useful for our analysis. We grounded our research in the following theoretical propositions:

- Commonly held notions of disability and ability are historically and culturally contingent (Davis, 2010).

- Disability is created by notions of normalcy and ability that are imposed in order to separate or exclude certain segments of the human population from others (Davis, 2010).
- Images help theorize normalcy and disability at a subconscious level (Titchkosky, 2009).

We situate ourselves as a diverse group of scholars in terms of age, race, culture, ethnicity, and ability status. When speaking and writing about disability, we collectively have personal experiences, family ties, and professional work that connects us to this study. These experiences provide us with an entry point into an understanding of ableism. However, none of us purports to be an expert. Aubrecht (2014) reminds us, as advocates of disability studies, we must acknowledge that ableists hold numerous suppositions of what people are supposed to be.

To address this concern, we initially read the books and then wrote a series of reflections related to the meaning we each inferred, based on our own life experiences. This process served two purposes. First, it allowed for the documentation of our aesthetic responses to visual texts (Rosenblatt, 1995). Second, sharing our reflections with one another allowed us to recognize points of departure in each researcher's reading and to consider why those differences existed.

Throughout this process, we continued to engage in deep reflection—writing, sharing, and revisiting our responses to each book. Ongoing reflection helped us to recognize patterns that resonated or created tensions with each of us individually and as a group. Additionally, reflecting repeatedly caused us to carefully consider how our own personal biases, beliefs, and worldviews might influence the study. Below, we outline some of our specific identity markers in an effort to provide transparency:

- Desiree Cueto – Northeastern African American, School Counselor, Professor, 40s, Dyslexic.
- Susan Corapi – American/Canadian, Multi-ethnic, Librarian, Professor, Bilingual (French), lived abroad in France, Côte d'Ivoire and Canada, 60s.
- Megan McCaffrey – Midwestern Caucasian, Reading Specialist, Librarian, Professor, 50s.

Text Selection

This study grew out of a collaborative project in which our group explored global representations of disabilities in 11 picturebooks. Because of our interest in global titles, we revisited catalogues published by the International Board on Books for Young People (IBBY), listing the titles housed in the IBBY Collections for Young People with Disabilities in the Toronto Public Library. We continued our search by reviewing books that won the Schneider Family Award and titles submitted to the Charlotte Huck Award committee. However, after a preliminary review of titles, we elected to limit our data to books written and published in Western/Global North countries. We realized that much of what we understood about the disability experience was located in Western conceptions of normalcy and wellbeing. Given the importance of critiquing the books within specific social, historical and cultural contexts, we eliminated non-Western books.

It was during the collecting phase that we noticed the dearth of titles addressing psychosocial and emotional impairments—effectively making these impairments less "visible" for readers. Since our intent was to challenge inequity by raising key critical questions about ableist norms, we decided to narrow our study to representations of mental illness—a category of disability that is often uncomfortable to address. We further limited our study to representations of depression, based on the prevalence of diagnoses reported by the World Health Organization (2017).

We read professional reviews (*Kirkus, Booklist, Horn Book, School Library Journal*, etc.) and insider reviews of the books, submitted on websites for school counselors and parents working with children and adolescents with depression. Eventually we selected titles in which the main character was the one dealing with depression instead of other family members, so we eliminated well-known titles like *The Color Thief* (Peters & Peters, 2014) and *Virginia Wolf* (Maclear, 2012). We also sought current depictions of depression—books published between 2015 and 2017—so we eliminated Shaun Tan's visual depiction of depression in *The Red Tree* (2001). Finally, we gave additional weight to books that were written and/or illustrated by insiders—those who indicated that they had been diagnosed with depression or mental illness. In the end, our text set consisted of these four books:

1. *Meh* is a wordless book, portraying a boy's journey through sadness and depression to hope and happiness. Deborah Malcolm is a Scottish illustrator who decided on the book's topic because she had suffered from depression and wanted to use imagery to describe the experience so others could understand it more.

2. *The Princess and the Fog* is the story of a young princess who experiences a fog that makes her feel alone, slow, sad, and tired. Through the efforts of her parents, classmates, knights, a druid, and a wise woman, the princess regains her happiness and learns to manage the fog. English author/illustrator Lloyd Jones acknowledges his own struggles in an author's preface, stating that he learned to live with the fog rather than suffer from it.

3. *Sadly the Owl* loves line-dancing in his red boots, however his dancing is hampered by a cloud that will not retreat. German/Canadian author Linnie von Sky writes out of her own experience of learning to live with and manage depression.

4. *Willy and the Cloud* is one of the most recent in award-winning English author/illustrator Anthony Browne's stories about Willy the Chimp. Browne often places Willy in difficult emotional situations (e.g., loneliness

in the 1991 *Willy and Hugh*, or being bullied in the 1984 *Willy the Wimp*). In *Willy and the Cloud* Browne adds another exploration of childhood experiences and emotions as Willy is shadowed by a cloud of depression.

Data Analysis

Our exploration unfolded through the study of ableist norms as visually depicted in the books. In our analysis, critical disability theory offered a lens for examining how illustrations of depression come to have meaning in children's literature. We read the illustrations alongside the scholarship of critical disability theorists: Tanya Titchkosky (2007; 2009), Leonard Davis (2014; 2010), Tom Shakespeare (2008) Dan Goodley (2013), Stephen Hinshaw (2008), and James Cherney (2011). Drawing on this body of research, we looked specifically for visual symbols or metaphors that might (re)produce stigma and bias. Additionally, we focused on the treatment of characters with depression.

Our analysis was guided by analytical tools from Painter, Martin, and Unsworth (2013). Mechanisms within the interpersonal metafunction were useful to our consideration of the relationships between characters as well as with the reader. Specifically, looking at focalization (from whose perspective is the reader seeing?), pathos and affect (the level of detail used to depict characters), and ambience (the emotional mood of the illustration, shaped by color and graduation of size and proximity) helped to expose static or binary representations and to uncover concepts of normalcy advanced by the illustrations. As we read, we coded dominant and disruptive representations of depression, and explored:

- The impact of a static or primary image that dominates the representation of depression.
- How various illustration techniques detract from or perpetuate concepts of normalcy and ableist ideologies.
- The potential of illustrations to present new or alternative ways of understanding depression.

After revisiting dominant codes, we arrived at an overarching trope of *Dark Clouds as Enduring Metaphors for Depression*. By closely analyzing the ways illustrators depicted dark clouds in relation to a central character and in the context of the composition, we developed three thematic subcategories: *Dark Clouds as Markers of Difference, Dark Clouds as Signs of Inaccessibility,* and *Dark Clouds as Symbolic Journeys*.

Dark Clouds as Markers of Difference

Davis (2004) suggests that characters are imagined as normal unless otherwise noted, and, when it comes to disability books, tend to center disability as a problem. At the same time, he points out that the possibility exists for challenging the "imagined normal" (p. 68). In this section, our analysis focuses on the use of dark clouds to depict the onset of depression. Across the text set, we find dark clouds signal which character is marked or different. We also find variations in the illustrations of clouds, as well as how they work with other elements to contribute to a nuanced understanding of depression.

All four books begin with a character who appears to be enjoying a "typical" life. For example, in *Willy and the Cloud*, the reader's eyes are first drawn to a happy Willy, on the right side. The anthropomorphized chimpanzee is wearing a brightly colored sweater vest and slacks, which stand in contrast to the solid white background. Not until the reader returns to the written text on the left side are our eyes drawn upward to the tiny rain cloud floating above. Browne's use of white space on the next two pages keeps the reader focused on movement of the cloud toward Willy. On pages 6–7, unmediated side views expand across a series of four framed panels, inviting readers to observe for themselves Willy's inability to escape the growing cloud—no matter how fast he runs. Browne's use of human characteristics in generic style illustrations to portray the growing concern on the chimp's face evokes an empathetic stance from the readers (Painter et al., 2013, p. 33). In the last of the four panels, a much heavier rain cloud casts a dark shadow over the chimp, the sweater's vibrant colors become muted, Willy's stride shortens, and his posture slumps. Interpreting this through a critical disability framework, we find that the elements Browne uses add depth of meaning to the dominant image of the dark cloud, which alone, would problematically introduce depression. The cloud, in this instance, functions alongside other elements to invoke the reader's sense of what it is like to experience the onset of depression for Willy.

Much like Willy, *Sadly the Owl* begins with the sun streaming through the windows, and a young owlet donning his bright red boots. A series of vignettes introduces the reader to the everyday happenings in Sadly's life. The focalization is primarily unmediated—from the side, from a distance or with a panoramic view. This places the reader as an observer, not as a participant in the story (Painter et al., 2013, p. 19). The reader is only clued in that something is wrong when Sadly wakes with a small raincloud floating above his head. While many stories, including *Willy and the Cloud* use a more generic style of art, closing the gap between human emotions and emotions on the animals' faces, *Sadly the Owl* does not. O'Mara uses minimalist style illustrations to convey the cloud's effects— subtle changes in Sadly's posture and half-closed eyelids communicate his sadness. The written text, by Linnie von Sky, explains what Sadly is experiencing, "The cloud had no intention of leaving and the harder Sadly worked to outsmart it, the darker it grew" (p. 10)." However, these words are not fully realized in the illustrations. The minimalist style combined with more traditional representation of the dark cloud and other static visual elements, positions the story as more of a gentle commentary on depression instead of one in which the reader develops empathy for the character (Painter et al., 2013, pp. 32–34). Referring to Davis's

(2004) argument, the more static image of the cloud serves primarily to identify depression as a problematic "thing" that possesses an individual character. When depression is constructed in this way, it keeps readers from continuing to critically examine what depression means (Titchkosky, 2007).

Some books present alternatives to the dominant dark raincloud by illustrating it in different forms. The remaining two books represent depression as an all-encompassing smoke cloud and a cloud of fog. In so doing, the illustrators provide deeper insight into the depression experience. Moreover, by placing the reader inside the experience, these illustrators work toward altering the "imagined normal" (Davis, 2014).

On the first page of *Meh*, the reader is introduced to a boy who stares up at a kitten-shaped cloud. The familiar child-world is vibrantly colored in a rainbow palette against a white background. However, when the smoke cloud begins to prey, the bright color disappears, and the ambience becomes muted (p. 10). The reader's gaze shifts from one of observation to mediated inscribed. In this case Malcolm visually positions the reader to focus on the boy's outstretched hands as the smoky cloud spills to the edge of the paper (p. 11) (See Figure 8.1).

This technique draws the reader into the boy's experience. As he sinks into the cloud of smoke, he looks up, hands extended, making an appeal to the reader for help. Malcolm's minimalist, almost animé style keeps the reader focused on the depressive episode depicted through greyscale. Close-ups of the boy's face allow Malcolm to communicate a wide range of emotions. His skin and clothing have progressively grayed out (p. 12), leaving him sad and helpless (pp. 13–14). Malcolm alters the traditional dark cloud to create a visual understanding of the pervasiveness of depression. Her example shows how even a slight variation to the norm of cloud = depression can upset the status quo and lead to new ways of seeing.

In *The Princess and the Fog*, the endpapers start the narrative with grayed background and cloud-shaped scribbles. The title page continues the theme with "FOG" in oversized black font. Positioned as a fairy-type tale, the focalization is unmediated, so the reader takes an objective stance and just observes what happens to the princess. Unlike the other three books, the fog is introduced as a character from the first page when a tiny scribble of fog emerges from behind tall buildings on the evening horizon. The princess, who is staring out of the castle window, does not see the fog enter her world. In a series of small vignettes, Jones invites the reader to view snapshots of the princess's life pre-depression. Then, at the onset of the princess's depression, the fog creeps onto the right bottom corner of the page. Only the reader is made aware of its presence. The next spread intersperses illustrations with short texts that read: "It happened slowly. So slowly that nobody really noticed, at first … One by one, dark clouds came to the princess, following her and gradually gathering around her head" (pp. 12-13). On a double spread Jones uses a gallery of royal portraits and a change from vibrant saturated colors to dark muted colors to reflect the gradual shift in the princess's mood and her withdrawal from her community. The princess's latest portrait lies

FIGURE 8.1 Mediated Image of Meh, Drawing the Reader into the Depression (Malcolm, 2015)

Source: Meh: A Story about Depression by Deborah Malcolm. Copyright © Thunder-Stone Books, 2015.

shattered and the princess is huddled in the corner feeling alone, "even when she wasn't" (p. 15). Jones uses the walls of the room to focus the reader's eye on the princess, who has become barely recognizable beneath the fog. These illustrations provide insight into the overtaking nature of depression. Similar to *Meh*, altering the image of the traditional raincloud in this book has a greater impact on the reader's understanding of depression, thus encouraging empathy rather than pity or judgement.

Dark Clouds as Signs of Inaccessibility

Titchkosky (2011) writes that exploring access is a way to understand how we live together as a society. She argues that reading disability through access encourages reflection on social interactions, responses to difference, and reframing thinking about diverse lived experiences. As representations of depression extend beyond its onset, illustrators in this text set rely on the dark cloud metaphor to depict the isolation characters feel from their community. The clouds, in these instances, act as an access symbol. This visual depiction of isolation/inaccessibility from other characters is evident in two of the books, *Willy and the Cloud* and *The Princess and the Fog*.

The works of Anthony Browne have long functioned as a commentary on the human condition. In *Willy and the Cloud* Browne uses the book format to help the reader understand the isolation Willy feels under the shadow of the cloud. In the spread on pp. 8–9 the strong line created by the book gutter separates Willy from the other primates. Willy is on the recto page, dwarfed and in the distance, his back to the reader. On the verso page, the smiling gorillas fill the foreground and background. In contrast to Willy who is huddled, wrapped in a blanket, the gorillas are basking in the sun, relaxed and socializing. Browne's depiction can be read as both revealing and troubling. On the one hand, if read uncritically, the contrasting images reinforce an ableist perception of disability as outside of the margins. According to Titchkosky (2011), when disabilities are viewed as not belonging, those with disabilities are "essentially excludable" (p. 39). However, the contrasting images also advocate a critical response—summoning the reader to consider how it feels to be Willy. The next image on page 10 uses elements of graduation to strengthen the sense of Willy's isolation. The entire page is filled with a brick wall (with many bricks having cloud shapes on them). Willy is micro-size on the bottom of the page, the cloud hovering over his head and casting a shadow (Figure 8.2).

On this same page, Browne again invites a critique connected to access in the form of the gaze. At the top of the page, one small window in the wall shows a puzzled face observing Willy. This use of perspective to show the able-body gazing down on the disabled body begs critique. Chemers (2008) writes that the abled make an impairment a disability by projecting their view of it as different. In order for this image to not be problematic, however, it must be read as a commentary on the way society views difference.

Lloyd Jones in *The Princess and the Fog* depicts the isolating nature of depression by changing the fog. It becomes more solid, hovering around the princess's head, separating her from her community. Eventually the fog becomes so large and dense that the princess retreats to a corner of her room. Jones uses graduation (repetition of an image) to visually depict the princess's growing isolation. A series of nine images in which she is sitting on her throne (pp. 18–27) reinforces the way she isolates herself, repeatedly rejecting activities that used to give her pleasure. She also refuses the efforts of others to help, responding to their suggestions with a large "NO" speech bubble. Revisiting access, Titchkosky (2011) writes that,

FIGURE 8.2 Willy, Isolated by the Cloud and the Graduation of the Wall (Browne, 2017)

Source: *Willy and the Cloud.* Copyright © 2016 by Anthony Browne. Reproduced by permission of the publisher, Candlewick Press, Somerville, MA on behalf of Walker Books, London.

Exploring some of the ways of depicting who disabled people are supposed to be will provide access to the social practice of drawing boundaries around forms of participation. "Who?" serves as a space of question that draws boundaries around who is in and who is out.

(p. 30)

Read through this lens, the interactions between the princess and her community produce boundaries between normal happiness v. abnormal unhappiness. Davis (2014) discusses that the notion of happiness as a goal of Americans is one that positions depression as something to be fixed. Jones reinforces this binary through a contrast in vibrancy that shows the change in the princess's mood. The first throne spread (pp. 18–19) begins with a bright daylight scene (verso) and changes to a dark muted scene (recto) showing the immobilization of the princess. It is not until she begins talking (non-isolating interaction) to everyone in the community, that she returns to health and happiness.

Dark Clouds as Symbolic Journeys

One technique the illustrators used to show transitions over time was to change the shape, density, and color of the clouds. In each book, the closing illustrations signified either an end or a continuation of the character's journey. We centered our analysis in this section on the fixed or cured trope. Titchkosky (2007) writes that, to the ableist, disabled means a problem that prevents the possibility of taking part in a normal life. We considered how the changing nature of the clouds either challenged or perpetuated ableist ideologies. We paid particular attention to the final illustrations and whether or not depression was represented as a problem in need of fixing.

As Willy's story arc climbs and falls, Browne uses graduation of size and proximity to represent changes in Willy's emotions. The cloud evolves from a small white cumulus to an enormous broiling thunderhead and then to a gentle rain, eventually disappearing altogether. At a pivotal point in this transition Willy takes action by shaking his fist at the cloud and calling the police, whose reaction marks him as laughable. Browne stretches the cloud across the page and uses close-ups to draw the reader into Willy's frustration and anger with the oppressive cloud. However, Willy's shout has the desired effect; the cloud dissipates in a rain shower, and the chimp's head-to-toe shots reappear.

Meh's journey has a similar conclusion, though the journey is darker. Deborah Malcolm's goal in writing *Meh* was to visually describe a depressive episode, helping readers to emotionally grasp the feelings. She positions the reader as a distant observer but uses close-ups at pivotal moments when the boy battles the darkness. The journey through depression is led by a feline, first represented only by small paw prints, and gradually increasing in size from a kitten to a tiger. In the final interaction with depression both boy and tiger roar, and the reader is brought in for a close-up in a mediated focalization to see through the boy's eyes the beauty of his release back into a color-filled world.

In both stories the characters experience an emotional journey but conclude with the color in life suddenly returning. In contrast, the stories of the princess and the owl avoid the sick/well binary that could be construed from the stories of Willy and Meh. In *The Princess and the Fog*, the fog is a dynamic character, changing across the book from small and wispy to a large mass, to an overwhelming mass extending to the ceiling. Even after the fog disappears, it sneaks back into the princess's life, illustrating Jones's point that the journey with depression is recurring (Figure 8.3). In *Sadly the Owl*, O'Mara changes very little

FIGURE 8.3 Princess on the Journey of Managing Depression (Jones, 2015)
Source: The Princess and the Fog: A Story for Children with Depression, by Lloyd Jones. Copyright ©Jessica Kingsley Publishers, 2015. Reproduced with permission of the Licensor through PLSclear.

about the size and color of the cloud as a constant presence, even at the end as it kisses Sadly goodnight. Both stories visually emphasize the ongoing nature of the journey with depression.

The fixed or cured trope is evident in Willy and Meh's journeys. Willy's world is vibrant and saturated until the cloud greys his world. The conclusion of the story is white-washed, indicating the drenching of the sun and the absence of a cloud. Willy's breakthrough is sudden and total. The final page shows a happy Willy reintegrated into the broader community where "EVERYONE was happy!" (p. 25) This ending feels all the more problematic because, up to this point, the illustrations gave hope that readers would leave with a deeper understanding of the importance of difference. According to Brown (2001), normality becomes the supreme goal for many stigmatized individuals until they realize that there is no precise definition of normality except what they would be without their stigma (p. 187). The same is true in *Meh* in which the vibrant world of the boy is suddenly covered by the cloud shadow, rendering his skin tones and clothing as gray as his world. As the boy climbs, walks, reflects, and works, the shadow becomes less black and whiter with a sudden shattering of the shadow and a return to a color-filled world.

In contrast, the princess's fog decreases slowly while she talks to many people and keeps her "team" on call in case the fog reappears. There is no sudden cure. Sadly has the same sort of experience. As he tries out the doctor's prescriptions his mood gradually improves. Davis (2014) discusses the positioning of depression as an illness that has a cure. The princess's slow, but certainly not permanent, return to a happier self communicates to the reader that depression has not disappeared due to a dose of medicine. Stories like *The Princess and the Fog* acknowledge the hard work required to manage depression.

Final Reflections

Perhaps more than anything, this chapter points to the need for more dialogue about the way notions of (dis)ability are shaped. Titchkosky (2009) contends that our imaginations are conditioned by the cultures in which we live, which shapes the way we imagine disability. When children engage with picturebooks, illustrations become part of their culture and shape their imaginations. As such, they serve as visual guides for understanding what is normal or abnormal and who should be included or excluded. For this reason, it is important to provide students with tools. Reading illustrations about specific disabilities through the lens of Critical Disability Studies opens the door for a more thoughtful consideration of different ways of being in the world. At the same time, considering the systems illustrators employ allows students to think about how they are being positioned and what subtle messages are being conveyed. These approaches to reading disability, particularly representations of mental illness, encourage a deeper understanding of and empathy toward fictional characters, thereby increasing the chance that this interaction will extend to real life.

The pervasive image of the dark cloud of depression has endured across a wide range of texts for children. The results of our analysis point to the need for illustrators to consider new or alternative ways of representing depression—preferably creating images that support an understanding of mental illness as a social construct. By expanding or recontextualizing the dominant cloud metaphor, illustrators can provide openings for new conversations about what it is like to experience depression. Yet, while their illustrations may represent a variety of different cloud formations, this single metaphor continues to contribute to limited understandings of the condition. When static images, based on the medical model of disability, are uncritically adopted, it limits the types of new knowledge readers are able to produce. While we do not suggest that illustrators refrain from using cloud metaphors completely, we do hope to advance the significance of adding alternative visuals to the lone representation of depression.

References

Aubrecht, K. (2014). Disability studies and the language of mental illness. *Review of Disability Studies*, 8(2), 1–15.

Barnes, C. (1996). A legacy of oppression: A history of disability in western culture. In L. Barton & M. Oliver (Eds.), *Disability studies: Past present and future*. Leeds, UK: Disability Press.

Barnes, C. (2007). Disability, higher education and the inclusive society. *British Journal of Sociology of Education*, 28(1), 135–145.

Brown, S.C. (2001). Methodological paradigms that shape disability research. In G.L. Albrecht, K.D. Seelman, & M. Bury (Eds.), *Handbook of disability studies* (pp. 145–170). Thousand Oaks, CA: Sage.

Campbell, F.K. (2008). Refusing able(ness): A preliminary conversation about ableism. *M/C, Journal of Media and Culture*, 11(3).

Chemers, M.M. (2008). *Staging stigma: A critical examination of the American freak show*. New York: Palgrave Macmillan.

Cherney, J.L. (2011). The rhetoric of ableism. *Disability Studies Quarterly*, 31(3). http://dx. doi.org/10.18061/dsq.v31i3.1665

Corker, M. & Shakespeare, T. (2002). *Disability/postmodernity: Embodying disability theory*. London: Continuum.

Church, I. (2018). The picture of madness–Visual narratives of female mental illness in contemporary children's literature. *Children's Literature in Education*, 49(2), 119–139.

Davis, L.J. (2004). Nude Venuses, Medusa's body, and phantom limbs: Disability and visuality. In D.T. Mitchell, J.I. Porter, & S.L. Snyder (Eds.), *The body and physical difference: Discourses of disability* (pp. 51–70). Ann Arbor: University of Michigan Press.

Davis, L.J. (2010). *The disability studies reader* (3rd ed.). New York: Routledge.

Davis, L.J. (2014). *End of normal: Identity in a biocultural era*. Ann Arbor: University of Michigan Press.

Goodley, D. (2013). Dis/entangling critical disability studies. *Disability and Society*, 28(5), 631–644.

Hinshaw, S.P. & Stier, A. (2008). Stigma as related to mental disorders. *Annual Review of Clinical Psychology*, 4, 367–393.

Hosking, D. (2008). Critical disability theory. Paper presented at the 4th Biennial Disability Studies Conference, Lancaster University, 2–4 September.

Meekosha, H. & Shuttleworth, R. (2009). What's so "critical" about critical disability studies? *Australian Journal of Human Rights*, 15(1), 47–75.

Painter, C., Martin, J.R., & Unsworth, L. (2013). *Reading visual narratives: Image analysis of children's picture books*. Sheffield, UK: Equinox.

Pratt, L.A., Brody, D.J., & Gu, Q. (2017). *Antidepressant use among persons aged 12 and over: United States, 2011–2014*. U.S. Department of Health and Human Services, NCHS Data Brief no. 283. Retrieved from https://www.cdc.gov/nchs/products/databriefs/db283.htm

Rosenblatt, L. (1995). *Literature as exploration.* New York: Modern Language Association.
Shakespeare, T. (2008). Debating disability. *Journal of Medical Ethics*, 34(1), 11–14.
Titchkosky, T. (2009). Disability images and the art of theorizing normality. *International Journal of Qualitative Studies in Education*, 22(1), 75–84.
Titchkosky, T. (2007). *Reading and writing disability differently: The textured life of embodiment.* Toronto: University of Toronto Press.
Titchkosky, T. (2011). *The question of access: Disability, space, meaning.* Toronto: University of Toronto Press.
Wahl, O.F. (2003). *Media madness: Public images of mental illness* (2nd ed.). New Brunswick, NJ: Rutgers University Press.
World Health Organization (2017). *Depression and other common mental disorders: Global health estimates.* Geneva: WHO.

Children's Literature References

Browne, A. (2017). *Willy and the cloud.* Somerville, MA: Candlewick Press.
Browne, A. (1991). *Willy and Hugh.* New York: Knopf.
Browne, A. (1984). *Willy the wimp.* New York: Knopf.
Jones, L. (2015). *The princess and the fog: A story for children with depression.* Philadelphia, PA: Jessica Kingsley.
Maclear, K. (2012). *Virginia Wolf.* Illus. by I. Arsenault. Toronto: Kids Can Press.
Malcolm, D. (2015). *Meh.* Las Vegas, NV: Thunder Stone Books.
Milne, A.A. (1926). *Winnie-the-Pooh.* Illus. by E.H. Shepard. New York: Dutton.
Peters, A.F. & Peters, P. (2014). *The color thief: A family's story of depression.* Illus. by K. Littlewood. Chicago: Whitman.
Tan, S. (2001). *The red tree.* Melbourne: Lothian.
von Sky, L. (2015). *Sadly the owl: An untold tale.* Illus. by A. O'Mara. British Columbia: Silk Web Publishing.
Willis, J. (2003). *Misery Moo.* Illus. by T. Ross. London: Andersen.

9

GRANDMA AND THE GREAT GOURD

A Comparison of Images in an App and a Picturebook

Deanna Day

Picturebooks have changed immensely with the digital revolution. The arrival of the tablet and iPad has encouraged the transformation of many picturebooks into book apps—digitally produced books that are downloadable and contain inter-activity and additional content or features. Book apps typically have home screens, navigational icons, different reading paths, music or sound and games that complement the book. This chapter uses critical multicultural analysis or CMA (Botelho & Rudman, 2009) as a framework to analyze the illustrations in the picturebook *Grandma and the Great Gourd: A Bengali Folktale* retold by Chitra Banerjee Divakaruni and illustrated by Susy Pilgrim Waters (Divakaruni, 2013) as well as the illustrations in the interactive app *Grandma's Great Gourd* (Literary Safari, 2016a).

Parents, classroom teachers, and librarians often purchase book apps for children. Popular book apps such as *Pete the Cat* (HarperCollins, 2012), *Don't Let the Pigeon Run This App!* (Willems, 2012), or *The Three Little Pigs: A 3-D Fairy Tale* (Nosy Crow, 2011) are read and enjoyed in classrooms, libraries, and homes. Young children play or read book apps for entertainment and to build literacy skills. During the school day book apps are read aloud and students have access to them during their literacy block to explore during silent reading. Since book apps are so frequently purchased and used by parents, educators, and librarians as part of young children's literacy development, it is crucial that they are closely investigated.

Colleen O'Connell, the director for digital books at HarperCollins, shares the planning process that goes into transforming a traditional book into an app: "All apps start with the same high-quality assets that are required of our print books: a great story, strong narrative, and excellent art" (Wooten & McCuiston, 2015, p. 27). She explains that a mixture of audio, animation, narration, and inter-activity brings the book to life. The digital enhancements may range from simple movement, user-initiated actions or game-based experiences. McCuiston emphasizes that every addition should enhance the story and give the reader a sense of participation. My interest was in analyzing and comparing the story experiences offered by the picturebook *Grandma and the Great Gourd* and the digital book app *Grandma's Great Gourd*.

Theoretical Framework of Critical Multicultural Analysis

Botelho and Rudman (2009) maintain that critical multicultural analysis acknowledges that all literature is a cultural and historical product, revealing how power relations of class, race, and gender work together in text and image in society. Stories offer a selective version of reality, told from a particular viewpoint by the author. Readers are positioned to respond in particular ways through the genre, language use, point of view, and other literary devices. Botelho and Rudman suggest that being *critical* means reading beyond the text and making connections between the local, sociopolitical, personal and political—grounded in historical analysis. Being *critical* involves paying attention to the power imbalance in society and how language shapes perceptions and social processes. *Multicultural* acknowledges the multiple histories among us, the diversity and fluidity of our cultural experiences and the unequal access to social power. *Analysis* means examining how cultural characters transpire and proliferate (Rudman & Botelho, 2005).

Children's books are windows into society and the complexities of power relations (Botelho & Rudman, 2009). Foucault (1995) explored power relations and suggested questions such as: Who exercises power? How does power happen? Who makes decisions, prevents or forces? Botelho and Rudman suggest exposing power by looking at how it is exercised, circulated, negotiated and reconstructed, because we live in a raced, classed, and gendered society. They created a continuum of how power is exercised through domination, collusion, resistance and agency. For my research I specifically looked at how the main character, Grandma, revealed agency within the two texts. Agency is initiation and power and resides in all classes, genders, and ethnicities. Agency is recognizing constitution and resisting, subverting and changing the discourses.

Critical multicultural analysis is also a multi-layered lens that is recursive in nature (Botelho & Rudman, 2009). At the center of this analysis is focalization of the story with additional layers: the social processes among the characters, the closure of the story, the genres as social constructions, the sociopolitical context, concluding with the historical context. As I analyzed *Grandma and the Great Gourd* and *Grandma's Great Gourd* I asked, whose story is this? From what point of view? Then I looked at the main character and wondered how power was exercised? Who had agency? Who spoke and acted? Next, I examined the ending of the folktale thinking about how Divakaruni closed the story. I wondered about assumptions embedded in the story and whether the story was open or closed. Then, I examined the genre as a social construction, pondering the position of the characters within these texts. How do folktales organize the reader's perceptions of reality? When contemplating the sociopolitical contexts I deliberated about the cultural statements to which these texts were responding. I researched reviews of both the hardback book and the digital book app to discover sociopolitical contexts and cultural themes. Finally, I studied the historical context, exploring the historical developments around the cultural themes. What prevailing dominant ideologies were translated into these texts? Gathering these layers together within critical multicultural analysis makes the discourses of race, class, and gender more visible. The critical multicultural analysis tenets that were most relevant to my study were power, class and gender.

Literature Review

A few articles describe how picturebooks changed with the evolution of the book app[lication] (Al-Yaqout & Nikolajeva, 2015; Yokota & Teale, 2014). Apps incorporate specific digital affordances. These include frequently altered font with the text placed at the bottom of the screen. Also, instead of turning the pages in a book, readers press or tap an arrow or swipe to go to the next page. Often only one page of the original picturebook is shown on a tablet at a time, losing the two-page spread and visual stretch of the book. In addition, there is sometimes cutting or resizing of the illustrations to fit them on the iPad screen, as well as the fact that the paratextual elements (front and back covers, endpapers, title page) are not always retained in apps.

Because these innovations are fairly recent, there is a scarcity of research into the accuracy and faithfulness of the apps to the original books. For instance, *The Fantastic Flying Books of Mr. Morris Lessmore* (Joyce, 2012) is one picturebook and book app that has been the focus of several articles. Both Schwebs (2014) and Serafini, Kachorsky and Aguilera (2015) looked at the features of the picturebook, film, book app, and augmented reality app. Serafini et al. (2015) found that each instantiation brought the story to life in a different way and the technological dimensions added to the narrative dimensions. Schwebs (2014) investigated the aesthetic affordances between four different versions of the Joyce book. He found that the verbal and visual forms between the different instantiations created a multi-sensuous experience, revealing a complex aesthetic convergence. None of these authors looked at culture from a critical lens in the digital instantiations.

Text Selection

The picturebook *Grandma and the Great Gourd: A Bengali Folktale* and the interactive digital book app *Grandma's Great Gourd* were chosen for critical analysis because they take place in India and discuss a South Asian culture. Furthermore, there are very few global digital book apps and this one has not been analyzed in children's literature or technology research.

As Rosenblatt (1938) suggests, every reader comes to a text with a unique history. Thus, I aesthetically examined the picturebook and the digital app differently from other readers because of my own middle-class European-American background and my education in art and literacy. I am an outsider to Indian culture, language, and region and had to consciously step away from my background, misconceptions, biases, and judgments while reading this book in the two forms. Prior to analysis of these two books, I read and explored children's books from India and researched Indian culture and history to gain a better understanding. Despite my best efforts, my outsider critical lens held me back, and I realized I needed to read the picturebook and digital book app with cultural insiders to gain their perspectives as part of my analysis process.

Grandma and the Great Gourd tells the story of an old woman who lives in a small village in India next to a deep, dark jungle. One day Grandma receives an invitation to visit her daughter who lives on the other side of the jungle. As she travels, she encounters a clever red fox, a shaggy black bear, and a sleek striped tiger. Each animal is hungry and eager to eat Grandma, but she shows them how skinny she is and convinces them to wait until she returns. When it is time for Grandma to go home, she hides in a large gourd to disguise herself. The fierce creatures do not know what to make of a gourd that sings, rolls, and bounces; thus, Grandma is able to outsmart them.

Literary Safari created the book app *Grandma's Great Gourd* based on the picturebook. The app integrates music and movement with a multimedia experience. Children can take a virtual field trip to explore food, art, animals, language, and clothing from the region of Bengal. In addition, there is a physics game where players launch Grandma in her gourd through the forest. Literary Safari is committed to presenting diverse cultures in their stories and encouraging children to see and experience the world's citizens as they are in real life.

The book's author, Chitra Banerjee Divakaruni, was born and raised in India. She is a well-known author of adult literature as well as several young adult novels. Divakaruni writes in realistic, historical, magical realism, myth, and fantasy genres. The picturebook illustrator, Susy Pilgrim Waters, grew up in England and is a designer and painter of textiles and furniture. Waters illustrated Divakaruni's young adult novel covers and describes her artistic style as expressionistic, graphic, layered, hand drawn and painterly. Divakaruni retold *Grandma and the Great Gourd,* writing about the country of her origin and the culture of her childhood, for an American audience. Literary Safari's founder, Sandhya Nankani, was born in Ghana and raised there and in India until middle school when she moved to the U.S. Nankani has more than a decade of experience creating educational content for *Scholastic Education* and *Weekly Reader.*

A number of websites such as Kirkus, Horn Book and Booklist have reviewed either the picturebook or the app, but none have evaluated both. For example, the online review source Common Sense Media said the app was an engaging story with beautiful graphics that dives into a world and culture that is not often represented (VanderBorght, 2016). Yet, this review source concentrated on the evaluation of the digital features present in the book app, paying no attention to the literary quality of the story. Surprisingly, Meyers, Zaminpaima and Frederico (2014) found that digital apps or games are often reviewed positively with little mention of the story content.

Research Methodology

Over the course of eight weeks, I immersed myself in the words and illustrations of both texts, using Rosenblatt's (1938) transactional theory of reading. I read the picturebook silently and aloud numerous times, trying to make sense of the story, thinking about the main character, Grandma, and the animals she meets, appreciating the colorful illustrations and enjoying the story. I did the same with the digital book app. I tinkered with the different ways to read and experience the app, playing the rolling gourd game, viewing the videos, and having fun.

As I aesthetically enjoyed these two texts many questions came to mind: Are book apps exact replications of picturebooks? Should they be? Do the artistic techniques, mediums, musical scores and voice artists in digital book apps divert or engage readers? Are the illustrations in the picturebook the same as in the book app? How do digital apps reveal cultural aspects? Over time the focus of my research became: What cultural attributes are revealed, particularly power, class, and gender, in the illustrations in the picturebook *Grandma and the Great Gourd* and the digital book app *Grandma's Great Gourd*?

To study the illustrations closely I moved them out of the confines of the hardcover book and photocopied each page of the picturebook in color from the cover to the end pages. This storyboard was then taped together and displayed page-by-page horizontally on a large wall in my home. The storyboard helped me notice and identify fundamental illustration elements I didn't see when I turned the pages of the book. For example, as soon as the storyboard was on my wall I realized that Susy Pilgrim Waters, the illustrator, repeatedly used circles. I noted other elements of design such as line, color, light/value, and texture. On sticky notes I posted the design principles I found in the illustrations, such as balance, movement, rhythm, repetition, proportion, and unity.

Next, I created a document with two columns in which I word-processed the picturebook text in the first column and the narrative text for the digital book app in the second column. For each double page spread I described the illustration. For the book app slides I noted the illustrations as well as the movement, sound, and speech bubbles. Creating this document took a considerable amount of time but doing so helped me complete an in-depth analysis of the structures of language and the illustrations, noticing recurring themes. I found the majority of the sentences in the digital book app had been simplified or shortened. The first double page spread in the hardback book contains 97 words, whereas the four slides in the digital book app that depict the same scene contain 63 words.

Approximately one third of the words were deleted in the digital book app version.

At this same time, I reviewed the scholarship on Indian folklore (Maitra, 2007) and read other Bengali folktales, such as *The Old Woman and the Red Pumpkin* (Bang, 1975) and *Tales from Thakurmar Jhuli: 12 Stories from Bengal* (Majumdar, 2012). Oral folktales such as *Thakurmar Jhuli,* known as *Grandmother's Bag of Tales,* were collected by Dakkhinaranjan Mitra Majumdar and published in a book in 1907. He also collected and published folktales, fairy tales and poems about grandfathers and maternal grandmothers/grandfathers. The original *Thakurmar Jhuli* stories were narrated by grandparents to provide moral and religious instruction to young minds (Maitra, 2007). Divakaruni, the author of *Grandma and the Great Gourd,* remembers her grandfather retelling this Bengali tale when she was a little girl (Krishnaswami, 2014).

Another layer of analysis included making screen shots of the digital book app slides, printing them in color and adding them vertically underneath each double-page spread of the picturebook storyboard on my wall. This visual representation of both text illustrations helped me juxtapose and analyze them using Painter, Martin and Unsworth's (2013) tools of visual analysis.

Adichie (2009) discussed the dangers of a single story to depict a culture and how this can create stereotypes rather than eradicate them. With this thought in mind, I shared *Grandma and the Great Gourd* with neighbors, parents, and colleagues from India. Each shared similar stories about Hindu gods and fantastical animals. They noticed the bright colors in the picturebook and told me about Indian folk art and Warli paintings. Two parents encouraged me to download and read *71 Golden Tales of Panchatantra* (Govindan, 2011) that contains some *Thakurmar Jhuli* tales.

Findings

Analyzing the two texts, *Grandma and the Great Gourd* and *Grandma's Great Gourd,* side-by-side through the lens of critical multicultural analysis helped me generate intertextual connections, disconnections, and questions. All of this allowed me to attend to the cultural perspectives in the illustrations, looking closely at culture, power, class, and gender (Botelho & Rudman, 2009). The findings are organized around the paratextual elements, the inside elements, and the additional content, discussing the CMA tenets throughout.

The Paratextual Elements in Grandma

Paratextual elements are important functions in picturebooks because they consist of everything besides the text. These components include the dust jacket, front and back covers, endpapers, title page, flyleaf, copyright page, and any other special features that set the stage for reading (Galda, Cullinan, & Sipe, 2010).

FIGURE 9.1A Picturebook Cover (Divakaruni, 2013)

Some book apps such as *Rules of Summer* (We are Wheelbarrow, 2013) have kept all the paratexts, yet in the digital book app *Grandma's Great Gourd* they have been altered or removed.

The first paratextual attribute is the cover in picturebooks or the icon in digital book apps. The cover of *Grandma and the Great Gourd* has an orange background with the title, author, and illustrator at the top, and geometric patterns around the words and on the sides of the book (see Figure 9.1A). A Bengal tiger and a black bear are hiding in green foliage, and Grandma stands out in a white sari. There are floral motifs scattered around the forest in orange, pink, red, and blue. These aspects of nature and the forest animals showcase Indian culture (Maitra, 2007). In contrast, the digital book icon is very simple with two large golden gourds and Grandma hiding between them (see Figure 9.1B). Some book app icons contain

FIGURE 9.1B Digital Book Icon (Literary Safari, 2016a)
Source: From *Grandma's Great Gourd*, copyright © 2016 Literary Safari.

shortened titles, yet *Grandma's Great Gourd* omitted the title, author, and illustrator, ignoring an essential part of the paratext (Al-Yaqout & Nikolajva, 2015).

The front and back covers of the picturebook foretell that a tiger, bear, and fox will appear in the story. Grandma has wrinkles in her forehead and a straight worried mouth, noting she will be leaving on a dangerous adventure. In contrast, the digital book app cover doesn't give viewers any sense of what the story will be about, except that Grandma is happy. Both the picturebook cover and digital icon are visually appealing, but the global setting and context is erased from the app icon. Grandma could be living almost anywhere. Young viewers won't be able to predict the characters Grandma meets because the app icon focuses on the middle of the book, not the journey Grandma takes to see her daughter, the animals she meets, or the theme of the story.

Through my analysis I noticed that the digital app omits other paratextual elements such as the dust jacket and end papers. Both texts contain a title page or home screen that are noticeably diverse. For example, the app's home screen is indigo blue with the title in the left hand corner in orange and green font. In the middle of the slide an icon moves side-to-side to a musical beat and is labeled "Read." Readers can touch this icon to read the story or swipe the page to the left to reveal additional icons "Roll," "Record," and "Explore." In contrast, the title page of the hardcover book shows a large orange circle surrounded by smaller circles with the title, author, illustrator, and publisher information. This large circle mimics the sun that is popping up over the trees in the background.

The copyright page is at the very end of the picturebook and contains dedications from the author and illustrator, Library of Congress information, and a summary. For the digital book app there is a small tree icon in the right hand corner of the home screen. When the tree is tapped, the words "*Grownups only! Press and hold!*" appear. Next, a slide describes the different attributes of the app, a brief review of the picturebook and credits—acknowledging the app developer, producer, creative director, music, and voiceover, as well as many advisors. Literary Safari is stating that copyright information is for grownups only and that children will not be interested in the individuals who wrote and illustrated the book or those who made the app. For more information on the Grown Up Guide see Literary Safari (2016b).

A common literacy practice in classrooms, libraries, and homes is to read aloud a picturebook cover, title page, and copyright information, especially the dedications. Literacy learning is a sociocultural practice that occurs through participation and placing culture at the center of learning (Botelho & Rudman, 2009). Paratextual elements engage children in the reading experience and help them look forward to the story, predicting what might happen. Since some of the paratextual elements are missing in the digital book app, or are for adults only, the reading and cultural experience for children will be different. Al-Yaqout and Nikolajeva (2015) note that the lack of paratexts in book apps interferes with the aesthetic experience of the narrative story. In addition, Botelho and Rudman (2009) maintain that any reading approach that excludes the social and political dimensions of reading, such as removing the paratextual elements for children to engage in, reproduces dominant power relations.

The Inside Elements in Grandma

The page layouts of picturebooks are important visual features affecting how children read and enjoy texts. Picturebook app developers are restrained by the size of the screen, whereas print books can come in a variety of shapes and sizes. In the hardcover book *Grandma and the Great Gourd* there are 15 double-page spreads with two single pages for the title page and the copyright information, whereas the digital book app has more than 100 slides. I was surprised to learn in my analysis that none of the slides in the digital book app are exact replications of the picturebook illustrations. I expected the app to emulate the picturebook both visually and verbally, but this was not the case.

The first page of the picturebook begins: "Once upon a time, in a little village in India, there lived an old woman whom everyone called Grandma. She loved gardening and had the best vegetable patch in the village." A colorful double-page spread in bold shades of orange and ochre depicts Grandma sitting in front of her hut with garden vegetables surrounding her. Grandma's two dogs, Kalu and Bhulu, are by her side with peacocks and elephants in the background. Some of Grandma's garden is under the sentences. In contrast, the first page in the digital book app begins with "A little village in Bengal," and the illustration depicts five ginger-colored huts with a light blue background. Palm trees sway to flute music in front of blue acacia trees and a rotating sun.

Colors express beauty and emotions such as joy, fear, or sadness. Painter et al. (2013) state that dark and light pigments reveal and display moods. The overall color scheme in the picturebook is oranges, reds, and pinks as revealed on the cover and the first double-page spread (see Figure 9.2). Whereas the digital book app slides mostly reveal cool colors of light blue and green, portraying a toned-down visual experience. The bold warm colors surrounding Grandma in the picturebook signify the vibrant culture of the country of India and characterize power, permanence, and presence (Botelho, Young, & Nappi, 2014; Maitra, 2007). The reduced color palette of soft colors in the digital app signals a different mood (Painter et al., 2013).

The value and vibrancy in the digital book app illustrations seem to come from the music and light/darkness. In the second double-page spread Grandma receives a letter from her daughter asking her to visit. As Grandma embarks on her journey to her daughter's home there are a couple of slides in the digital book app that display a daunting forest with dark blues, greens and grays. The music becomes slow and repetitive. The dark background colors change the ambience, making it very clear to viewers that Grandma is hesitant to travel through the forest. These slides appear each time Grandma is about to meet a forest animal. They are not in the picturebook.

Grandma is the main character in both the picturebook and digital book app. There are no male characters except for the animals—Grandma's loyal dogs and the forest animals. Elderly women, especially widows in mourning clothing such as a white sari, are not common in western folktales or fairy tales. *Thakurmar Jhuli* stories are known to be the thoughts, fantasies, beliefs, and/or feelings of women in rural West Bengal. Before India achieved independence from Britain, many widows were ostracized and banished from their families and expected to mourn until the end of their lives. They left behind their colorful saris, jewelry, and hair, becoming invisible within society (Gorney, 2017). In some rural villages of West Bengal families still shun and send widows away, but this is not the case with Grandma. *Thakurmar Jhuli* tales preach gentleness, meekness, submission, passiveness, compliance, and docility, along with responsibility and bravery (Maitra, 2007). Grandma's posture, facial demeanor, and actions in the picturebook and the digital book app confirm this socio-cultural ethos.

In the succeeding page spreads and digital slides, Grandma's dignity is stifled as she wears white and is depicted as frail and skinny with a timid posture, showing passiveness and docility. As she meets the hungry animals for the first time, she is spaced out from them with a frown on her face, concerned eyebrows, and worried eyes. Grandma's eyes only gaze out directly to readers when she meets the bear, pleading with them to help her. When Grandma meets the tiger in the hardback book, the perspective and power change because she is situated in front of the tiger and viewers see a close-up of her from the chest up. Grandma's face still portrays nervousness as she looks at the tiger, but her size demands respect. Even though Grandma is apprehensive each time she meets the forest animals, she shows agency in her words, "If you're planning to have me for breakfast that's a terrible idea. See how skinny I am? I'll be a lot plumper on my way back from my daughter's house."

When Grandma leaves her daughter's home on page 8, rolling through the forest in a hollowed-out gourd, she faces her return journey with power and agency. The expression on her face is completely different—her eyes gaze directly out at readers, her mouth is smiling, and she has defined pink cheeks (Painter et al., 2013). Maitra (2007) wrote that *Thankurmar Jhuli* addresses courage with bravery, and these Indian cultural attributes are shown in the second half of both the picturebook and digital book app illustrations.

The picturebook includes many geometric patterns and symbols within the pages that enhance the collage illustrations. The region of West Bengal is known for kantha embroidery and quilts that reflect life, traditions, and cultural ideals that express happiness, sorrow, and imagination. Additionally, alpona painting is a traditional Indian folk art that is created on floors and flat surfaces in homes or on streets with rice-paste. This ancient practice is done among women and includes patterns such as butterflies, flowers, fish, cows, and haystacks (Tripathi, 2013–2018). Susy Pilgrim Waters, the illustrator, doesn't have an Indian background, but she takes care to use alpona and kantha art styles through the depictions of floral patterns and geometric shapes in the hardback picturebook. The front cover shown in Figure 9.1A reveals circles, stars, flowers, ferns and leaves. Interestingly, the digital book app has removed the majority of these intricate floral motifs and symmetrical shapes (see Figure 9.2B). In addition, Waters created block prints or stamped designs in the borders of the picturebook, a process found on textiles and fabrics in Bangladesh. Most of these block prints have been removed in the book app, but a few were retained.

It is helpful to look closely at the same scene from the picturebook and the digital book app where Grandma has safely returned back to her village and is thanking her dogs for saving her life. The picturebook illustration in Figure 9.2A contains red block print leaves at the top of the page, with crimson stars scattered whimsically around Grandma and her loyal dogs. On the right-hand side of the double-page spread are floral leaf patterns with lumbering elephants in the background. These symmetrical and intricate patterns are not in the same scene in the book app shown in Figure 9.2B. The removal of these cultural motifs from the app illustrations is problematic because children miss out on the cultural art styles—alpona paintings, kantha embroidery and block prints.

In both the picturebook and the digital book app Grandma lives in a hut by herself. She lives in a rural village in the region of West Bengal where she grows

FIGURE 9.2A Picturebook Illustration (Divakaruni, 2013) on the Left
Source: From *Grandma and the Great Gourd: A Bengali Folktale* © 2013 by Chitra Banerjee Divakaruni. Illustrations © 2013 by Susy Pilgrim Waters. Reprinted by permission of Roaring Book Press, a division of Holtzbrinck Publishing Holdings Limited Partnership. All Rights Reserved.

her own vegetables, gathers her own food, and cooks her meals outside. Traditional literature was orally transmitted across generations and is deeply rooted in beliefs, values, and morals. *Grandma and the Great Gourd* seems to be a contemporary retelling, echoing a time past. Widows typically lost their property and were banned from seeing family. Yet, in these two texts Grandma has her property and can communicate with and visit her daughter. Poverty is evident, possibly even romanticized, but not emphasized in the storyline or illustrations in either version of the story (Botelho & Rudman, 2009). The focus of both texts presents Grandma as a resilient and resourceful independent woman, resisting the economic oppression.

Folktales or fairy tales are told in a certain way where readers expect a clear ending. At the conclusion when the clever fox opens the gourd and Grandma falls out she says, "You caught me fair and square. I guess you deserve to eat me up." But Grandma doesn't give up and asks to sing a song that alerts her dogs to chase the fox away. Viewers/readers witness Grandma exercising power and trickery over the forest animals through her words and the illustrations. Botelho et al. (2014) noted that all book endings solidify a historical and sociopolitical message. With this particular folktale, action and creativity, as well as family, save Grandma. Furthermore, Grandma isn't silenced as many widows were during colonial rule or in rural areas in India today because she has agency and power. Grandma's two loyal dogs also return a good deed, thus teaching a moral lesson to children.

FIGURE 9.2B Digital Book App Slide (Literary Safari, 2016a).
Source: from *Grandma's Great Gourd* copyright © 2016 Literary Safari.

The Additional Content in Grandma

Digital book apps provide additional affordances such as interactivity and content that picturebooks are not able to support. These interactive ingredients may be music, sound effects, and motifs. Apps also utilize zooming in and out, still and moving images, as well as panning. When parents or teachers share digital book apps with children they usually linger on the illustrations, point, and give names to objects, ask questions and encourage children to participate in the app (Schwebs, 2014). Researchers such as Hamer (2017) and Sargent (2013) believe these interactivities may influence the reading of the story and the meaning–making process.

The digital book app, *Grandma's Great Gourd*, contains movement, music, and sound effects. When Grandma is walking through the forest to her daughter's home, she walks across the screen *"khut-khut-khut"* to drum and flute music. Each time Grandma meets an animal in the jungle, the animal bounces up and down, signaling an interactive hotspot. Since Grandma is scared her heart makes sounds such as *"dhuk-dhuk"* and *"dhip-dhip,"* and the text is enlarged for readers. In addition, Grandma sometimes bounces, and when she is tapped a speech bubble appears with dialogue. On Grandma's return trip through the forest, when she is hiding in the gourd, it bounces and rolls in a somersault across the screen. All of these sound effects and movements complement the content of the picturebook, yet also alter it because they expand the story. Hamer (2017) noted that these features invite readers to engage with the performative elements of the narrative.

With digital book apps viewers often have many choices. In *Grandma's Great Gourd*, a child can choose "Read by Myself" or "Read for Me" modes where the text is highlighted. In addition, all sound and music can be turned off and there is a choice to "Record" and customize the narration of the story with sound effects. Viewers have the option of slowing down the reading by skipping scenes or jumping ahead in the story. When Grandma is about to enter the forest for the first time, viewers see all three animals hiding in the foliage. Painter et al. (2013) note that the appearance of these characters, such as the forest animals, invites readers to have fun and signals them to choose the animal they want Grandma to meet. The storyline in the digital book app is not linear like the picturebook where Grandma meets each animal in a certain order. As Sargent (2013) suggests, these interactive features invite children to become active participants in the narrative construction of the story.

When Grandma reaches her daughter's home, she works in the garden by digging, watering and sprinkling the ground with fertilizer to help the vegetables grow—typical labor for females in rural areas. In the picturebook this is described in one double-page spread. In the app 19 slides slow down this scene with animation, movement, and a game. The vegetables, along with flowers and designs, fall from the sky, encouraging children to touch them to make them explode. When children tap on a shovel, holes are dug in the ground. When the watering can is tapped, seeds are watered and grow into sprouts and larger plants. None of these actions, such as the vegetables growing in the garden and the explosion game, are a major part of the picturebook but are embellished in the digital book app. In fact, in some ways, these slides take away from the theme of the picturebook— Grandma developing power, agency, and outsmarting the forest animals.

Another interactive feature in the app is a gourd game where players launch Grandma in her gourd through the forest and unlock different gourds. VanderBorght (2016) remarked that the weakest part of the app was this game because the execution is awkward and there isn't any physics learning. Sargent (2013) noted that games in apps are sometimes designed for immersive play, rather than reinforcing or enhancing the narrative content. Hamer (2017) discussed replayability—when a child replays a game, such as launching the gourd over and over during an extended period of time. The gourd game may have replayability for very young children, keeping them engrossed in the screen, but after playing it multiple times it is more for entertainment rather than enhancing the narrative story.

The supplementary features in the "Explore" section of the app include a world map and videos of India's art, how to wear a sari, the wildlife in the Sundarbans, how to say "grandma" in different languages, and a recipe for rice treats. These features enrich the story content and are culturally authentic, and none of them are included in the hardback book. When children view these videos and multimedia elements they will learn more about the Bengali region, gaining additional cultural experiences.

Discussion

Literature helps children appreciate human knowledge, offering experiences beyond their actual understandings and giving them possibilities for new adventures. Through both the picturebook *Grandma and the Great Gourd* and the digital book app *Grandma's Great Gourd*, young children's worldviews might be transformed. Both titles are told well with interesting onomatopoeic sounds such as having the dogs say "*gheu-gheu*" or the giant lizards "*khash-khash.*" Both are culturally authentic and introduce a traditional folktale different from western tales, with a main character who is spunky, full of life, and able to outsmart the animals by telling them to wait to eat her. Before Grandma leaves her daughter's home, she takes action by hiding in a large hollowed out gourd to disguise herself. Grandma is a positive role model for children because of her power and agency.

The picturebook *Grandma and the Great Gourd* could be read aloud and enjoyed by preschool to intermediate-age children. Yet the digital book app is geared to very young children, aged 2–5. The sentences have been revised and the text has been shortened. In addition, the copyright information is for "*Grownups only!*" Literary Safari, producers of the app, seem to assume that digital book apps need to contain simple language and that young children aren't interested in the paratextual elements such as the author, illustrator, or the people who made the app, yet if the sentence, language structure, and paratextual elements had remained the same as in the published picturebook, perhaps the app would reach a larger audience.

The animation of the water sprinkling and the vegetables growing in the garden scene may keep young children engaged, but it interrupts the story and exaggerates one scene that is not important to the theme of the book. Moreover, *Thakurmar Jhuli* or *Grandmother's Bag of Tales* (Majumdar, 1907) were told to provide moral and religious instruction, advocating for gentleness, meekness, submission, passiveness, compliance, and docility, along with responsibility and bravery (Maitra, 2007). The animated games seem to go against the goal of Indian folktales and subtract from the major theme of power and agency. Yokota and Teale (2014) maintain that the interactive features in digital book apps need to align with the content and integrity of the story.

One possible reason the illustrations in the digital book app were modified, softened, and toned down was to make them less busy for children who would be listening, viewing, and playing the app. It looks like Susy Pilgrim Waters, the picturebook illustrator, tried to stay true to the folk literature and Indian culture by using artistic elements from kantha embroidery and alpona paintings, but these have been removed or toned down in the digital book app. Even children aged 2–5 appreciate cultural art and could easily have appreciated and learned from the same illustrations in the picturebook.

The supplementary features of the app such as the world map, videos, and recipes add cultural information to the story that is not available in the hardback picturebook. In fact, the app appears to put more focus on learning about a culture and less on experiencing a story. The app could have been strengthened by adding a link to the author's and illustrator's websites and a video interview of both. Opportunities for word exploration would have also strengthened the app so that children could tap on a word, such as "tamarinds" or "Dervish," and have it pronounced or defined. A feature that would have made the app more diverse would have been an added option to hear the book read in Bengali so that children from India or Bangladesh could have their language affirmed and English learners could acquire Bengali vocabulary.

Few critical analyses of book apps and their picturebook counterparts have been completed. Understanding and contrasting the visual aspects of each medium is valuable because they are becoming increasingly relied upon by parents, teachers, and librarians as part of literacy instruction. When I think about the illustration elements that were revised in the digital book app—changing the overall color scheme from warm oranges, reds, and pinks to cool colors and deleting the many floral patterns and geometric shapes that were borrowed from kantha embroidery and alpona paintings—it appears that the app was made to look aesthetically pleasing rather than authentic. Furthermore, it looks like generic illustrations were chosen for the digital book app because American children would be reading, viewing, and playing with it.

Hutcheon's (2013) *A Theory of Adaptation* states that adaptations of media, such as books apps, are recreations rather than reproductions and should be regarded as autonomous works and interpreted and valued as such. Even though there are significant visual and textual variations between the picturebook and the digital book app, both contribute to the storytelling of an engaging cultural folktale. I believe both stories have strengths even though they have very different purposes.

Final Reflections

Engagements with high quality literature and digital book apps can introduce children to the power of literature, the importance of recognizing the social and cultural contexts that brought the literature into being, and the contexts that shape their responses. Reading books/apps and transacting with literature holds the possibility for transforming lives, communities, and societies.

Missing from this analysis are the thoughts of children, teachers, and librarians on this unique folktale. Hearing their perspectives, voices, and opinions would strengthen this analysis. Future research needs to include sharing both picturebooks and apps with children so as to obtain their perspectives. Examining how children read and interact with the two types of text could also inform literacy practices, providing insight into opportunities for children to critically engage with these texts. In addition, it may help to interview the author, illustrator, and publisher of the app to understand their perspectives on their work. More research needs to be conducted on how emerging readers are influenced by the technological aspects of digital book apps. The interactive affordances may influence or develop the meaning-making processes.

The picturebook *Grandma and the Great Gourd* and the digital book app *Grandma's Great Gourd* are both tactile texts, bringing a variety of verbal and visual forms in a multi-sensory experience to share a Bengali folktale for children. Both books provide an aesthetically engaging and interactive experience. Yet, after reading and analyzing both renditions, I must conclude that the digital book app is teaching and developing a set of stories (games, map, videos, etc.) that detract from the main theme of the folktale. The digital book app *Grandma's Great Gourd* is a teaching tool, teaching about culture, whereas the picturebook *Grandma and the Great Gourd* is a strong narrative presenting a story about a culture.

References

Adichie, C.N. (2009). The danger of a single story. Ted Talk. Retrieved from https://www.ted.com/talks/chimamanda_adichie_the_danger_of_a_single_story

Al-Yaqout, G. & Nikolajeva, M. (2015). Re-conceptualizing picturebook theory in the digital age. *Nordic Journal of ChildLit Aesthetics*, 6, 1–7, http://dx.doi.org/10.3402/blft.v6.26971

Botelho, M.J. & Rudman, M.K. (2009). *Critical multicultural analysis of children's literature: Mirrors, windows, and doors*. New York: Routledge.

Botelho, M.J., Young, S.L.B., & Nappi, T. (2014). Rereading Columbus: Critical multicultural analysis of multiple historical storylines. *Journal of Children's Literature*, 40(1), 41–51.

Foucault, M. (1995). Strategies of power. In W. Truett Anderson (Ed.), *The truth about the truth: De-confusing and re-constructing the postmodern world* (pp. 40–45). New York: G.P. Putnam's Sons.

Galda, L., Cullinan, B., & Sipe, L. (2010). *Literature and the child*. Belmont, CA: Wadsworth/Cengage.

Gorney, C. (2017). For widows, life after loss. *National Geographic*. Retrieved from https://www.nationalgeographic.com/magazine/2017/02/global-images-of-widows-india-bosnia-uganda-discrimination-exile/

Hamer, N. (2017). The design and development of the picturebook for mobile and interactive platforms. In N. Hamer, P. Nodelman, & M. Reimer (Eds.), *More words about pictures* (pp. 63–80). London: Taylor & Francis.

Hutcheon, L. (2013). *A theory of adaptation*. New York: Routledge.

Krishnaswami, U. (2014). Interview: Chitra Banerjee Divakaruni on books for young readers. Jaggery. Retrieved from http://jaggerylit.com/issue-3-summer-2014/chitra-banerjee-divakaruni-on-books-for-young-readers/

Literary Safari Inc. (2016a). *Grandma's great gourd*. Mobile application software. Retrieved from www.literarysafari.com

Literary Safari, Inc. (2016b). Grownup guide. Retrieved from www.grandmasgourd.com/grownupguide

Maitra, L. (2007). 100 years of *Thakurmar Jhuli (Grandmother's Bag of Tales)*: From oral literature to digital media—Shaping thoughts for the young and old. *Indian Folklore Research Journal*, 4(7), 77–95.

Meyers, E.M., Zaminpaima, E., & Frederico, A. (2014). The future of children's texts: Evaluating book apps as multimodal reading experiences. *iConference*, 916–920.

Majumdar, D.M. (1907). *Thakurmar Jhuli* (Bengali). Kolkata, India: Mitra and Ghosh.

Painter, C., Martin, J.R., & Unsworth, L. (2013). *Reading visual narratives: Image analysis of children's picture books*. Sheffield, UK: Equinox.

Rosenblatt, L. (1938). *Literature as exploration*. New York:Appleton-Century.

Rudman, M.K. & Botelho, M.J. (2005). Shock of hair: Hair as a cultural theme in children's literature. *The Dragon Lode*, 24(1), 11–19.

Sargent, B. (2013). Interactive storytelling: How picture book conventions inform multimedia book app narratives. *Australian Journal of Intelligent Information Processing Systems*, 13 (3), 29–35.

Schwebs, T. (2014). Affordances of an app: A reading of The fantastic flying books of Mr. Morris Lessmore. *Nordic Journal of ChildLit Aesthetics*, 5, 1–11, http://dx.doi.org/10. 3402/blft.v5.24169

Serafini, F., Kachorsky, D., & Aguilera, E. (2015). Picture books 2.0: Transmedial features across narrative platforms. *Journal of Children's Literature*, 41(2), 16–24.

Tripathi, A. (2013–2018). Alpana. *Important India*. Retrieved from https://www.importa ntindia.com/135/alpana/

Turrion, C.J. (2014). Multimedia book apps in a contemporary culture: Commerce and innovation, continuity and rupture. *Nordic Journal of ChildLit Aesthetics*, 5, 1–7, http:// dx.foi.org/10.3402/blft.v5.24426

VanderBorght, M. (2016). *Grandma's great gourd*. *Common Sense Media*. Retrieved from http s://www.commonsensemedia.org/app-reviews/grandmas-great-gourd

Wooten, D.A. & McCuiston, K.F. (2015). Children's literature book apps: Exploring new paths for books and literacy development. *Journal of Children's Literature*, 41(2), 26–30.

Yokota, J., & Teale, W.H. (2014). Picture books and the digital world. *The Reading Teacher*, 67(8), 577–585.

Children's Literature and App References

Bang, B. (1975). *The old woman and the red pumpkin: A Bengali folk tale*. Illus. by M. Bang. New York: Atheneum.

Divakaruni, C.B. (2013). *Grandma and the great gourd: A Bengali folktale*. Illus. by S.P. Waters. New York: Roaring Brook Press.

Govindan, S. (2011). *71 golden tales of Panchtantra*. London: Unicorn Books.

HarperCollins. (2012). *Pete the cat*. Mobile application software. Retrieved from http:// itunes.apple.com

Joyce, W. (2012). *The fantastic flying books of Mr. Morris Lessmore*. Mobile application software. Retrieved from http://itunes.apple.com

Literary Safari Inc. (2016). *Grandma's great gourd*. Mobile application software. Retrieved from http://itunes.apple.com

Majumdar, M.D. (2012). *Tales from Thakumar Jhuli: 12 stories from Bengal*. Transl. by S. Ray. London: Oxford University Press.

Moonbot Studios LA. (2011). *The fantastic flying books of Mr. Morris Lessmore*. Mobile application software. Retrieved from http://itunes.apple.com

Nosy Crow. (2011). *The three little pigs: A 3-D fairy tale.* Mobile application software. Retrieved from http://itunes.apple.com

We are Wheelbarrow. (2013). *Rules of summer.* Mobile application software. Retrieved from http://itunes.apple.com

Willems, M. (2012). *Don't let the pigeon run this app!* Mobile application software. Retrieved from http://itunes.apple.com

PART IV

Visual Images and Ideologies

10

HOLY MOLÉ! AND THE REPRODUCTION OF A COLONIALIST PERSPECTIVE

Carmen M. Martínez-Roldán and Denise Dávila

Interrogating children's literature about Latin American cultures is essential in today's diverse society. More than 63 percent of the 57.5 million Hispanics in the United States are of Mexican origin and nearly a quarter (24.3 percent) of U.S. elementary, middle, and high school students are identified as Hispanics (U.S. Census Bureau, 2017). However, of the U.S. children's books published in 2017, only 6 percent featured significant Latinx content and 3 percent were by Latinx authors and/or illustrators (Cooperative Children's Book Center, 2018). Because picturebooks provide an aesthetic experience that contributes to children's socialization and treatment of others, it is crucial that bookmakers (authors, illustrators, and publishing teams) create books for young audiences that include relatable characters and visual elements while offering windows into dignified representations of diverse sociocultural groups and communities (Sims Bishop, 1990). It is equally important that teachers have the tools to help students develop the kinds of critical visual literacies to analyze the texts and images they consume.

This chapter presents a critical content analysis of the visual images in the picturebook *Holy Molé!: A Folktale from Mexico*, written by Caroline McAlister and illustrated by Stefan Czernecki (McAlister 2006). The Library of Congress (LOC) information for this book states that the story is a "retelling of the traditional Mexican tale explaining the origins of molé [sic]." Although the LOC entry suggests that *Holy Molé!* retells a traditional Mexican folktale, the story overlooks the Indigenous, pre-Columbian origins of mole and reinforces a colonialist ideology that erases and appropriates the contributions of Indigenous communities to Mexican culture. Our study examines the ways the visual and narrative strategies in *Holy Molé!* challenge or/and reproduce colonialist ideologies. We analyze how the illustrations in *Holy Molé!* position readers relative to the story's Indigenous and European characters and relative to mole, a culinary staple of Mexican culture.

The text of *Holy Molé!* retells a contemporary, twentieth-century urban legend that attributes the creation of mole to a culinary mishap that occurred in a Spanish monastery kitchen during Colonial times. According to her author's note, McAlister expanded upon the legend by adding a young protagonist to the picturebook. Carlos is an orphaned Indigenous Mexican boy who works in the monastery. On the day the Brothers (Catholic missionaries) are preparing a meal for the Viceroy's visit to colonial Mexico, hungry Carlos tries to grab a raisin bun from the kitchen floor. In doing so, he up-ends the kitchen worktable. The chopped spicy chilies, which were intended for a dinner sauce, and the chocolate and cinnamon that were reserved for dessert fly across the kitchen and land in a pot of savory turkey stew. In this adaptation of the urban legend, Carlos' misstep produces an exquisite blending of flavors, which people know today as mole.

Since the contemporary story privileges the Spanish colonizers and minimizes the Indigenous pre-Columbian peoples of Mexico, we preface our analysis with a brief examination of the stereotype of "el indio" relative to Spanish colonial imperialism in Mexico. Then, we describe the critical theoretical perspectives that informed our study. After, we highlight the methods we employed to conduct our critical visual analysis of *Holy Molé!*, in which we focused on the visual graduation, illustration style, and narrative tools in the picturebook. We present examples of our analysis in the Findings section of the chapter and conclude with a summary of our arguments and a set of implications from our analysis.

Socio-historical and Cultural Aspects of the Context

Māori scholar Linda Tuhiwai Smith of New Zealand (2012) points out that colonial imperialism was facilitated to expand the European economy and control of resources. As a result, colonialism involved the appropriation of Indigenous lands and the subjugation or extermination of Indigenous peoples. By positioning Indigenous peoples as ignorant savages who were not fully human, Europeans justified the enforcement of their colonizing policies and actions. For instance, the Burgos legislation, developed by Spain in 1512, outlined how to treat Indigenous people based on the assumption that they were by nature inclined to a life of sin. This legislation regulated the Spanish–Indigenous relationships for three decades. Regardless of whether they saw Indigenous people as sinful or good savages, the Spanish conquerors regarded themselves as the dominant "Us" group and positioned the native peoples of Mexico as the inferior "Other" (Said, 1979) and the poor Indians ("los inditos") as needing to be civilized.

At the same time, the Spanish developed a racial caste system that privileged fair-skinned individuals above dark-skinned individuals and that sometimes made exceptions for persons with a certain socioeconomic stature (Vinson, 2018). The stereotypes that promoted the racial caste system persisted for centuries. Even after the 1810 Mexican War of Independence from Spain and the recognition of Indigenous groups as members of Mexican society, the stereotypes of el indio continued into the twentieth century. They included the image of *los inditos* as humble, obedient, submissive Indians (Pérez Montfort, 2007), an image that long benefited the elite groups in power. Moreover, the emergence of cinematic media reinforced the colonial stereotype of the good Indian as a passive, quiet victim abused by powerful men (Méndez & Huerta Figueroa, 2015). Twentieth-century popular culture included other harmful images of Indigenous people as sneaky tricksters (e.g., the image of *el Indio pata rajada*/the [barefoot] Indian with a cut foot) and bandits (e.g., *el Indio ladino*/robber) (Pérez Monfort, 2004; 2007).

In recent years, contemporary Mexican scholars have contested popular narratives that attribute the origins of mole to Spaniards and that reinforce the historical positioning of Mexico's Indigenous peoples as the Other. For example, Cristina Barros (2004), a researcher, writer, and culinary specialist in Mexican food, has traced the origins of mole through Mexican cultural and historical knowledge. She found that pre-Colombian mole, which was known as *mulli* (a word used by the Indigenous Nahua people) and *chiles* (chili peppers) were among the ingredients that appeared in the sixteenth-century publication *Historia general de las cosas de la Nueva España/ General History of Things in New Spain,* penned by Franciscan missionary Bernardino de Sahagún sometime between 1540 and 1585. This friar interviewed many Aztec informants who described their different types of stews as variations of *mulli* (or moles): the *patzcalmollo, chilcuzmulli, mazaxocomulli, huauhquilmolli,* and *izmiquilmolli.* The Aztecs prepared moles for the gods and honored the lives of deceased people with the preparation of the *totolmole* and/or *mole de guajalote.* Today there are more than 40 types of moles, which reflect Indigenous people's culinary contributions to Mexico's national identity (Pérez Montfort, 2004).

Barros (2004) observed that despite the primary documents describing Bernardino de Sahagún's sixteenth-century account of the origins of mole, the pervasive urban legends that attribute mole to a monastic, colonial endeavor neither honor Mexican cuisine nor acknowledge the extraordinary creative cooks who, starting in pre-Hispanic times, have created infinite combinations of this dish.

Theoretical Framework

As a response to the problematic urban legends, our critical content analysis of *Holy Molé!* is framed by postcolonial theory (Tyson, 2011) and decolonizing research (Smith, 2012; Swadener & Mutua, 2008). It is also informed by the critical perspectives advanced by Latinx epistemologies (e.g., Delgado-Bernal, 1998; 2002) and draws from literary theory on narrative aesthetics (Nikolajeva, 2005).

Critical Perspectives and Decolonizing Research

Our theoretical lens aligns with those of decolonizing researchers who look beyond spatial and temporal elements to recognize the devastating material consequences and effects of colonialism on culture (Swadener & Mutua, 2008). The need to develop decolonizing Indigenous methodologies has resulted, in part, from the way research in Indigenous communities has been implicated in the production of theories that have dehumanized Indigenous peoples and have continued to privilege Western ways of knowing, while denying the validity of Indigenous knowledge, language, and culture (Smith, 2012). Decolonizing and critical researchers seek to "produce research knowledge that documents social injustice, that recovers subjugated knowledges, that helps create spaces for the voices of the silenced to be expressed and 'listened to,' and that challenges racism, colonialism and oppression" (p. 198).

We integrate decolonizing and postcolonial theories in two ways. First, we situate our study within Latinx/Chicanx epistemologies, which challenge the traditional notions of what counts as knowledge, what systems of knowledge are valued, who can generate knowledge about minoritized communities, and how this knowledge is or is not legitimized (Delgado-Bernal, 1998). These epistemologies validate knowledge that is grounded in the experiences of Latinx communities. Second, our study adopts Tyson's (2011) postcolonial framework for analyzing literature in order to understand how stories reproduce a colonialist or anticolonialist ideology. As described by Tyson, employing a postcolonial lens requires researchers and readers to examine how we define ourselves relative to others, considering the interplay between race, ethnicity, class, religion, gender, sexual orientation, and so forth.

Narrative Theory

This next section provides an overview of our adoption of narrative theory as part of a postcolonial framework. In short, the meaning-making processes of writers, illustrators, and readers are indivisible from the local, social, cultural, historical, and global contexts (Galda & Beach, 2001; Martínez-Roldán, 2016; Tyson, 2011). Therefore, it is necessary to consider the multidimensional ideologies that influence the creation, marketing, consumption, and interpretations of folk stories, which have been attributed to a particular ethnic group, as in the case of Holy Molé!

Bookmakers' ideological perspectives are often revealed through the narrative agents of a book, such as the real author and the implied-author (Nikolajeva, 2005). The real author is the person who actually writes the book's manuscript, authors' notes, and acknowledgements. The implied-author reflects the reader's image of the author based on the ideologies woven into the text. The ideal audience reflects the writer's ideological perceptions of their prospective readers. Finally, the real reader is the child or adult who actually engages with the book. We assume that just as there are narrative agents, there are also visual agents at work in picturebooks. They include the real illustrator as well as the implied-illustrator, whose ideologies are imbued in the illustrations and represent the real readers' conceptions of the artist.

Concepts of the real illustrator and implied-illustrator figured prominently in Dávila's (2012; 2015) examination of children's picturebooks about the celebration of el Día de los Muertos in local communities of the U.S., Mexico, and Central America. For example, Dávila (2012) observed that the illustrations of the non-fiction picturebook, *Día de los Muertos*, written by Ann Heinrichs and illustrated by Mernie Gallagher-Cole (2006), suggest that the implied-illustrator was complicit with a colonizing view of ancient Mesoamerican spiritual traditions by visually conflating el Día de los Muertos with the Christian/Catholic traditions (All Hallows Eve), All Saint's Day, and All Soul's Day. Next, Dávila (2015) found that the images in some of the popular realistic-fiction picturebooks about el Día de los Muertos indicate that the implied-illustrators "assumed the mantle of a tourist photographer" (p. 79). For example, despite the fact that shopping is never mentioned in the narrative texts, the illustrations of some of the realistic-fiction picturebooks feature colorful outdoor markets, which are popular with tour groups. These images treat the ideal audience like a group of vacationers who want to visit the kinds of picturesque sites featured on postcards. As a result, the implied-illustrator positions the realistic story characters as exotic Others who are part of a scenic tour rather than real people with rich, complex lives and traditions. The illustrations reinforce a harmful colonialist perspective by which the realistic characters are commodities for tourists' voyeuristic consumption rather than equals to the actual readers/consumers of the books. These concepts are relevant to our discussion of *Holy Molé!*

In sum, five key theoretical tenets inform our analysis:

- Latinx epistemology—culturally and linguistically relevant ways of knowing and understanding that are grounded in the sociohistorical experiences of Latinxs and the experiences of their communities (Delgado-Bernal, 1998; 2002).
- Colonialist ideology—"the colonizer's belief in their own superiority over the colonized, who were usually the original inhabitants of the lands the colonizers settled in or invaded" (Tyson 2011, p. 248).
- Subalterns—persons who occupy the bottom rungs of the colonialist social ladder. They are positioned as the Other by members of the colonizing culture (Tyson, 2011).
- Otherism—the dominant group ("us") as the norm and those who are different ("them") as inferior, exotic, uncivilized, or even dangerous (Nodelman, 1992; Said, 1979; Tyson, 2011).
- Narrative theory—ideologies of the writer and illustrator are regarded as imbued in the text and illustrations of a picturebook (Nikolajeva, 2005).

Methodology

Our study employs analytical tools from Painter, Martin, and Unsworth's (2013) systemic-functional semiotics framework. In tandem with our use of these tools,

we followed the procedures of critical content analysis as a research method
(Short, 2016). The introductory sections of this chapter describe the first phases of
the procedures in which we (a) selected a text and a critical theoretical framework
for our study, (b) explored the historical and sociocultural aspects of *Holy Molé!*,
(c) examined other studies that analyze the textual and visual content of picturebooks about Mexican culture, and (d) identified the theoretical tenets to frame
our close reading of *Holy Molé!* In the forthcoming findings and discussion section, we address the outcomes of our subsequent procedures in which we
(e) examined the representations of power and agency in the book, (f) applied the
theoretical tenets in our iterative close reading of *Holy Molé!*, (g) developed
themes that represent our analysis using the tools of systemic-functional semiotics,
and (h) chose visual elements and metafunctions of the picturebook as exemplars
of our theoretically-based research process. Following the guidelines set forth by
Painter et al. (2013) during our procedures, we focused on how the illustrator's
visual choices in *Holy Molé!* positioned readers relative to the characters and
relative to the writer's overall adaptation of the urban legend. Within these
positional relationships, which reveal an interpersonal metafunction, we examined
the visual systems of social distance (through an analysis of the illustrators' visual
style) and visual graduation, which upscales and downscales images.

Social Distance and Illustrator's Style

Writers and illustrators set up potential affective relationships between the reader,
text, and illustrations of a picturebook through the depiction of characters. Painter
et al. (2013) explain how a naturalistic style of illustration, which provides realistic
details and representations of the characters, invites readers to become involved
with the characters as actual persons who've had actual life experiences, while the
non-realistic minimalist style positions readers as voyeurs of the characters, who are
treated as objects of detached amusement. A "caricaturesque" visual style assumes
readers will not have empathy and will view the characters as Others, although it
may be used also as a social commentary (p. 35).

Visual Graduation

Visual graduation relates to the upscaling and/or downscaling of images, which
convey attitudinal meanings and reveal underlying ideologies on the part of the
bookmakers. As an illustrative tool, visual graduation establishes a visual lens
through which the ideal audience will view each character. It positions readers to
relate to the images in specific ways to solicit certain emotions. Visual graduation
employs three different types of image quantifications: (a) number, in which
upscaling is represented by high (repetitive) quantities of the same image and
downscaling is represented by low quantities of an image, (b) mass, in which,
comparatively larger images in a frame represent upscaling and comparatively

small images suggest downscaling, and (c) extent, in which the image that takes up the most available space is upscaled and the image that takes the least amount of available space is downscaled (Painter et al., 2013). Our analysis also considers how ideational meanings are represented by individual images and narrative sequences. Ideational meaning is drawn from the descriptions of the identities and attributes of the protagonist and the tracking and sequencing of the protagonist's appearance relative to the other characters in the story.

We then apply narrative theory to examine the interpersonal positioning of readers relative to the writer/illustrator, the implied-author/illustrator, and the ideal audience for *Holy Molé!* Our analysis addresses how the illustrative spreads and text position readers to assume certain ideological attitudes towards the characters. Last, we attend to the use of color in relationship to this ideological positioning of readers.

Our Positioning

Our interest in understanding representations of Latinxs in children's literature reflects our own epistemological positions and experiences as Latinx educators. Born in Puerto Rico, a territory and colony of the United States, Carmen has been keen to analyze the representations of colonized populations in children's literature. Born in California to a bi-racial Latinx family, Denise never saw families like hers in the school curriculum, let alone children's literature. Both authors are committed to decolonizing research and the affirmation of Indigenous epistemologies in their research and teacher education programs.

Findings and Discussion

In this section, we describe the ways in which the writer and illustrator of *Holy Molé!* position their ideal audiences relative to the characters, both Indigenous and Europeans, and to the culinary staple of Mexican culture known as mole.

Visual Graduation Positions Protagonist as Subaltern

In *Holy Molé!* the illustrator makes extensive use of the strategies of visual graduation. We argue that Czernecki's visual choices depict the story's young protagonist Carlos as a subaltern to the adult characters.

In our discussion, we follow the chronological presentation of texts and images in *Holy Molé!* We begin with the book's cover art. It features an upscaled, close-up view of Carlos with a pot of poultry stew. As suggested by the book title, the pot appears to contain mole. The illustrator's use of visual graduation by extent produces an image that nearly fills the entire cover of the book. Carlos is dressed as a campesino with a downscaled Zapata-style sombrero, hinting to the reader that he is Mexican. He appears to taste the contents of the pot like chefs do.

Readers who are not familiar with the traditional clothing of campesinos might assume that Carlos is dressed in a chef's uniform. The upscaling of Carlos' head and body in the image suggests that he will be a protagonist in the story. While the book's cover art suggests that Carlos will star in a leading role, the subsequent title page shows a very tiny barefoot Carlos with an empty bowl. His presentation is reminiscent of the *Indio pata rajada* insult. The image on the title page disrupts any notion that Carlos is dressed in chef's clothes (see Figure 10.1).

A folktale from Mexico

Caroline McAlister
Illustrated by Stefan Czernecki

Little Folk
ATLANTA

FIGURE 10.1 Carlos as Pata Rajada on Title Page
Source: Holy Molé!: A Folktale from Mexico by Caroline McAlister and illustrated by Stefan Czernecki. Text Copyright © 2007 Caroline McAlister. Illustrations Copyright © 2007 Stefan Czernecki. Published 2007 by August House Publishers, Inc.

The title page illustration alludes to popular images of hungry children with empty bowls often used by charities for raising funds for food donations. Via the downscaled image by extent, which takes little space on the page, readers are positioned to pity Carlos as a small, impoverished, hungry child who is at the mercy of others.

On the first page of the story, the illustrator reintroduces Carlos through upscale graduation by extent, in which the child's image fills the page (see Figure 10.2).

Carlos squatted under the kitchen table as he cleaned the monastery floor.

He heard someone enter the room.

FIGURE 10.2 Carlos' Subaltern Positioning
Source: Holy Molé!: A Folktale from Mexico by Caroline McAlister and illustrated by Stefan Czernecki. Text Copyright © 2007 Caroline McAlister. Illustrations Copyright © 2007 Stefan Czernecki. Published 2007 by August House Publishers, Inc.

However, the upscaling neither enhances Carlos nor suggests that he has power, as the size increase would afford. To the contrary, the image shows Carlos on the ground, kneeling, cleaning the monastery floor. It underscores his subaltern position, especially as the line representing his lips is downturned, indicating unhappiness.

The graduation choice of upscaling the image of a subservient boy raises questions about Carlos' relationships with the church members living in the monastery. The image suggests that the barefoot young boy engaged in slave-like labor for the missionaries.

Carlos reappears in a double-page spread (pp. 4–5), in which Czernecki uses visual graduation differently. For instance, he used upscaled quantification by number in showing four adult friars towering over a small Carlos (downscaled not only in terms of number but also of mass), who is significantly smaller in size. In fact, only part of Carlos' head (and hat) appears in the spread, which suggests that the child is of marginal importance relative to the missionaries. The images also speak to the distribution of power in the colonial monastery, in which young Carlos has very little. The inclusion of other children, pupils, or kitchen helpers could have visually suggested a more balanced distribution of power.

In the next spread (pp. 6–7), the barefoot Carlos re-emerges with his arms positioned behind his back, listening attentively to Brother Pascual. Using downsized quantification of mass, Czernecki depicts Carlos significantly smaller than Brother Pascual. The depiction is reinforced by the text in which Brother Pascual refers to Carlos as "little kitchen boy" and orders the child to help make tortillas for a high-ranking official. The monastery will receive a visit from the Viceroy, a direct informant to the Spanish Crown.

Moving between gradations, in the succeeding spread (pp. 8–9), the illustrator returns to a larger, upscaled presentation of Carlos, described in the accompanying text as "an orphan boy" who helped in the kitchen in exchange for "scraps of food" (p. 9). Unfortunately, the potential for a visually positive representation of Carlos is lost when Brother Pascual tells the child to "stay out of sight" when the Viceroy arrives (p. 9). In this scene, the dialogue minimizes the child in the same way that the stereotypes of "el indito" and "el pelado" have historically marginalized Indigenous persons of Mexico. The interplay between the text and images of the first few pages of the book reinforces the racial colonial caste system between the Spanish Viceroy, the missionaries/friars (of Spanish, Spanish American, and/or Mestizo heritage), and the Indigenous persons of Mexico. Applying narrative theory, imbued in the text is the implied-author's complicity with the colonial caste structure by which the Indigenous child's hunger is secondary to pleasing the European-Spanish social class.

The next time Carlos appears is on pages 14 and 15. While the child's upscaled image fills most of the page, Carlos looks as though he is tumbling to the floor. The child's fall is magnified by the illustrator's choice of extent graduation. The accompanying text states that Carlos, "was waiting to sneak a bit of something sweet ..." So, when "he spied a raisin bun that had fallen on the floor," Carlos "darted out to grab it" (p. 15). In other words, the implied-author indicates that the Indigenous child had a premeditated plan to engage in sneaky behavior when the opportunity presented itself. The text points to the author's (McAlister's) image of her ideal audience that would disapprove of an Indigenous child who sneaked, spied, darted-out, and grabbed whatever he wanted. In addition, the text reinforces contemporary twentieth-century racist stereotypes of the "sneaky Mexican," the "trickster Mexican," or the "Indio ladino" (robber). These negative images of Mexicans were popularized in the 1960s and 1970s advertisements for Frito-Lay's corn chips. In the print ads, the gun-wielding "cunning, clever, and sneaky" Frito Bandito "loves crunchy Fritos corn chips so much, he'll stop at nothing to get yours." (See the popular Frito-Lay™ "Frito Bandito" television commercial on Youtube).

On the next spread (pp. 16–17), both Carlos and Brother Pascual lie on the floor with equal upscaled extent images. The text suggests that Carlos has collided with Brother Pascual (p. 17). The narrative implies it was the child's fault that the meal preparations were "ruined" and that the friars' opportunity for garnering favor with the king was "spoiled" (p. 19). These words offer little empathy for a child who was hungry and desperate for food. Nothing in the text suggests that the incident was an accident. In fact, Carlos accepts that he will be punished for his actions. The text tells the reader that Carlos feels a lump in his throat and worries that he will be given nothing to eat by the brothers. It seems that the implied-author was more complicit than outraged with the notion of withholding food from a hungry child.

As a point of commentary, we are intrigued by McAlister's presumptions about the Spanish missionaries while writing the narrative for *Holy Molé!* Certainly, we acknowledge that historical documents describe how the mission system in California, which was under Spanish and, subsequently, Mexican rule until the 1848 Treaty of Guadalupe Hidalgo, forced Indigenous peoples into labor, sometimes via corporal punishment (Archibald, 1978). However, the back matter of *Holy Molé!* does not include any factual information or references to substantiate McAlister's presentation of the friars as perpetrators of child neglect. We also find it noteworthy that neither Czernecki nor McAlister adopted an anti-colonialist stance to depict an empowered Carlos and offer a counter-narrative to the abuse of an Indigenous child. We speculate that since McAlister took the "storyteller's liberty of adding the character of Carlos in order to capture a child's perspective," as described in her author's note at the end of the text, she was fully aware of her positioning of an Indigenous child as a sneaky, willful servant to persons of European descent. Hence, we are disturbed by the subtext of McAlister's narrative in which the friars essentially starved and enslaved an orphan.

In the next spread (pp. 18–19), the illustrations feature a fearful Carlos and an anxious Brother Pascual after their collision. In the center of the spread is an upscaled image of the pot, which has greater mass and, thereby, importance in this kitchen scene. Surrounded by the ingredients that flew into the turkey stew,

Brother Pascual appears to pray. Frightened Carlos appears to worry about being starved as punishment.

Following the collision, an unnamed, fair-skinned friar is featured in the next page spread alongside Carlos and a downscaled version of the pot of stew (pages 20–21). The friar is larger than Carlos, who is depicted exactly as he appears on the book's cover, except with his eyes closed. Sometimes, people close their eyes when they are enjoying their other senses, like that of taste. While this scene seems to visually elevate Carlos to the position of chef, the un-named brother tells Carlos to get away from the pot and to stop causing trouble. This friar's reprimand reinforces the writer's suggestion that Carlos' behavior was deviant rather than a symptom of hunger and desperation. Carlos, however, seems to be oblivious to the scolding and instead focuses on tasting the food, exclaiming how delicious it tastes: "Ummm! !*Rico!*" His comment prompts the brothers, in the next spread, to try the food.

On pages 22–23, Czernecki uses upscaling by quantity. Four friars surround a downscaled Carlos, who is located in the center of the spread adjacent to an upscaled pot of mole. All of the characters encircle the mole, highlighting its importance.

In the subsequent spread (pp. 24–25), a downscaled Carlos is depicted behind the Bishop as the friars bring the food to the awaiting Viceroy (see Figure 10.3). For the very first time in the sequence of images, Carlos appears without his sombrero. We cannot tell whether the illustrator's intention was to demonstrate Carlos's obedient sign of respect for the Viceroy, or to indicate the child's deep concern and fear about the Viceroy's perception of the dish.

In the next spread (pp. 26–27), the illustrator's use of color reinforces the representations offered through his use of visual graduation up to this point. Czernecki shows the dark-skinned Brother Pascual bowing in front of the fair-skinned Viceroy. Here, Czernecki's application of skin tone aligns with the colonial caste system. His color selections position Carlos as the exotic Other among the lighter-toned characters and normalize the colonial racial caste system. By contrast, depicted with the lightest complexion, the Viceroy is the most symbolically powerful character in the story. Fortunately for Carlos and Brother Pascual, the Viceroy enjoys his meal and proclaims "I give the cook my highest praise" (p. 27). In response, Brother Pascual tells the Viceroy that truly, "All praise belongs to *Him* above" (p. 27, emphasis added). McAlister's use of a capital H for "Him" suggests it is God who deserves all praise.

However, what the Viceroy does not know, revealed in the next page spread (pp. 28–29), is that Carlos is seated on a beam "above in the rafters" (p. 29). Czernecki's illustration shows an upscaled, smiling Carlos in a physically elevated position "*above*" the other characters with a bowl filled with mole (see Figure 10.4). The interplay between the dialogue and the image could be interpreted as a commentary on how Carlos was positioned throughout the retelling of the urban legend as an Indigenous person. With this scene, we could not help but ask, "Was there an ideological shift in the story?"

Trembling, they carried the
stew to the dining room
'where the Viceroy waited.

FIGURE 10.3 Carlos behind the Bishop
Source: Holy Molé!: A Folktale from Mexico by Caroline McAlister and illustrated by
Stefan Czernecki. Text Copyright © 2007 Caroline McAlister. Illustrations Copyright
© 2007 Stefan Czernecki. Published 2007 by August House Publishers, Inc.

Up above in the rafters, Carlos was glad to be out of trouble. He ate until he could eat no more. After all, the meal was *un puro milagro*, a complete miracle. He could not count on such luck every day.

FIGURE 10.4 Carlos Elevated "Above"
Source: Holy Molé!: A Folktale from Mexico by Caroline McAlister and illustrated by Stefan Czernecki. Text Copyright © 2007 Caroline McAlister. Illustrations Copyright © 2007 Stefan Czernecki. Published 2007 by August House Publishers, Inc.

Our question was quickly answered. The narrative goes on to state that Carlos was happy to be "out of trouble" (p. 29), evading the friars' punishment for his previous behavior. The hungry child ate until he was full. The text explains that it was a "miracle" the dish was so appetizing and that Carlos "could not count on such luck every day" (p. 29). To summarize, had it not been for the culinary miracle, the Indigenous child would have endured further abuse and humiliation on the part of the Spanish missionaries.

Sadly, the bookmakers passed over the opportunity to challenge Carlos' subservient position as a colonized subject in the final scene of *Holy Molé!* Hidden in the rafters, Carlos is invisible. He consumes the mole secretly and remains barefoot, impoverished, and dependent on the friars for food. The final scene's narrative reinforces rather than critiques the colonial caste system. In the end, the writer offers little hope that Carlos's living conditions and quality of life would change under Spanish rule. There is no transcendence of the colonial ideologies imbued in the contemporary text and illustrations of *Holy Molé!*

Minimalist Visual Style Reduces Characters to Typecasts

Corresponding with our analysis of the visual graduation and ideological underpinnings of the narrative, in this section we discuss the minimalist qualities of *Holy Molé!* Here, we begin with the book's title, which inappropriately applies an accent mark to the word mole (i.e., molé). We interpret this grammatical blunder in the same way we interpret visual images in comics that reduce real people to caricatures. The error suggests that McAlister and her editors were unaware of basic Spanish grammar and pronunciation and did not bother to consult a Spanish language expert when they published the book. Otherwise, they would have known that mole is neither pronounced nor spelled with an accent on the last syllable. The visual presence of the arbitrary accent mark signals that language accuracy is not important when retelling stories about Mexican history and culture. It reinforces that the bookmakers' ideal audience for *Holy Molé!* excludes people who speak, read, and/or write in Spanish.

Akin with the erroneous title, the visual representations of the book's characters do not include accurate facial or body proportions as evident in the figures. The artist used large circles to represent human characters' heads and small circles with pupils and brows for eyes. Although two of the characters have mustaches, the faces have minimal details and are presented only in side and front profiles. Consequently, the visual description of emotion is highly schematic, affording few degrees of happiness, sadness, and surprise, as is emblematic of the caricaturesque/minimalist style (Painter et al., 2013).

We propose that in *Holy Molé!* the illustrator's use of the caricaturesque/minimalist style subtly promotes two problematic social narratives. First, the cartoon-like representation of the characters distances readers from the actual people who lived in Mexico during Colonial times. Positioned as objects of detached amusement, the caricatures also reinforce the contemporary social narrative that Indigenous communities were comprised of exotic Others who no longer exist. Second, the lack of emotional range in the illustrations reduces the characters to typecasts, as opposed to real people. When combined with the bookmakers' selection of narrative text, visual graduation, and color density, the lack of emotional depth in the characters' depictions reinforces Carlos' subaltern position to the friars, and the friars' subaltern position to the Viceroy, advancing, instead of challenging, a colonialist ideology.

Final Reflections

In this chapter, we have applied a postcolonial lens to examine the visual and narrative strategies that McAlister and Czernecki employed in the picturebook *Holy Molé!* Informed by analytical tools from Painter et al., (2013) and Nikolajeva (2005), our analysis revealed some of the ways in which the bookmakers ascribed certain ideologies to their ideal audience of readers and reinforced harmful stereotypes and social narratives about the Indigenous peoples of Mexico. We have argued that the text and illustrations reproduce colonialist ideologies and position Indigenous persons as subaltern characters and comical typecasts. We wonder why the publishers chose not to include more dignified representations of Indigenous characters.

From our perspective, children's publishers should vet with informed stakeholders both the texts and the illustrations they produce for public consumption. In *Holy Molé!*, Carlos' contribution to the mole was miraculous, accidental luck. The bookmaking team dismisses the history of pre-Columbian gastronomy that evolved into mole, a staple of Mexican cuisine. Certainly, the team could have presented a story in which Carlos had agency and was equipped with sources of knowledge that were unknown to the friars. Instead of perpetuating an unfounded myth, they could have celebrated the actual pre-Columbian origins of mole via an intelligent and confident Indigenous child.

In the end, our analysis begs the question, "Whose knowledge counts?" We encourage educators to consider which narratives become salient in the classroom. Is it a twentieth-century urban legend retold by a bookmaking team of persons who are culturally distant from the Indigenous Mexican community and culinary traditions? Or, is it the story of mole that is documented in primary sources and retold by culinary experts within the Mexican community? As described by Smith (2012), Indigenous people "understand and have a shared language for talking about the history, the sociology, the psychology and the politics of imperialism and colonialism as an epic story telling of huge devastation, painful struggle and persistent survival" (p. 20). Our hope is that our analysis will prompt educators to critically evaluate simplistic reproductions of cultural stories and attend to problematic issues raised by the bookmakers' visual and narrative choices in producing children's literature for and about culturally diverse groups and audiences.

References

Archibald, R. (1978). Indian labor at the California missions: Slavery or salvation? *The Journal of San Diego History*, 24(2). Retrieved from https://sandiegohistory.org/journal/1978/april/labor/

Barros, C. (2004). Los moles: Aportaciones prehispánicas. In Consejo Nacional para la Cultura y las Artes (Eds.), *El mole en la ruta de los dioses, Cuadernos 12, 6to Congreso sobre patrimonio gastronómico y turismo cultural. Memorias* (pp. 19–27). Puebla, Mexico: Coordinación de Patrimonio Cultural, Desarrollo y Turismo.

Cooperative Children's Book Center (2018). Publishing statistics on children's books about people of color and first/native nations and by people of color and first/native nations authors and illustrators. Retrieved from: https://ccbc.education.wisc.edu/books/pcstats.asp

Dávila, D. (2012). In search of the ideal reader for children's non-fiction books about el Día de los Muertos. *Journal of Children's Literature*, 38(1), 16–26.

Dávila, D. (2015). Deadly celebrations: Fiction picturebooks and el Día de los Muertos. In L. Clement & L. Jamali (Eds). *Global perspectives on death in children's literature* (pp. 74–86). New York: Routledge.

Delgado-Bernal, D. (1998). Using a Chicana feminist epistemology in educational research. *Harvard Educational Review*, 68, 555–582. doi:10.17763/haer.68.4.5wv1034973g22q48

Delgado-Bernal, D. (2002). Critical race theory, Latino critical theory, and critical raced-gendered epistemologies: Recognizing students of color as holders and creators of knowledge. *Qualitative Inquiry*, 8, 105–126.

Galda, L. & Beach, R. (2001). Theory and research into practice: Response to literature as a cultural activity. *Reading Research Quarterly*, 36(1), 64–73.

Martínez-Roldán, C.M. (2016). When entertainment trumps social concerns: The commodification of Mexican culture and language in *Skippyjon Jones*. In H. Johnson, J. Mathis, & K. Short (Eds.), *Critical content analysis of children's and young adult literature: Reframing perspectives* (pp. 61–76). New York: Routledge.

Méndez, A. & Huerta Figueroa, S.K. (2015). Analizan estereotipos sobre los indígenas en el cine mexicano de ficción. *Boletín del Instituto Nacional de Antropología e Historia*, 272. Dirección de medios de comunicación. Retrieved from http://inah.gob.mx/es/bole tines/3497-analizan-estereotipos-sobre-los-indigenas-en-el-cine-mexicano-de-ficcion

Nikolajeva, M. (2005). *Aesthetic approaches to children's literature: An introduction*. Lanham, MD: Scarecrow Press.

Nodelman, P. (1992). The other: Orientalism, colonialism, and children's literature. *Children's Literature Association Quarterly*, 17(1), 29–35.

Painter, C., Martin, J.R., & Unsworth, L. (2013). *Reading visual narratives: Image analysis of children's picture books*. Sheffield, UK: Equinox.

Pérez Monfort, R. (2004). El mole como símbolo de la mexicanidad. In Consejo Nacional para la Cultural y las Artes (Eds.), *El mole en la ruta de los dioses, Cuadernos 12, 6to Congreso sobre patrimonio gastronómico y turismo cultural. Memorias* (pp. 71–85). Puebla, Mexico: Coordinación de Patrimonio Cultural, Desarrollo y Turismo.

Pérez Monfort, R. (2007). *Expresiones populares y estereotipos culturales en México. Siglos XIX y XX. Diez Ensayos*. México, DF: Centro de Investigaciones y Estudios Superiores en Antropología Social.

Said, E.W. (1979). *Orientalism*. New York: Random House.

Short, K. (2016). Critical content analysis as a research methodology. In H. Johnson, J. Mathis, & K. Short (Eds.), *Critical content analysis of children's and young adult literature: Reframing perspective* (pp. 1–15). New York: Routledge.

Sims Bishop, R. (1990). Mirrors, windows, and sliding glass doors. *Perspectives: Choosing and Using Books for the Classroom*, 6(3), ix–xi.

Smith, L.T. (2012). *Decolonizing methodologies: Research and Indigenous people*. London: Zed Books.

Swadener, B.B. & Mutua, K. (2008). Decolonizing performances: Deconstructing the global postcolonial. In N.K. Denzin, Y. Lincoln, & L.T. Smith (Eds.), *Critical and Indigenous methodologies* (pp. 31–43). Thousand Oaks, CA: Sage.

Tyson, L. (2011). *Using critical theory: How to read and write about literature*. New York: Routledge.

U.S. Census Bureau (2017, August 31). Hispanic Heritage Month 2017. Release number: CB17-FF.17. Retrieved from https://www.census.gov/newsroom/facts-for-features/2017/hispanic-heritage.htm

Vinson, B. (2018). *Before mestizaje: The frontiers of race and caste in colonial Mexico*. New York: Cambridge University Press.

Children's Literature References

Heinrichs, A. (2006). *Día de los Muertos/All Souls Days*. Holidays, festivals, and celebrations series. Illus. by M. Gallagher-Cole. Chanhassen, MN: The Child's World.

McAlister, C. (2006). *Holy Molé!: A folktale from Mexico*. Illus. by S. Czernecki. Atlanta, GA: August House.

11

POSTWAR IMAGES

Japanese Ideologies of National Identity in Picturebooks

Junko Sakoi and Yoo Kyung Sung

World War II books set in Asia are not as widely available in the United States as books written by European and American authors about World War II events in Europe (Lyn, 2009). While there are some stories set during the time of the Japanese occupation of different Asian countries along with personal accounts, only a few such books have been written for children (Wang, 2000). The picturebooks that have been published are set in Hiroshima and Tokyo, even though Hiroshima and Nagasaki are the "once-destroyed" cities targeted by atomic bombs.

Hotta (1991) says "creating these books [war literature] is part of the healing process for Japanese authors and illustrators" (p. 157). Unlike Western countries that treat topics like death and war in children's texts with social caution (Hunt, 1994), Japanese war books are written to encourage healing and to offer warnings not to repeat the war again (Hotta, 1991). Japanese World War II literature meets different social needs from other nations because the Japanese have different complexities in interpreting their war experiences.

This study investigates visual and textual war images in translated picturebooks in relation to Japan's postwar national identities. The main research questions are: How are World War II experiences in Japan portrayed in picturebooks? What messages about Japanese nationalism are evident in the books? The study seeks to explore Japanese understandings of World War II through children's books about the "once-destroyed cities," because stories of Hiroshima and Tokyo dominate books in English about Asian experiences of World War II.

Japan's Colonial History and Nationalism

While the history of Western conquests of other nations and their colonial histories are well documented, Japanese colonialism is under-represented in world history. Japan's imperialism is grounded in a national ethos before and during World War II. Japan's coloniality began within the country through the colonization of the islands of Ryûkyûans in Okinawa and the Indigenous Ainu in Hokkaido as *naichi*, internal colonies (Mason, 2012, p. 20). Assimilation, discrimination, and exploitation were forced upon residents and citizens in these areas (Inoue, 2013; Imanishi, 2007). After more than 200 years of national isolation (1639–1854), the Japanese began colonizing outside the country, with the aim to become a modernized state by establishing international relationships with the allied Western powers of imperialism (Tujioka, 1973).

To counter the military and economic pressure from Western countries, the Japanese government implemented the *fukoku kyohei* policy, fortifying the country and strengthening the military. Japanese imperialism was fueled by the fear of a national security crisis caused by the West. Additionally, it was triggered by the desire to use people and resources from neighboring Asian countries for Japanese needs of military power and natural resources. Japanese aggressions were characterized as military commitments and territorial extension (Duus, Myers, Peattie, Zhou, & Japan-United States Friendship Commission, 1996, p. xiii). By the end of World War I, the empire of Japan included Taiwan, Korea, Pacific island (Nan'yō) chains, the southern half of Sakhalin, and participation in an unequal treaty system with China (Young, 1999). In 1943, the Japanese Empire occupied the five original colonies of Korea, Taiwan, Karfuto, the Kwantung Territories, and Nanyo, and had expanded to ten other territories: Manchukuo (Northeast China), Borneo, the Dutch East Indies, Burma, the Philippines, French Indochina, Timor, Thailand, and Malaya (Duus et al, 1996). Consequently, imperialism, the so-called hegemonist, colonialist, and militarist perspective of Japan, became Japan's major national identity as "the Western country in Asia" (Miller & Asia-Pacific Center for Security Studies, 2004). Colonial rule over all territories except for the Japanese mainland was renounced by Japan in 1945 following World War II. Today, however, international conflicts, such as disputes over territories with Russia, Korea, and China, are occurring because of Japanese imperialism and colonialism (Nogami, 2014).

Nationalism is integrated into people's everyday lives and influences their identity and ideology through its invisibility (Billig, 1995). McVeigh (2001) reported that both hard and soft nationalism exist in Japan, influenced by historical events, ideological preferences, international developments, and geographical conditions. Hard nationalism is more obvious and political. For example, some politicians and right-wing organizations deny Japan's wartime atrocities, such as the Nanjing Massacre in China in 1937. Hard nationalism is reflected in the Imperial Shrine of Yasukuni, in which approximately 2.4 million war-lost souls are enshrined, including 1,000 war criminals from World War II (Yasukuni Shrine, 2008). Soft nationalism consists of four sub-categories of nationalism: economic, educational, cultural, and peace (McVeigh, 2001).

In this study, picturebooks are interpreted through the lens of peace nationalism. The concept of peace nationalism grew out of the atomic bombing of Japan, resulting in a war-renouncing Constitution, one-country pacifism, denial of the right of belligerency, and denial of international politics under the US–Japan Security Treaty. Dower (1999) states, "Defeat, victimization, an overwhelming sense of powerlessness in the face of undreamed-of-weapons of destruction soon coalesced to become the basis of a new kind of anti-military nationalism" (p. 493). In other words, passive nationalism exhibits Japanese victimhood through an anti-war and anti-military ideology, which likely resulted from being the first and only people in the world to experience atomic bombs. Peace nationalism is exemplified in the great symbol of Japanese victimization from the atomic bombing, the Yasukuni Shrine, which also includes leaders and supporters who waged World War II with imperialist ideology (McVeigh, 2001). Even though national debates in Japan are now occurring regarding proposed constitutional revisions to revive the Japanese military or the return of a "normal" Japan, peace nationalism has remained one of the significant faces of Japan.

Theoretical Frameworks

This study employs several critical theories to examine Japanese nationalism, including homogeneous ideology and post-war escapism. Postcolonialism (Said, 1994) enabled us to explore Japan's postwar attitudes that focus on Japanese victims in texts for young people. Peace and educational nationalism construct an imagined community (Anderson, 2006) that does not reflect the whole of society. In taking a peace nationalism stance, Japan focuses on its public face, which does not fully include the aftermath of World War II beyond Japanese territories in Asia where postcolonial conflicts remain.

Postcolonialism thus explains the consequences of World War II that led to unsolved global tensions and continuing conflicts in foreign relations faced by the Japanese government. Walker (2001) points out that, "the history of Japan is the history of the expansion of the living sphere of the Yamato (ethnic Japanese) people" (p. 7). Japan's invasion of Asian nations resembles those of Western empires who conquered Indigenous peoples. Japan's colonialism can be viewed as Japan's "perception of racial (ethnic) difference" as informed by "economic motives" and reinforced and reproduced by technological and military hegemony (Xie, 2000, p. 7). Public post-war rhetorics often do not include social others, non-Japanese victims, from colonies in the nation of Japan.

Japan's national victimhood seems to imply the presence of primarily Japanese members in their nation, defined by Anderson (2006) as "an imagined political community" (p. 49). A nation is an imagined, ideological construction because "the members of even the smallest nation will never know most of their fellow-members, meet them, or even hear of them, yet in the minds of each lives the image of their communication" (p. 49). Anderson's treatment of nations as imagined communities projects nations to the level of the imagination, underscoring their socially constructed nature. Postcoloniality in Billig's (1995) analysis of banal nationalism demonstrates that the workings of nationalism operate largely in the background unnoticed; the ideology is pervasive in postmodern social life. The concept of the imagined community helped us examine Japanese national ideology to determine how Japan as a nation desires to be represented in the global community, particularly by the West.

Said (1994) argues the structure of colonialism and the social relationships between the colony and colonizer reveal how the colonial relationships and practices of the past persist today. Ideology is produced and demonstrated through various mediums. Japanese peace nationalism amplifies the Japanese social mindset of postcoloniality that still regards war victims from other Asian nations as the colonized. In the Asian colonial context of the postcolonial period, homogeneous cultural perceptions of the other have been generated. Kikuchi's (2004) concept of "Oriental Orientalism" explains the creation of another other in Asia with the articulation of cultural differences between Japan as "Self" and Asia as "Other," through which Japan dissociates itself from Asia by differentiating and Orientalizing cultures in Asia. Therefore, superior and civilized Japan has the responsibility to take proper leadership and protect the interests of uncivilized colonial people, thus justifying Japan's colonization (Kikuchi, 2004). Even within modern Japan, a social hierarchy exists among the people Japan colonized, such as Koreans, Chinese, and Taiwanese, based on Japanese superiority.

World War II in Children's Books

World War II as a focus was uncommon in global children's literature until the 1970s because of different social ideologies about whether war was an appropriate topic for young readers. Hunt (1994) notes social attitudes regarding World War II in U.S. children's books mirror changes in societal views of the war over the past 50 years. During the 1940s, children's literature in most Western countries did not acknowledge the war. Americans struggled with the idea of illustrating scenes of war for children, so the subject of death and suffering was handled with caution (Hotta, 1991). Except for books imported from other countries, the death of a child was nearly non-existent in U.S. children's literature (Ordal, 1983; Hotta, 1991). Consequently, American books in the 1940s avoided war stories by turning wartime reality into fantasy or not mentioning the war. Gradually, children's fiction in the U.S. moved from excluding the war to educating young readers (Hunt, 1994). Even in England, the war was rarely the subject of British children's literature until the early 1970s when novels about the war were written by authors who were children at the time of the war (Pinsent, 2012).

In contrast, Japanese post-war children's books, such as *Hiroshima No Pika* (Maruki, 1981), which portrays a young girl's experience during the bombing of Hiroshima, are unique in that these books were not only written for Japanese children but also published outside of Japan and translated for non-Japanese readers. These books made an international impact on global audiences as exceptional literature at a time when many Western authors were hesitant to tackle war topics in children's texts (Hotta, 1991). McCallum (1999) notes, "representations of sub-jectivity in fiction are always based on the ideological assumptions about relations between individuals, and between individuals, societies and the world" (p. 7). We argue that Hiroshima-centered post-war narratives represent ideological assump-tions about relations between individual Japanese people, Japanese citizens and the government, the Japanese military, and different parts of the world.

Hasegawa (1981) critiqued *Faithful Elephants: A True Story of Animals, People, and War* (Tsuchiya, 1988), a story written in Japanese and published in Japan about zookeepers at the Ueno Zoo who put three elephants to death as a humane act to protect people from danger in Tokyo during World War II. Hasegawa found distorted historicity that disguised the intentions of Japanese authorities regarding the order to kill the animals. He concluded that the mis-representation was associated with Japanese military propaganda designed to evoke people's hatred of the enemy. In addition, Kawabata and Vandergrift (1998) compared the Japanese and English versions of *Faithful Elephants* and found several textual and visual differences between the two texts. The subtitle of the English version claims it is a "true story" but leaves readers unaware of the con-troversy surrounding the Japanese version. Additionally, the English text clearly states that the animals were killed by "command of the Army" (p. 8), while the Japanese version avoids designating any responsibility by emphasizing the need to protect people from danger.

Kogochi (1979) identified three categories of World War II literature in Japan: (1) children as evacuees, victims of air raids or the atomic bomb, or offspring of occupying soldiers and Japanese women; (2) the difficult daily lives of soldiers and the conditions of prisoner-of-war camps and battlefields; and lastly, (3) depictions of friendship between enemy children and soldiers. Japanese children's books con-tained a wide range of topics and themes about World War II. In contrast, most translated books focus on young evacuees or victims rather than Japanese soldiers. Such subtle dynamics in the texts extend McVeigh's (2001) concept of soft nationalism that makes the historical war position of the Japanese military unclear.

Postcolonial Studies on National Ideologies

Scholars of children's literature (Bradford, 2007; Sung, 2009; Yenika-Agbaw, 2008) conduct postcolonial studies on how Western national ideologies and atti-tudes are embedded in children's literature within the West–East binary or the colonizer (Western) and the colonized (Africa). These studies analyze cultural misrepresentations resulting from postcolonial beliefs that Western cultures are superior and that inferior East or colonized African or Indigenous nations need the West's help to articulate cultures and lands of the inferiors (Said, 1978).

A few studies found marks of Japan's imperialism through picturebooks. Sung (2012) explores the journey of Korean victims developing resilience after sexual slavery by the Japanese military during World War II, fighting against the national silence maintained by the Korean government as well as the Japanese government. Several studies of Japanese nationalism exist in Japanese children's literature. Sung and Sakoi (2017) found that the ancient yet contemporary Ainu culture (Indigenous people in Hokkaido) is mostly available in folklore but not in historical or contemporary realistic fiction for children. Japan's imagined nationhood explains Japanese national ideology, which defines who the Japanese people and their cultures are.

Methodology

This study uses tools from Painter, Martin, and Unsworth (2013) to conduct a critical content analysis of the visual images in four translated World War II nonfiction and fiction picturebooks. The analysis procedures included three steps: (1) identifying visual and textual modes embedded in the texts, (2) creating a multimodal transcript, and (3) conducting a descriptive analysis to determine thematic patterns. The key questions about the functioning of these modes include: What modes make a text cohesive? What themes and categories are signified through these modes? Where and how are readers positioned as viewers? This analysis of the modes informed our major research questions about victimhood and national ideology in Japanese children's books.

Text Selection and Authorship

The four picturebooks examined in this study were *Hiroshima No Pika* (Maruki, 1981), *My Hiroshima* (Yamamoto, 1987), *Shin's Tricycle* (Kodama, 1995), and *Faithful Elephants: A True Story of Animals, People, and War* (Tsuchiya, 1997). These books were selected because they are well known, widely available, and frequently used as anti-war books in post-war education in Japan and the U.S. This section provides a story plot with brief author information for each book.

Hiroshima No Pika was written and illustrated by Toshi Maruki and is based on a true story that Maruki heard from a female survivor of the atomic bomb. It was published in Japan in 1980 and won the Ehon Nippon Prize (Japan Picturebook Award) for the best picturebook in Japan. In 1981, it was selected by the School Library Association for recommended reading for elementary students. An English version was published in the U.S. in 1980 and gained international recognition when it won the Mildred L. Batchelder Award for translation in 1983.

My Hiroshima was first published in English in Australia in 1987 and then was translated into Japanese and released in Japan in 1988. It is an autobiographical account of author Junko Morimoto's story as a Hiroshima atomic bomb survivor. Morimoto and her family survived, but she witnessed devastation and horror, such as death and the destruction of her home city, Hiroshima.

Shin's Tricycle was first published in Japan in 1992 and then translated into English and released in the U.S. in 1995. The story was written by Tatsuharu Kodama, who was born in Hiroshima and lived through the war. The book's illustrator, Makoto Ando, is Taiwan-born Japanese. This is the true story of Nobuo Tetsutani, a Hiroshima atomic bomb survivor, and his three-year-old son, Shin, who was killed when the bomb dropped.

The original Japanese version of *Faithful Elephants*, created by author Yukio Tsuchiya and illustrator Motoichiro Takebe, who both have war memories, was published in 1970. The English edition, published in 1988 in the U.S., was translated by Tomoko Tsuchiya Dykes and illustrated by Ted Lewin. The story is based on true events about starving the elephants at the Tokyo Ueno Zoo in 1943. The National School Association selected this book for required basic reading for young children in Japan.

Data Collection and Analysis

We analyzed five components in the multimodal transcript drawn from Painter et al.'s (2013) analytical tools: (1) the relationship between characters and audiences, (2) color modes and character gazes, (3) characters' gestures and action processes, (4) the mood of the settings, and (5) characters' positions in the scenes. We created a multimodal transcript chart with columns for the transcript, subcategories, main characters, and themes. On the left side of each chart, page numbers were marked. For the multimodal transcript, images and words were coded under each metafunction of interpersonal, ideational, compositional, and linguistic (Painter et al., 2013).

The gaze-based relationship between characters and readers was investigated in addition to the meanings of colors, which helped to identify the meanings that characters produce with their actions, behaviors, postures, and positioning, as well as the meanings that symbolic attributes generate in relation to circumstances and characters. For example, in our analysis of page 2 of *Shin's Tricycle*, participants such as Shin (protagonist), Kimi (Shin's best friend), and the rest of the family members were first identified. After that, the characters' actions and interactions and relationships were analyzed by asking why and how they act and talk. Any directionality of the characters' gazes was studied in relation to the physical environments in which the characters were situated and positioned on the page. The characters' perspectives in relation to the audiences' stances in scenes were also examined. On page 2 of *Shin's Tricycle*, Shin and Kimi show their faces to readers, considered an invitation to connect with Shin and Kimi.

Next, colors were explored, including what colors were used in what ways and what meanings these colors construct. Warm colors like red, orange, and yellow create comforting feelings and moods and build a sense of connection between the characters. Written words related to the images were also coded. For example, "my son," "red tricycle," "Shin was three," and "best friend" were coded.

These words represent the characters' identities, such as age and family structure, their relationships, and symbolic attributes. After this coding process, the multimodal codes were categorized into groups informed by patterns and commonalities. Consequently, two themes emerged: (1) individual experiences as victims, and (2) the social and political institutional experiences of victimization. There are also five subcategories (Table 11.1).

The history of the colonizer and the colonized has a great impact on the stances of each of us as researchers in terms of our analysis of these four picturebooks. Junko grew up in Japan, read these stories, watched anime and films, and had discussions with peers in and out of school. The Hiroshima atomic bombing is an integral unit of the social studies curriculum in Japanese elementary and secondary schools. Junko does not recall being given space to ask questions, such as who gets to speak and why, and felt guilty about questioning her country's history. Junko was taught as a citizen with a Japanese national identity. Yoo Kyung is a Korea-born U.S. immigrant who was raised in South Korea, where critical stances on political issues of the lost sovereignty of Joseon (the previous dynasty of Korea) to the Japanese government are a significant educational ethos in public education. Junko and Yoo Kyung's nationalities and cultural backgrounds influenced and shaped the research questions and critical perspectives for this analysis.

Japanese Nationalism as Victimhood

In the analysis of four picturebooks, two major themes were found for victim-based identities that demonstrate Japanese nationalism within a peaceful victimhood culture. These themes are (1) the individual experiences of victims, and (2) the social and political institutional experiences of victimization. The first suggests that readers develop a sense of the victimhood of vulnerable social groups, such as mothers, babies, children, families, elderly people, and animals. The second indicates that readers feel a sense of the despondent victimhood of the cities of Hiroshima and Tokyo, and for Japan as a collective national identity.

TABLE 11.1 Overview of Themes, Main Categories, and Subcategories

Themes	Main Categories	Subcategories
Individual experiences as victims	Symbolize vulnerable groups as innocent victims	Vulnerable social groups Ordinary family time and space.
The social and political institutional experiences of victimization	Symbolize bombs victims, symbolic attributes, and anti-war messages as innocent victims	Atomic bomb victims Symbolic attributes as national identity Anti-war messages

The Individual Experiences of Victims

An emphasis on the individual experiences of victims occurs when vulnerable social groups are highlighted in books. Through observation of their daily lives, usually portrayed before the impending bomb explosion, readers are invited to recognize the innocence and vulnerability of these individuals as symbolic victims of the war.

Vulnerable Social Groups

The picturebooks highlight individuals from social groups often viewed as vulnerable by society, such as children, babies, and animals. In *Shin's Tricycle*, the story initially focuses on a little boy named Shin, his parents, and his friend, Kimi. In the family backyard, they play together, read books, and ride Shin's precious red-colored tricycle, a birthday gift from his uncle. Shin's mother watches over them while holding her baby. Each character displays emphatic expressions as they show their faces to viewers from oblique angles. *My Hiroshima* presents a young girl's daily life before the atomic bombing. She spends her time drawing at home, playing with her friends, watching fireworks with her family, and attending school. As she looks away from viewers, readers get a glimpse of her archetypical child's life.

In *Faithful Elephants*, three elephants, a favorite for children, are illustrated in full in several pages, with an emphasis on their faces. The zookeepers have significant patterned postures, such as despondently and hopelessly facing the ground and watching the elephants, while looking away or hiding their faces from readers. These postures indicate their powerlessness in the society to change the situation and keep the elephants alive. This emphasis on these vulnerable social groups by highlighting their facial features and postures from oblique angles across the stories symbolizes their weakness.

Ordinary Family Time and Space

Across the books, highlighting the image of a family gathering at a particular time and place encourages readers to connect with the families in the books. In *My Hiroshima, Hiroshima No Pika,* and *Shin's Tricycle*, a family is illustrated at the center of a page and invites readers to develop a closer relationship. A young girl's family photo is shown in sepia tones at the beginning of *My Hiroshima* to introduce her family members. In the photo, she and her parents, two sisters, and one brother wear winter kimonos and school uniforms and directly make eye contact with readers. The symbolic attributes, such as a sepia-colored photo, winter kimonos, and school uniforms, allow readers to reference the time period as before the bombing when the family had a peaceful life.

In *Hiroshima No Pika* and *Shin's Tricycle*, the families gather in a living room. In *Hiroshima No Pika*, the parents and their little daughter wear special clothing to protect them from an atomic bomb as they eat breakfast. They are excited about sweet potatoes, which they seem not to have eaten for a long time, perhaps since the war started. The family in *Shin's Tricycle* are in the living room where Shin is begging his parents for a tricycle for his birthday. They are trying to dissuade him because getting something new during wartime was difficult.

These representations of ordinary family time and space create a sense of closeness with the families and encourage personal connections. Thus, the picturebooks highlight the war experiences of vulnerable social groups, such as families, by emphasizing their facial features and postures. This positioning is also a basis for readers to develop a sense of victimhood towards those children and families.

The Social and Political Institutional Experiences of Victimization

In three of the picturebooks, the atomic bomb falls on Hiroshima midway through the book. This moment shifts readers' stance from observing the scenes to participating in them. In addition to the main characters, who represent vulnerable social groups, more characters appear as victims to emphasize the city of Hiroshima and the mushroom cloud. This imagery can enhance the social and political institutional experiences of victimization.

Collective Victimhood as National Identity

In *My Hiroshima*, a young girl, a mother with a dead baby on her back, and a little child are highlighted as survivors. They show their faces with emphatic expressions from oblique angles. Similarly, in *Hiroshima No Pika*, a young girl and her mother, half naked, are seen escaping from the fire, along with other wounded people, toward the riverbank. They eventually reach the river, which is filled with wounded and dead people and animals, and they sit on the ground hopelessly, directly making eye contact with readers. Afterwards, they move toward the sea.

Another image highlights vulnerable people, including two dead babies, their dead mothers, and a surviving half-naked old woman and a little girl by the seashore. The old woman gives a rice ball to the girl, and then dies. Emphasizing the number of wounded, dying, and dead people, including babies, mothers, children, old people, and animals, in the background aside from the main characters symbolizes the number of innocent Hiroshima atomic bomb victims, again enhancing readers' sense of collective victimhood identity at the institutional level.

Victimized Symbolic Attributes as National Identity

Several symbolic attributes, such as Hiroshima City, the Hiroshima Atomic Bomb Dome, the mushroom cloud, and the tombstone for the animals killed at the Tokyo Ueno Zoo, are also highlighted in the books. These visual images may trigger readers to make a significant connection between these symbolic icons and the war or the atomic bombing. Furthermore, because these icons are located or occurred in Hiroshima or Tokyo, readers further symbolize the locations as innocent areas of victimization. These attributes seem to strengthen a national identity of collective victimhood on the part of readers.

In *Shin's Tricycle*, an image shows Shin's father carrying the badly wounded Shin on his back to the riverbank (see Figure 11.1). A tall building appears in the background, later recognized as the only building left standing after the bombing. Today, this building is known as the Hiroshima Peace Memorial or the Atomic Bomb Dome in Japan. At the end of the book, an image shows present-day Hiroshima City, along with the Atomic Bomb Dome. This time, the Dome is large and located in the center of the page. The Dome also appears in *Hiroshima No Pika* and *My Hiroshima*. In *Hiroshima No Pika*, for instance, it is illustrated as small, yet it significantly stands out in burned-down Hiroshima City. Highlighting the Atomic Bomb Dome seems to be an attempt to symbolize Hiroshima as victimized.

My Hiroshima's opening scene depicts a mother in a summer kimono holding a little girl and looking at Hiroshima City from a distance; her two little children,

FIGURE 11.1 Wounded and Dead People in the Hiroshima Atomic Bombing (Yama-moto, 1987)
Source: Shin's Tricycle by Tatsuharu Kodama and illustrated by Noriyuki Ando. Copyright © Walker & Company.

also wearing summer kimonos, are playing with a fan and a windmill, with their backs to the city. This portrayal invites readers to observe the city over the mother's shoulder from a higher horizontal angle. The long shot of Hiroshima, along with the defenseless people in it, emphasizes the vulnerability of the city. Several symbolic items, such as a kimono, the fan, and the windmill, signify summertime. The atomic bomb was dropped on the city on August 15th, so these items signal summer, a time of more vulnerability, while also showing Hiroshima in the background to emphasize the susceptibility of the city.

My Hiroshima and Shin's Tricycle illustrate the moment the bomb was dropped on Hiroshima in a two-page spread with fully saturated and vibrant colors and little to no written text. In My Hiroshima, for instance, the two-page spread is divided into three horizontal panels. It has no words, thus inviting readers to focus on the images. The black and dark brown colored images at the top and bottom present people's struggles with air raids by showing only their hands, without any other body features. A white-colored mushroom cloud in the clear blue sky over Hiroshima is illustrated in the center and is conspicuous between those framed dark-colored images. This image generates a strong sense of fear, anxiety, and terror and symbolizes the helplessness of the people and of Hiroshima.

Faithful Elephants shows the tombstone of the killed animals at the Tokyo Ueno Zoo on page 6. 動物よ安らかに ("Animals, Rest in Peace") is inscribed in Japanese on the stone. The representation of the tombstone, along with cultural icons, such as paper cranes and cherry blossoms, emphasizes the setting of Tokyo, Japan's capital city. These images may draw upon readers' sympathy and give them a sense of the victimization of Tokyo and the country of Japan in general, as well as of the zoo animals beloved by children.

Anti-War Messages

Anti-war messages are included in the written texts, along with the use of symbolic attributes and an emphasis on vulnerable groups, such as the Atomic Bomb Dome and children in all four picturebooks. This tactic also creates a strong sense of victimhood as a social and political institutional experience. In My Hiroshima, a large black-and-white photograph of the Atomic Bomb Dome and a number of people around the Dome, perhaps taken years after the war, appears on the very last page of the book. At the bottom of the photo, an anti-war message is written in caps as follows: "LET ALL THE SOULS HERE REST IN PEACE. FOR WE SHALL NOT REPEAT THE EVIL" (n.p.). In Shin's Tricycle, Shin's burnt-out tricycle is displayed at the Peace Museum in Hiroshima, and a family, including the father, the mother, and their young daughter, examine it. Along with this image, an anti-war message is given from Shin's father's point of view using the word "children" several times (p. 29) and phrases associated with young children, such as "innocent people" and "tricycle."

The anti-war message in *Hiroshima No Pika* says, "'It can't happen again,' she [mother] says, 'if no one drops the bomb'" (p. 43), along with an image of the Hiroshima Lantern Ceremony held every August 6th as a memorial ceremony for the souls of the dead from the bombing. In a red and orange illustration, the bomb survivors, four girls and one boy in summer kimonos, sit close together at the riverbank and float lanterns on the water (see Figure 11.2). Many people gathered at that site right after the bomb was dropped. The names of atomic bomb victims and vulnerable groups, such as あかちゃん (a baby), お母ちゃん (mom), and おとうさん (dad), are inscribed in Japanese on each lantern. One girl faces readers, directing them to other victims with her gaze and posture.

In *Faithful Elephants*, after the elephants die, one zookeeper implores, "Stop the war! Stop the war! Stop all wars!" (p. 27). In the image (see Figure 11.3), the zookeepers express their sadness and anger in various ways while elephant bodies on the floor imply the cause of such emotive statements in visual and textual texts. The anti-war message across these dramatic portrayals in *Shin's Tricycle*, *Hiroshima No Pika*, and *Faithful Elephants* present people and animals in Japan as victims. Delivering anti-war messages from the victim-survivors' perspectives fosters a victimhood ideology of Japanese nationalism.

FIGURE 11.2 Characters' Gaze and Posture in the Hiroshima Lantern Ceremony (Maruki, 1981)

Source: Hiroshima No Pika by Toshi Maruki and Iri Maruki. Copyright © Komine Shoten Company. English translation copyright © HarperCollins, 1982.

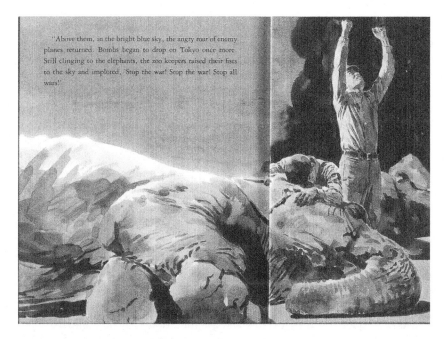

FIGURE 11.3 Sadness Expressed through Characters' Gestures and Elephants' Embodiments: "Stop the War!" (Tsuchiya, 1970)
Source: Faithful Elephants: A True Story of Animals, People and War by Yukio Tsuchia, Tomoko Dykes, and Ted Lewin. Text copyright © 1951 by Yukio Tsuchiya. Illustrations copyright © 1988 by Ted Lewin. English Translation and Introduction copyright © 1988 Houghton Mifflin Harcourt.

This analysis examined two facets of Japanese nationalism embedded in picturebooks for young readers: the individual experiences of victims and the social and political institutional experiences of victimization. The exaggeration of focalization, gestures, and postures and the positioning of victimized social groups and communities establishes their vulnerabilities as innocent war victims. Consequently, readers foster empathetic and sympathetic feelings, which enhance a victimhood identity and shapes a concept of nationhood as that of victim.

Discussion and Implications

This study revealed images of vulnerable social groups, symbolic icons, and settings across four translated World War II picturebooks. Their visual evidence implies Japan's post-war imagined nationalism, which reflects being the victim of the world's first atomic bomb attacks and does not include any reference to Japan's role as a colonizer-aggressor. The messages are perhaps consciously or unconsciously constructed and reinforced by the authors as part of the national ideology in which they live and which is enhanced through the intertextuality of these four picturebooks. John Stephens (1992) defines intertextuality as "the production of meaning from the interrelationships between audience, text, other texts, and the sociocultural determinations of significance" (p. 84). In other words, intertextuality uncovers the hidden echoes of Japan's imagined nationalism embedded in the images across the books. This approach may encourage readers to develop empathy, sympathy, and feelings of pity. Subsequently, it could also strengthen the symbolism of innocent war victims with respect to characters and to the Japanese people and the country of Japan. However, the Japanese national identity as the colonizer or war aggressor is not present in children's texts. Hiroshima stories are retold to U.S. readers disconnected from the Japanese attack on Pearl Harbor and the colonization of Asian countries by Japan, even though the negative consequences of Japanese expansion were extensive.

Depictions of a nation solely as victim in children's books ignores historical knowledge of Japanese occupations in the World War II era. Even though there are still active protests in different locations in postwar Asia, World War II experiences are continuously retold by European and American authors, and the Asian experiences in this conflict remain obscure facts.

Through reading historical fiction and examining the actions of characters, readers can explore issues of diversity and gain historical awareness (Sliwka, 2008). The historical fiction picturebooks in this study convey history through the lens of Japan's soft and hard nationalism. Kawabata and Vandergrift (1998) note, "Myth is much stronger and longer lasting than fact" (p. 9). While these picturebooks play important roles in historical awareness, if soft nationalism is embedded in texts, history becomes myth, so that Japan's soft nationalism is continuously constructed and promoted through such stories. Focusing on victimization and romanticizing World War II experiences may create social resilience and help readers overcome the collective national trauma that Japan has suffered for more than seven decades from the bombing; however, this collective national trauma does not include the many victims of Japanese aggression during that war.

Final Reflections

Children's literature is an artifact of cultural identity, and national identity is enhanced and promoted through literature (Kelen & Sundmark, 2013). The critical analysis of visual images in these texts creates understandings of the deep meanings of the Japanese government's controversial actions against the people of Japan and other Asian countries. Imperialism and postcolonialism lenses display connectivity between historical and current perspectives on Japan's actions as a nation. Kelen and Sundmark (2013) note that nations demand faith and loyalty on the part of their subjects, and these demands are usually delivered through appeals to emotions rather than to reason.

The emotional appeals in these picturebooks are not inclusive when members of the nation are part of an imagined community. The victims of the bombing include many people not acknowledged in these books. For example, the monument to Korean victims at the Hiroshima Peace Memorial Park notes that 10 percent of those who died in that bombing had Korean lineage, around 20,000 Koreans, with thousands more killed in the Nagasaki bombing (Taylor, 2016). Vulnerable victims in these picturebooks construct an ideological post-war Japanese nationhood and lead to further victimization of forgotten "Others" by excluding them from contexts of global conflict.

This study has revealed the significance of children's books that help readers analyze the meaning of (in)visible history. We hope that more children's authors will tell stories of the silenced histories of people and nations. Visual images that portray chaos and atrocities during World War II are powerful means of projecting a hidden ideology that quickly produces emotional reactions but is a myth without any basis in history. After all, resilience cannot fully or authentically take place when the partial truth attempts to be the whole truth.

References

Anderson, B. (2006). *Imagined communities*. London: Verso.

Billig, M. (1995). *Banal nationalism*. London: Sage.

Bradford, C. (2007). *Unsettling narratives: Postcolonial readings of children's literature*. Ontario: Wilfred Laurier University Press.

Dower, J. (1999). *Embracing defeat: Japan in the wake of World War II*. New York: Norton.

Duus, P., Myers, R., Peattie, M., Zhou, W., & Japan-United States Friendship Commission (1996). *The Japanese wartime empire, 1931–1945*. Princeton, NJ: Princeton University Press.

Hasegawa, U. (1981). ぞうもかわいそう：猛獣虐殺神話批判 (The elephants are also to be pitied: A criticism of the myth of animal slaughter). *Children's literature criticism quarterly*, Charter Issue, 4-16

Hotta, A.M. (1991). The suffering child's plea for peace in Japanese picture books. *Children's Literature Association Quarterly*, 1, 154–160.

Hunt, C.C. (1994). U.S. children's books about the World War II period: From isolationism to internationalism, 1940–1990. *The Lion and the Unicorn*, 18(2), 190–208.

Imanishi, H. (2007). 帝国日本と国内植民地：内国植民地論争の遺産 (Imperial Japan and colony: Consequence of internal colony contentious). *Language and Cultural Studies, Ritsumeikan University*, 19(1), 17-27.

Inoue, K. (2013). 明治日本の植民地支配：北海道から朝鮮へ (Japanese colony during Meiji era: From Hokkaido to Korea). Tokyo: Iwanami Shoten.

Inoue, K. (2013). 明治日本の植民地支配:北海道から朝鮮へ [Japanese colony during Meiji era: From Hokkaido to Korea]. Tokyo: Iwanami Shoten.

Kawabata, A. & Vandergrift, K.E. (1998). History into myth: The anatomy of a picture book. *Bookbird: A Journal of International Children's Literature*, 36(2), 6–12.

Kelen, C. & Sundmark, B. (2013). *The nation in children's literature: Nations of childhood*. New York: Routledge.

Kikuchi, Y. (2004). *Japanese modernization and mingei theory: Cultural nationalism and oriental orientalism*. London: Routledge.

Kogochi, T. (1979). The depiction of World War II in Japanese books for children. *Bookbird*, 17(4), 13–16.

Lyn, K.S. (2009). In search of the child: Children's books depicting World War II in Singapore. *Biblio Asia*, 5(2), 10–13.

Mason, M.M. (2012). *Dominant narratives of colonial Hokkaido and Imperial Japan: Envisioning the periphery and the modern nation-state*. London: Palgrave.

McCallum, R. (1999). *Ideology of identity in adolescent fiction: The dialogic construction of subjectivity*. New York: Routledge.

McVeigh, J.B. (2001). Postwar Japan's "hard" and "soft nationalism."Japan Policy Research Institute. Working paper 73. Retrieved from www.jpri.org/publications/workingpapers/wp73.html

Miller, J. & Asia-Pacific Center for Security Studies (2004). *The outlier: Japan between Asia and the West*. Honolulu, HI: Asia-Pacific Center for Security Studies.

Nogami, Y. (2014). 日本の領土に係わる問題と関係各国の歴史認識との関係:尖閣諸島、竹島、北方領土の事例研究 [Issues of Japanese colony and historical perceptions: The study of the Senkaku Islands, Takeshima, and the Northern Territories]. *The Japan Institute of International Affairs*, 1–40.

Ordal, C.C. (1983). Death as seen in books suitable for young children. *Omega: Journal of Death and Dying*, 14(3), 249–277.

Painter, C., MartinJ.R., & Unsworth, L. (2013). *Reading visual narratives: Image analysis of children's picture books*. Sheffield, UK: Equinox.

Pinsent, P. (2012). The child in British literature: Literary constructions of childhood, medieval to contemporary. In *The post-war child: Childhood in British literature in the wake of World War II* (pp. 212–224). London: Palgrave Macmillan.

Said, E.W. (1978). *Orientalism*. New York: Vintage.

Said, E.W. (1994). *Culture and imperialism*. New York: Vintage Books.

Sliwka, C. (2008). Connecting to history through historical fiction. *Language Arts Journal of Michigan*, 23(2).

Stephens, J. (1992). *Language and ideology in children's fiction*. London: Longman.

Taylor, A. (2016, May 25). The forgotten story of tens of thousands of Koreans who died in Hiroshima. *Washington Post*. Retrieved from https://www.washingtonpost.com/news/worldviews/wp/2016/05/25/the-forgotten-story-of-tens-of-thousands-of-koreans-who-died-in-hiroshima/?utm_term=.6db71e1d63ee

Tujioka, M. (1973). 日本資本主義と近代化 (一) [The capitalism and modernization of Japan]. *Hiroshima University of Economics*, 8, 113–134.

Sung, Y.K. (2009). Post-colonial critique of the (mis) representation of Korean-Americans in children's picture books. Unpublished dissertation, University of Arizona, Tucson.

Sung, Y.K. (2012). Hearing the voices of "Comfort women": Confronting historical trauma in Korean children's literature. *Bookbird: A Journal of International Children's Literature*, 50(1), 20–30.

Sung, Y.K. & Sakoi, J. (2017). Stories of the Ainu: The oldest Indigenous people in Japanese children's literature. *Bookbird: A Journal of International Children's Literature*, 55(1), 4–13.

Walker, B.L. (2001). *The conquest of Ainu lands, ecology and culture in Japanese expansion, 1590–1800*. Berkeley: University of California Press.

Wang, G. (2000). Memories of war: World War II in Asia. In P.H. Lim & D. Wong (Eds.), *War and memory in Malaysia and Singapore* (pp. 11–22). Singapore: Institute of Southeast Asian Studies.

Xie, S. (2000). Rethinking the identity of cultural otherness: The discourse of difference as an unfinished project. In R. McGillis (Ed.), *Voices of the other: Children's literature and postcolonial context* (pp. 1–17). New York: Routledge.

Yasukuni Shrine (2008). *About Yasukuni Shrine: History.* Retrieved from www.yasukuni.or. jp/english/index.html

Yenika-Agbaw, V. (2008). *Representing Africa in children's books: Old and new ways of seeing.* New York: Routledge.

Young, L. (1999). *Japan's total empire: Manchuria and the culture of wartime imperialism.* Twentieth-century Japan, 8. Berkeley: University of California Press.

Children's Literature References

Kodama, T. (1995). *Shin's tricycle.* Illus. by N. Ando. New York: Walker.

Maruki, T. (1981). *Hiroshima no Pika.* Boston: Lothrop, Lee & Shepard.

Tsuchiya, Y. (1970). かわいそうなぞう [Pitiful Elephants]. Illus. by M. Takebe. Tokyo: Kinnohoshi.

Tsuchiya, Y. (1997). *Faithful elephants: A true story of animals, people and war.* Illus. by T. Lewin. Trans. by T.T. Dykes. Boston: Houghton Mifflin Harcourt.

Yamamoto, J. (1987). *My Hiroshima.* Sydney: William Collins.

12

IMMIGRANT MEMOIRS AS REFLECTIONS OF TIME AND PLACE

Middle Eastern Conflict in Graphic Novels

Seemi Aziz

This study is a critical content analysis of the visual images in four graphic memoirs set in Iran, Libya, Syria, Palestine, and Lebanon. Through an interplay of words and images, these narratives depict the lives of children living under violence and conflict as hybrid personalities (Bhabha, 1994) where their identity and subjectivity come into question (Stephens, 2013). This study inspects the manner in which visual and written text in graphic novels reinterprets/or challenge a colonial mindset, and how these novels position the reader in regard to the depicted violence and conflict.

Comic books have been around for ages. Black and white comic strips adorn newspapers, drawing laughs and making candid political and social commentary more acceptable. Movies take these ideas and project them for a larger audience, heightening their impact for the public. Graphic novels are currently popular, building on this narrative discourse from popular films and comic books. The work of Eisner (2008) and McCloud (1993; 2006) provides insight into the art of comic books, bringing scholarly discourse through theoretical frames that expound on the genre as an art form and visual images as a strong medium of communication.

Children make sense of their worlds through the images that surround them and of cultures that differ from their own through images that frame and project these cultures. Critically reading images, thus, needs to be an integral part of education. Pearson (2005) argues that visual images in books "can tell difficult stories about the human cost of war; heroic and horrific acts of humankind, and sad and moving personal tales that make history more real to the reader in a strikingly visual format" (p. 31). Shared memories, oppression of children, and lived experiences within the graphic memoirs examined in this study render relevance to these profoundly personal narratives.

Theoretical Frame

This study is grounded in the assumption that regions that were once colonized carry within them reflections of previous colonizers and are viewed by the Western world through a lens that portrays them in a manner that creates a sense of "othering" for the inhabitants (Said, 1978; Loomba, 2005). Postcolonial theory draws on these suppositions to unveil how knowledge is constructed and circulated in dealing with global power relations. It also sheds light on how identities become hybrids as the process of colonization impacts the psyche of inhabitants of these regions (Bhabha, 1994). Postcolonialism is "the critical study of the effect of colonialism and colonial text on current societies" (Mills, 1997, p. 94). This study takes on the tenets of othering, hybridity, and imperial gaze to understand how readers make sense of texts, with gaze studied at the levels of the micro in daily life and the macro in global views.

The symbiosis of visual/textual discourse within graphic novels is strong and lends itself to studying the implications of colonial mindsets that permeate the modern world and challenge beliefs that colonialism has ended. To observe how the concepts of hybridization, imperial gaze, and othering are represented within these graphic novels, postcolonial theory is useful in exploring issues of oppression that speak to the power discourse that gives Western icons their prominence (Said, 1978; Foucault, 1972). Within this research I use the critical frame of postcolonialism as a careful analytic examination and reflection on the graphic memoirs based on the following theoretical tenets:

- Hybridization: Homi Bhabha (1994) refers to postcolonial subjects as people struggling with their subjectivity. They take on dual or multiple identities as they move through their lives within or outside of regions that were or are colonized. These subjectivities are forever fluctuating, never seamlessly attained, and thus are always hybrids.
- Othering: Edward Said (1978) in his seminal work, *Orientalism*, speaks to the perception of "othering" where the West looks at Eastern peoples as "others" or different from the norm of the West. Western mindsets highlight differences rather than similarities to set people apart when they present the East or Middle Eastern regions.
- Imperial Gaze: The Western/imperial gaze applies to discourse, seeing, and projecting of certain people from a perspective that looks down and vilifies them.

Methodology

In analyzing the graphic memoirs, critical content analysis along with analytical multimodal tools were used since the books tap into multiple senses for audiences through two modes of the communication. Short (2016) emphasizes that critical content analysis brings a critical lens to the study of texts in an effort to investigate the potential messages within those texts, mainly as related to power. The term critical is defined in this study as a critical reading and analysis of the texts to reveal concepts of hegemony and power through the lens of postcolonialism. These texts were part of specific sociohistorical contexts and so an important aspect of critical content analysis is to investigate not only the texts themselves, but also the surrounding contexts in regard to global events, policies, and social traditions.

This study speaks to and is framed by the research question: How do authors of graphic memoirs represent their own experiences of growing up within the Middle Eastern regions during a time of conflict?

The data is drawn from four graphic memoirs written and published in English-speaking countries, based on the following criteria: (a) published between 2000 and 2017, (b) identified as a graphic novel which is a memoir, and (c) set mainly in Middle Eastern regions and/or their constantly shifting borders. Three of the graphic memoirs selected for analysis are personal memoirs, while the fourth is an intimate family memoir of the author's father. These graphic memoirs were selected in order to have access to two modes of communication, verbal and visual, along with personal narratives based in the turbulent ways of life experienced by each protagonist. The study of regions of the Middle East connects to present day concerns about U.K. and U.S. policies on immigration and refugees, and sheds light on the lived experiences of children displaced by conflict and violence.

The analysis process began by collecting and reading book reviews for each title and compiling information on each author/illustrator and translator. Further, patterns across the texts were initially noted by examining images on book jackets along with the verbal/visual texts in each book. The texts were read and reread multiple times to pinpoint the strongest recurring patterns. These patterns were coded and used to develop categories that were studied in relation to the lives of the author/illustrators. Specific images that projected violence and subjectivity were selected for close analysis using analytical tools for visual images from Painter, Martin, and Unsworth (2013).

In Chapter 2 of this book, Painter argues that there are three kinds of meanings, purposes, and textual interplay that work simultaneously so that readers can make sense of the text. Within this study I used analytical tools from ideational meaning (representation of content or subject matter) and interpersonal meaning (roles and relationships between reader and writer, including attitudes and stances of both) to examine the visual and verbal data. The repeated juxtaposition of the verbal and the visual makes it possible for readers to create a connection between both. This analysis considers how ideational meaning is created by visual images and the sequencing of events. The focus on ideational meaning involves

describing and comparing/contrasting the identities and subjectivities of the protagonists and their connections to other characters.

Table 12.1 provides a brief description of each book along with a brief biography of each author/illustrator. *Note*: It was not possible to obtain permission to
include all of the interior images from the graphic memoirs that are described in
this chapter, but these works are widely accessible in bookstores and libraries.

TABLE 12.1 Descriptions of the Texts and Their Authors/Illustrators

Text	Book Description	Biography of Authors/Illustrators
1. AbdelRazaq, Leila (2015). *Baddawi*.	The author's father Ahmad grew up stateless in the Palestinian refugee camp of Baddawi in Northern Lebanon. AbdelRazaq writes about her father's lived experiences in this graphic family memoir, spanning the years 1959–1980.	AbdelRazaq is a Palestinian Muslim living in Chicago, where her art and work focus on social activism. She studied theatre and Arabic studies, and created Bigmouth Press and Comix, a blog, as a platform for women of color to connect and have a voice.
2. Abirached, Zeina, (2007/2012). *A Game for Swallows: To Die, to Leave, to Return.* Translated from the French.	This graphic memoir is based on the lived experiences of Zenia, a Lebanese Christian, who was a child during the civil war in 1984 Beirut.	Abirached is a Lebanese Christian now settled in France. She collected her childhood memories of Beirut to share the strength of family and community during civil conflict.
3. Satrapi, Marjane (2000/2003). *Persepolis: The Story of a Child-hood*. Translated from the French.	This novel is a pioneer in the field of graphic memoirs based in Middle Eastern regions. Satrapi writes about her experiences of living through two revolutions in Iran, recounting her experiences as a 10-year-old in 1980 until she leaves as a 13-year-old for Vienna.	Satrapi was born in Rasht, Iran, and is of Gilak and Qajars origin, growing up in Tehran in a middle-class family. Her parents were politically active and supported Marxist causes against the monarchy of the last Shah. When the Iranian Revolution took place in 1979, they were oppressed by the right-wing Muslims in power. She lived in Vienna and then in France.
4. Sattouf, Riad (2015). *The Arab of the Future: A Childhood in the Middle East, 1978–1984.* Translated from the French.	This memoir is about Sattouf's life in Libya, Syria and France through the eyes of a 2-year-old child with a French mother and a Syrian father. Sattouf highlights his experiences of living in different regions of the world.	Sattouf is a best-selling cartoonist and filmmaker who grew up in Syria, Libya, and France, and lives in Paris. The author of four comic series in France and a satirical weekly column in *Charlie Hebdo*, he also directs films. This book is his first to appear in English in a five-book series.

The analysis further uses the tools from interpersonal meaning through the close study of social relations. Choices made by illustrators generate connections or gaps that create a distance from which readers make sense of a text. The analytical tools of interpersonal meaning (Painter et al., 2013) relevant to this study are as follows:

- *Attitude* is the angle of face and angle of gaze and the way a reader is positioned in relation to power.
- *Proximity* is the relationship between characters and the locations of power represented through the positioning of characters in relation to each other.
- *Focalization* is positioning of the viewer/reader to assume a viewpoint through the study of the gaze of characters toward the viewer/reader and other characters, and the manner in which characters are placed within a picture plane.
- *Pathos* refers to the creation of empathy through facial expressions and style of the art.
- *Ambience* is the creation of emotional mood through color- or black and white images.

My interest in this analysis is due to the present political climate in relation to the Middle East and my own position as a researcher of Muslim representations within children's and young adult literature. As a Pakistani-American Muslim, who migrated to the U.S. as a woman in her 30s from Pakistan and who continues to return periodically, I feel that I am an insider, even though I do not belong to the specific Middle Eastern regions represented in these four graphic memoirs. Further, I deeply connect to the harrowing experiences of migrants as I went through similar conditions in losing my way of life due to unrest and civil war in East Pakistan (present day Bangladesh) as a child.

Socio-Historical and Cultural Aspects of the Text Settings

New Historicism argues that literature reflects the interests and biases of the period, and so connects to perspectives of past views and self-interpretations of an event. Texts are thus part of the everyday, embedded in the institutions and power relations of general culture (Malpas & Wake, 2013, p. 67). Further, meaning is derived by not separating literature from other forms of cultural and social interactions, but through awareness that a given period is understood as a site of conflict between competing interests and discourses. These ideological powers must be questioned and contested to explore the relationships of varied texts. Documents are viewed as interpreters of social control and political subversion and texts should be read as canonical texts, even those that are personal narratives or social media documents. According to New Historicism, literature reflects the interests and biases of the period it is written in. A work of literature is never created in a vacuum, but is influenced by forces both inside and outside of the author's life and experiences.

The four texts integral to this analysis are based in the Middle Eastern regions and the tumultuous historical events that impacted each narrative. The stories they project are those of children growing up under many kinds of oppression, which influenced who they became and how they interpreted their narratives for readers/audiences. Each of the narratives draws on the socio-political conditions of the regions they represent, so the historical contexts are regarded as artifacts within these narratives.

All four books depict a historical period of instability and violence within the Middle East, and so the young protagonists leave home because they have to, not because they want to. Each protagonist exists in a place of conflict and a constant feeling of insecurity without a stable home. Sattouf's father moves the family from place to place in the Middle East even though he has a chance to live in France; his own extended family takes his inherited land and home and sells them in his absence. Satrapi's personality and commitment to speaking truth to power forces her to leave her beloved homeland, parents, and grandmother for Vienna; her situation is that of homelessness due to her pursuit of education and a better life. Abirached's life propels her family to move for security reasons because of civil war in Lebanon. AbdelRazaq's father is Palestinian, living in a refugee camp in Lebanon. The name of his camp, Baddawi, comes from "Bedouin," meaning nomad. The Palestinian residents of this camp have been there since 1948 or since their birth, and they are not nomads by choice. They live in a permanent state of desiring to return home, even those who have never been home.

Oppression is also a strong constant within these narratives. The protagonists' circumstances, their own families/communities, and their governments oppress them. Their own people become their oppressors as occurs in Sattouf's experiences in Libya and Ahmad's in Lebanon. Due to their constant movement, these protagonists project strong dichotomies and binary positions in the manner in which they live and their constantly changing beliefs and faiths.

The oppressors' gaze plays a significant role in these narratives, as the protagonists' experiences expose regimes of hegemony. While Sattouf's family lived under the scrutiny of dictators such as Assad and Gaddafi, Satrapi existed under the regime change of the Shah of Iran and the Islamic revolution in Iran. Civil war between Muslims and Christians in Beirut is the focus of Abirached's experiences, where Muslims were regarded negatively. AbdelRazaq's father had his every move scrutinized in the refugee camp, with fences restricting his movements. Thus, these narratives project strong instances of political/societal oppression.

Historical and societal changes are markedly present in these books. The historical periods represented in these graphic novels project into the lives of the protagonists. Their memoirs thus become historical narratives and discourses. Each government's political and social oppression under which the protagonists and their families exist transforms them.

Portrayals of Lives in the Middle East

The research question on portrayals of Middle Eastern cultures was explored in the data through the lens of the critical theoretical frame of postcolonialism and using visual tools (Painter et al., 2013). Strong themes emerged from analysis of the patterns within these personal narratives. These patterns project dominant societal perspectives in the plot and storytelling, and crisscross the four graphic memoirs as identified by the frame of postcolonial theory and the tools of inter-personal and ideational meanings.

These graphic memoirs primarily use simple, minimalistic, stark black-and-white visual images, with a few washes of flat color, that include expressive dialogues in speech bubbles, leaving enough space for the reader to insert political and social commentary into the gaps. Painter et al. (2013) say that the perception of pathos created by "the minimalistic style requires us to be relatively detached observers of characters rather than to take them to our hearts. It is a style that suits a social commentary, often one deploying humor to carry its message" (p. 32). This style is thus suitable for these satirical/comic-like graphic novels. The memoirs are strong examples of social commentary on the regions as well as the circumstances of the families, with the visual images less impacted by the translations of these books from their original language into English.

The images bound within frames create boundaries that are permeated through continuing dialogue between characters. These memoirs particularly use sequencing in storytelling as a seamless way of integrating the words and images, showing strong control so each duels with the other, leading to a tension that creates further information or ideational meaning. Verbal dialogue is depicted in speech bubbles and internal expression is depicted as a narrator's voice in boxes above or below the frames. Thus, meaning is created through an amalgamation of inferred and real verbal/visual texts.

The iconic or stylized forms of the minimalistic drawings create pathos through facial expressions and the style of the art, while ambience is created through black-and-white images. These emphasize understanding through visual literacy rather than what is merely visible in the verbal/visual content. This style reinforces the ideational content of the narratives through a restricted use of color. The reader is propelled towards the context and the words through these minimalistic images. Empathy for the protagonists may be created through reader's lived experiences of the content but is not encouraged through the minimalistic images and lack of color. The subject matter of the narratives is fortified by the visual images and violence is expressed in most of the images. Where these images speak to the normalcy of everyday life within these regions, they also project the upheavals of living these lives and forming identities in times of conflict. In a visually effective manner, these narratives emphasize the context through satire.

Through minimal color and primarily black-and-white images, these narratives become compelling due to the interactions of verbal and visual content and their historical contexts. Further, the use of strong contrasts within these texts provides a dramatic quality that reinforces the serious historical content and context. The use of a reduced color palette signals literal removal from a familiar reality in contrast to the brilliant colors and realistic drawings found in most children's books. However, these texts are for more mature readers due to the seriousness of the subject matter that draws attention to the struggles of children left homeless due to war, genocide, and unrest.

Satrapi writes with bluntness and draws with expression in *Persepolis*. Her provocative and thoughtful dialogues emphasize her higher social status and her family's communist beliefs that challenged the increasingly prohibitive pressures of the Mullahs under the Shah's liberal rule. On pages 9, 14, and 26, she speaks truth to power through the interactions of her vibrant character with those around her. Her connections to her grandmother and God are clearly depicted in both the verbal and visual text. She writes her dialogues in capital letters. For example, she does not fulfill her promise to God that she will be a prophet, but then feeling guilty about this, says to God, "NO, NO I WILL BE A PROPHET, BUT THEY MUSTN'T KNOW." In the very next frame she says, "I WANTED TO BE JUSTICE, LOVE AND THE WRATH OF GOD ALL IN ONE" (p. 9). She projects a visual image of a thoughtful, strong, liberated young female supported by family, despite the violence gripping her nation and which is particularly directed toward women in that time period. Through oblique eye movements and the placement of the figures within the frame, Satrapi successfully conveys a perception of herself as a child.

Visual gaze plays a significant role in Satarapi's images. She conveys meaning through her simple but expressive eyes and the ways in which they guide and direct the reader to pay attention, along with the way her character responds to each situation. The cover image, Figure 12.1, depicts Satarapi looking straight at the audience to compel a reaction and to indicate her unhappiness through her expression and crossed arms. The Islamic patterns around the border also direct the viewer to Satarapi in the center of the cover.

Page 14 of *Persepolis* depicts violent images of unrest when a cinema was burned down with all the people inside. This image contains theatregoers who look like phantoms rushing toward the exit, with the caption, "The BCC said there were 400 victims. The Shah of Iran said that a group of religious fanatics perpetrated the massacre. But the people knew that it was the Shah's fault!" The doors were locked from the outside and the police did nothing to save the 400 people trapped within. While Satrapi converses with God, the Shah's people stage this event to blame the religious right. The concept of proximity comes into play with the image placing the reader in close proximity through close-ups of the violence in the bottom left and right images on both sides of the double-page spread. The images highlight power through proximity in bold images that cannot be avoided. It is evident that the person telling the story is placed outside of this horrendous act, with the reader positioned to assume a certain viewpoint of the images. The contrasting black backdrop and white images create strong

FIGURE 12.1 The Cover of *Persepolis* by Marjane Satrapi
Source: "Illustrations" from *Persepolis: The Story of a Childhood* by Marjane Satrapi, translation copyright © 2003 by L'Association, Paris, France. Used by permission of Pantheon Books, an imprint of the Knopf Doubleday Publishing Group, a division of Penguin Random House LLC. All rights reserved.

diagonal vectors in the final image on the right-hand page to show extreme action that presents the powerful oppressive government as being without law, order, or empathy, thus indicating who tells the story and who is seeing/witnessing the events as an example of the visual tool of focalization.

In *The Arab of the Future*, Sattouf creates perceptions of ambience or emotional mood by using light washes of color in otherwise linear minimalist images to express his varied childhood experiences in different parts of the world. The limited use of color adds to the images and provides clarity for the reader as to the time and the space the family occupies. France is represented with a blue wash, Libya is yellow, and Syria is pink. His images also reflect his negative views of his father's Middle Eastern background as his narrative shows almost no urban development and the dated clothing worn by his father's family is in contrast to his depictions of France. The cover of the book (see Figure 12.2) presents the

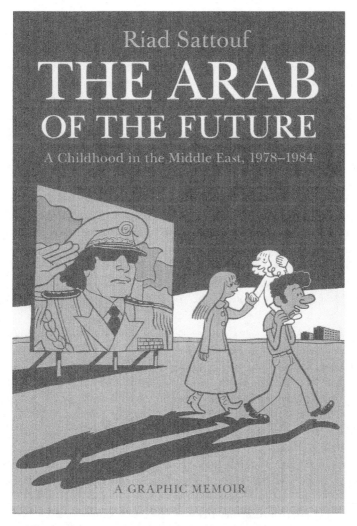

FIGURE 12.2 Cover of *The Arab of the Future* by Riad Sattouf
Source: "Cover," *The Arab of the Future*: A Childhood in the Middle East, 1978–1984. by R. Sattouf. Trans. from the French by S. Taylor. Translation copyright © 2015. Used by permission of Metropolitan, New York. All rights reserved.

diagonal dark shadows of the family as they walk, with the father carrying Sattouf on his shoulders. The child is focused on his mother, holding her hand, a fore-shadowing of the family relationships in the book. The oppression in Libya is portrayed through the image of Gaddafi on a large billboard in a full military uniform saluting his troops.

Within the book, Sattouf is first presented as a blond two-year-old carrying a pistol, facing the right side as if walking into the book with an intense expression in both eyes and face. This image is blue, set in France, as he takes the audience on this journey with him. The page with the most telling image is that on the recto page that says "Chapter 1" and has a yellow, white, and black (Libyan flag colors) diagonal image of the father as a dominant mass, almost filling the picture plane with oblique vectors, diagonal lines that project action. Sattouf is presented as sitting in his father's open left hand on the lower diagonal corner. The hand is the largest object within the frame as the father seems to offer his small, White, defenseless child for the reader to devour.

Most significant are the gaze and the expressions on the faces of the father and the son as they diagonally face each other. Sattouf has a shocked expression and his father is looking down at him in a confused but detached manner. This wordless image foreshadows and encapsulates the narrative where the father is represented as dragging his family around the world, especially the insecure world of the Middle East, without considering the impact on his French wife and White child. Physically, father and son could not look more dissimilar from each other. So even before the reader begins the main narrative, the audience is prepared for certain experiences due to these two initial images that frame the narrative without verbal dialogue. Within the verbal and visual text, Sattouf's disdain for his father's actions is clear throughout the narrative. The connection to oppression of a child by an adult is represented in that the adult holds the power to manipulate his child.

Abirached's book, *A Game for Swallows*, is printed on heavy glossy paper and includes intricate and expressive features on the faces of the characters to create ambience or mood. The author/illustrator creates ambience and high drama through the saturation of black contrasting with white. Her story is about the persecution of Christians in Beirut, Lebanon, but the challenges of survival seem to be the same as in the other three books. The use of intricate stylistic designs as frames infers the strong historical context of the family and a caring community that scaffolds and protects families as they undergo challenges that inevitably force them to leave their homelands for safer spaces. Whenever the parents of Zeina and her brother leave for the grocery store or to visit their grandmother, the children are protected by neighbors and friends. The images on the pages reflect insecurities that are life threatening as well as the support that keeps the family together unscathed. The cover (see Figure 12.3) depicts the influence of family, community, and friends in surrounding and protecting the two young children from harm, as well as the illustrator's use of highly stylized details of hair and clothing.

FIGURE 12.3 The Cover of *A Game for Swallows: To Die, to Leave, to Return* by Zeina Abirached

Source: A Game for Swallows: To Die, to Leave, to Return by Zeina Abirached. Copyright © 2007 by Editions Cambourakis. English translation copyright © 2012 by Lerner Publishing Group, Inc. Reprinted with the permission of Graphic Universe, a division of Lerner Publishing Group, Inc. All rights reserved. No part of this excerpt may be used or reproduced in any manner whatsoever without the prior written permission of Lerner Publishing Group, Inc.

The second image of the book is a double-page spread without human figures. The diagonal division of the page provides an oblique/diagonal vector which conveys a strong message, as do the written monologues above and below the images. The contrast of the zigzag line crossing the straight demarcation line represents paths that people take as they try to bypass a sniper who shoots to kill while people walk, run, jump, and climb to safely visit family and friends on the other side. At the bottom of the page the narrator states, "CROSSING THE HANDFUL OF STREETS BETWEEN US MEANT FOLLOWING COMPLICATED AND PERILOUS CHOREO- GRAPHY" (p. 17). This image firmly places the absent sniper as the villain. He belongs to the "other" group, Muslims, thus the reader is positioned in relation to who has power to tell a story. This visual image positions the reader by inferring a Muslim male as a terrorist, thus reinforcing a frequent stereotype in popular media.

AbdelRazaq emphasizes the displaced Palestinian experience through mini- mally detailed images in *Baddawi*. She chronicles her father's life in Lebanon near Tripoli, and his movement to Beirut and finally the U.S., emphasizing the day- to-day life of a stateless individual. The poignant beginning says, "Palestine is buried deep in the creases of my grandmother's palms, they once kneaded bread dough and sowed seeds of her homeland in my family's village." (p. 4). Abdel- Razaq focuses on the grandmother and the family as the narrative progresses. Gaze plays a significant role within the visual images in this narrative.

With the use of diagonal lines in the images shown in *Baddawi* (2015) Figure 12.4, the human figures are insignificant due to their size but the airplanes and the diagonally falling cluster bombs show the devastation they are causing through the same diagonal line dropping from top right going down to the left corner. The first image of a ball of bread, ready to be baked, is strategically placed to show that life in the region can go from the peace of everyday life to violence in a matter of minutes. Also, the airplanes are huge in the upper right image as they approach the target of innocent Palestinians. The placing of the images next to each other on a page places the reader outside of the experiences of Ahmad and his people, again creating a particular attitude by positioning the reader in relation to who has the power over the lives of the inhabitants of the camp.

The protagonists of these narratives project images of life in the Middle East through the memories of their lived every day experiences that include the con- stant threat of violence. Using visual tools within a theoretical frame as well as knowledge about the sociopolitical environment of the regions, the reader comes away with a deeper and stronger understanding of the texts and their overt and covert messages.

Perceptions of Othering through Hybrid Identity Formation

The protagonists develop a hybrid personality as they move from one region to another and learn to cope with ever-changing circumstances. Each of these author/illustrators eventually found their way to a Western nation that became viewed as saving them from violence and unrest.

The most relevant example is that of Sattouf, born to a French mother and a Syrian father who moved the family between France, Libya, and Syria. His

FIGURE 12.4 The Bombing of a Village in Beirut, Lebanon (AbdelRazaq, 2015)
Source: "Illustrations," from *Baddawi* by L. AbdelRazaq (2015). Used by permission of
Just World Books, Charlottesville, VA. All rights reserved.

father's idiosyncrasies represent what is viewed as a typical Middle Eastern male
through his actions and beliefs, thus reinforcing stereotypes about Muslim males
in general. Said (1978) says that Muslim or Middle Eastern males are represented
by Western discourse as selfish and opinionated, based on perceptions of a male-
dominated society. His father's family refers to Sattouf as a girl and a Jew due to
his light skin and long blond hair, and so shuns him.

Sattouf's connection to his grandmothers is special. He likes the smell of his
paternal grandma even though she does not stop his cousins from beating him up.
His maternal French grandmother is presented as liberated as she remarries in old
age, showing him how to live off the land and talking about death to him. He
learns to accept the eccentricities of his Middle Eastern family and hide behind his
paternal grandmother and mother, even though living in the Middle East leads

him to question his existence in both worlds and his hybrid identity. He represents himself as accepted by his French family while othered by his Middle Eastern family.

The young characters in each graphic novel gradually come to project agency in voicing their opinions, despite their varied circumstances. They develop identities subjugated and reactive to the oppressions within their everyday lives. They also cultivate a sense of self and agency through their uncertain existences. These protagonists often shift from direct speech to indirect narrator thoughts represented in either straight locked lines somewhere within the frame (Sattouf) or in separate frames (Abirached), indicating that this discourse represents the character's inner thoughts, as expressed by a narrator's voice. The protagonists face instances of discrimination within their circumstances and families as well as by the powerful dictatorships in their countries. They exist under constant threat from their people, sometimes their own families and other times the larger community.

History plays a strong part in these narratives, since the hegemony of each historical oppressor contributes to the formation of each character. It is difficult for a people's identity to be formed when there is confusion as to who they are and where they belong. The characters within these books reflect the progressive creation of identities and subjectivities embedded within the multiple cultures they inhabit.

Sattouf in his unbound first image at the beginning of the book (p. 3) illustrates an innocent two-year-old represented as "perfect" by his own adult voice. The last image of the book represents the same child looking back at the reader, while being led to a plane, with a shocked, tearful expression as he realizes he is being taken back to Syria by his father. His expression seems to be pleading with the audience/reader to save him. This last image of the book, like the opening image, is blue, black and white, signaling Sattouf's departure from his secure existence in France. Multiple images project Arab perceptions of the significance of family and the role of responsible males/sons in Arab traditions, which seems integral in the formation of Sattouf's hybrid identity and perceived subjectivity.

The concept of gaze is significant at both micro and macro levels within these texts. Within ideational meaning (Painter et al., 2013), visual positioning through gaze within these narratives is sometimes mediated so that the gaze is presented as taking on the point of view of the reader. There are also places where the visual positioning takes on the reader's perspective and audience stance is inferred. At the micro level within these narratives the character's gaze sometimes invites, and in some instances demands, the viewer's participation in the events. Satrapi and Abirached use sideways, playful glances to overtly invite the audience in, thus creating a boundary that is not easily discerned between laughing at and/or with the characters. At the macro level the regional upheavals and histories invite consideration of the lived sociopolitical experiences of the characters. This understanding of the systemic macro-aggressions is represented in all four of the novels through both forms of communication. Specific instances include when

Sattouf and Satrapi portray images of the government interference that infiltrates the everyday lives of citizens. Also, there is the inferred imperial macro lens shown through the verbal dialogues, the ways of living represented in the texts, and the images of dictators such as Gaddafi when Sattouf is in Libya and other Middle Eastern regions. The imperial viewpoint is further represented through the decision by the author/illustrators to write a memoir. The inner voice of the author/illustrators and the manner in which they look down upon their own culture and society is particularly strong in the verbal/visual texts of Satrapi and Sattouf.

Although the author/illustrators present narratives that reflect their lived experiences, they do so from a perspective of identities that have travelled through time and space to be inhabitants of the Western nations where they have opportunities to be heard by audiences. Sattouf's visual narrative, within the images that were analyzed in this study, seems to communicate a negative view of Middle Eastern people as backdated in the way that he represents family members, and his own father as an oppressor. Satrapi's visual narrative describes a protagonist who is a free-thinking independent female, in contrast to other females in Iran. She is viewed as an exception to the norm, giving an impression of writing from a perspective of Western females with a Western imperialist viewpoint.

Discussion

There is little doubt that these graphic memoirs have strong literary merit through their use of authentic dialogue, expressive characters, and strong but minimal visual setting. The format of a graphic memoir is suited to and helps communicate the serious subject matter within specific historical settings (Pagliaro, 2014). These strong points convinced me to look deeper into the minimalistic drawings and observe the images through the analytical tools of pathos, ambience, and gaze, as well as to look for visual patterns with the narratives. This analysis adds to deeper understandings of both verbal and visual texts in these graphic memoirs.

Foucault and Rabinow (1984) state that history is discontinuous, and the redefined role of power is a force that is everywhere. Literature is shaped by the ideas, beliefs, and desires of a society and is actively involved in sustaining or challenging them (Malpas, 2013, p. 68). No example of literature exists without connections to world events and history. Authors and illustrators create characters that are influenced by historical events and in turn influence the events surrounding them. Thus, the historical context of an event is an imperative and, "meaning emerges from languages, beliefs, practices, institutions, and desires of particular historically located cultures" (Malpas, 2013. p. 62). Therefore, text with context is essential to any kind of interpretation.

New Historicism argues that the lived through experiences of these authors are present within their narratives. Postcolonialism points out that power relations are systemic and embedded in institutions and society (Malpas & Wake, 2013). Texts reflect everyday lived experiences of protagonists and project a certain worldview.

Further, meanings in these narratives are derived from other forms of cultural and social interactions, a tenet of postcolonialism. By not separating literature from other forms of cultural and social interactions, narratives provide the possibility of being accepted as counter-narratives, of challenging what is commonly believed and accepted as representations of a culture. These counter-narratives help a given period to be understood as a site of conflict between competing interests and discourses. Historical, personal narratives can present lived experiences that reinforce the reality of political and social interactions within the regions, hence providing a necessary vision of the events within those nations at that given time. This potential of a personal narrative to serve as a counter-narrative for that time period, however, is not realized in the four graphic memoirs analyzed in this study.

The findings indicate that these authors use the graphic novel format as a social commentary on their home countries and the present and past circumstances in the Middle East by telling their own story, but without providing a more complex and empathetic view of the situations they lived through. Using their narratives as social commentary allows a one-sided point of view to be projected. These narratives do not dismantle the damaging tropes of commonly accepted worldviews of Middle Eastern regions and Muslims; rather, they reinforce them. These narratives lack multiple perspectives because they are memoirs and personal narratives, and so project a one-sided viewpoint that is heavily weighted by personal experiences and circumstances. This one-sided perspective becomes even more evident through analysis of the visual images.

Final Reflections

Critically reading these texts is necessary to appreciate the subliminal visual, metaphorical, and direct messages embedded in visual/verbal texts within the narratives. The play of power relationships that encompasses these mostly black-and-white texts projects the dominance of one kind of people from past to present that catapults them into a shaky future, pointing toward postcolonial concerns and issues. According to Painter et al. (2013), "Visual images are the most significant means for setting up an affective relationship between a child and book, an important step in coming to terms with the print medium" (p. 15). This statement speaks to the significance of images in picturebooks and graphic novels as a meaning-making process. Further, the protagonists project an imperialist viewpoint through their actions, narrative structures, and plots where they finally reach the shores of Western nations that provide them with a platform to voice their narratives and an agency to tell their tales.

Forced journeys are a way of life for many children today as they are rendered homeless through no fault of their own. Currently, there is an increase in young adult and children's books highlighting the struggles of immigrant and refugee children who live more than one life with multiple identities as they adjust to new regions and languages. This trend is accompanied by a demand to represent global cultures in a more respectful and empathetic manner so that the readers can better understand the characters' challenges. Literature provides a means for youth to connect with cultures and experiences outside their own world as well as to better understand the difficulties of their own lives.

Comparing these narratives to the present-day turmoil where refugees are not given access to a safe refuge leads to the observation that history repeats itself. These narratives project lives in a broken region of the world and reinforce ongoing concerns of the Middle East as a place of conflict and unease, making it a fertile ground for unrest and creating an influx of immigrants, who sometimes turn violent. Even though the families show no such aptitude in these graphic novels, they still represent a group of people viewed negatively in the Western world.

Children who grow up facing conflict, where they are rendered homeless, tend to embrace survival. Their identities are forever oscillating and they are never completely whole. This is a position directly opposite to that of many Western children who are the audience for these narratives. Each of these graphic memoirs projects a Middle Eastern society frozen in time, where oppression is the norm. This representation projects them as "other" and evokes feelings of pity or rein-forces stereotypes of Middle Eastern people as vicious, backward, thoughtless, and anti-Semitic.

Graphic novels can play a critical role in either giving voice to or silencing the "other," particularly within the previously colonized world (Said, 1978). These graphic memoirs provide a one-sided mirror, which reflects only some insiders, and a narrow window that provides glimpses of authentic subjective experiences of people within the regions and its cultures.

Painter et al. (2013) state that, "stories for children function not only as sources of pleasure and entertainment but also as a prime means for teaching the young ... Books carry not only implicit literacy lessons but implicit literary and social training" (p. 30). This study suggests that criticality can be brought into reading visual images and expand how to read graphic memoirs and novels within and beyond educational borders in a convergence of multimodality and history to expand global literacies. Critical texts such as graphic memoirs can foreground issues of representation and immigration as well as themes of vio-lence and conflict that are currently prevalent for Muslims and the regions that have mostly Muslim populations, especially during today's constantly changing social and political climate. A critical reading of graphic memoirs can provide the means of developing and drawing on multimodal practices for all students. By inviting dialogue to challenge the ways in which these stories depict the peoples and cultures of the Middle East, the possibility exists that students will also challenge these depictions in mainstream society, thus creating the potential for a more equitable future for the Middle East, Muslims, and immigrants in a new, safer land.

References

Bhabha, H.K. (1994). *The location of culture*. London: Routledge.

Eisner, W. (2008). *Graphic storytelling and visual narrative*. New York: W. W. Norton.

Foucault, M. (1972) *The archaeology of knowledge*. London: Tavistock.

Foucault, M. & Rabinow, P. (1984). *The Foucault reader*. New York: Pantheon Books.

Loomba, A. (2005). *Colonialism/postcolonialism, the new critical idiom* (2nd ed.). New York: Routledge.

Malpas, S. (2013). Historicism. In S. Malpas & P. Wake (Eds.), *Routledge companion to critical and cultural theory* (pp. 62–72). New York: Routledge.

Malpas, S. & Wake, P. (Eds.). (2013). *Routledge companion to critical and cultural theory*. New York: Routledge.

McCloud, S. (2006). *Making comics: Storytelling secrets of comics, manga, and graphic novels*. New York: HarperCollins.

McCloud, S. (1993). *Understanding comics: An invisible art*. New York: William Morrow.

Mills, S. (1997). *Discourse, the new critical idiom*. New York: Routledge.

Painter, C., Martin, J.R., & Unsworth, L. (2013). *Reading visual narratives: Image analysis of children's picture books*. Sheffield, UK: Equinox.

Pagliaro, M. (2014). Is a picture worth a thousand words? Determining the criteria for graphic novels with literary merit. *English Journal*, 103(4), 31–45.

Pearson, M.B. (2005). Speaking to their hearts: Using picture books in the history classroom. *Library Media Connections*, 24 (3), 30–32.

Said, E.W. (1978). *Orientalism*. Harmondsworth, UK: Penguin.

Short, K. (2016). Critical content analysis as a research methodology. In H. Johnson, J. Mathis, and K. Short (Eds.), *Critical Content analysis of children and young adult literature* (pp. 1–15). New York: Routledge.

Stephens, J. (2013). *Subjectivity in Asian children's literature and film: Global theories and implications*. New York: Routledge.

Children's Literature References

AbdelRazaq, L. (2015). *Baddawi*. Charlottesville, VA: Just World.

Abirached, Z. (2012). *A game for swallows: To die, to leave, to return*. Trans. from the French by S. Guavin. Minneapolis, MN: Lerner.

Satrapi, M. (2003). *Persepolis: The story of a childhood*. Trans. from the French. New York: Pantheon.

Sattouf, R. (2015). *The Arab of the future: A childhood in the Middle East, 1978–1984*. Trans. from the French by S. Taylor. New York: Metropolitan.

13

THE DE-QUEERING OF *HEATHER HAS TWO MOMMIES*

Mary L. Fahrenbruck and Tabitha Parry Collins

Children construct new understandings of people, places, cultures, and ideologies as they transact with the verbal and visual narratives found in picturebooks. Esposito (2009) explores the potential constructive power of picturebooks, stating "[w]hat we come to know is mediated by how it is represented" (p. 65). As such, it is imperative that the narratives in picturebooks portray a wide range of constructs rather than a single story.

Close examination of the verbal and visual narratives in children's picturebooks helps readers uncover the hidden ideologies embedded within the texts. This type of uncovering is difficult for young children, especially in visual narratives. Teachers must be intentional about the ways they help children uncover hidden ideologies in picturebooks. Unfortunately, educators (including ourselves) unknowingly pass over these hidden ideologies. As unintentional as teachers' actions may be, the consequences can be devastating for the very children with whom they share their love of stories.

The purpose of this chapter is to examine the ideologies embedded in the visual narrative of the newest edition of *Heather Has Two Mommies* (Newman, 2015), the story of a young child with same-sex parents. Teachers customarily use this story when they engage (typically) primary students in lessons or units that focus on self, families, or communities. *Heather* fits well with these topics, especially since nearly 2 million children come from homes headed by LGBTQ and same-sex parents (Child Welfare League of America, 2017). Sharing *Heather Has Two Mommies* has the potential to help young children understand that families come in varied configurations and the "the most important thing about a family is that all the people in it love each other," the theme of *Heather* (Newman, 2015, n.p.).

Some researchers (Esposito, 2009; Taylor, 2012) have taken issue with the verbal and visual narratives found in *Heather*. Because these researchers focus on the earlier publications of *Heather*, we wanted to explore the newest edition to see if the revised text and new illustrations are still problematic and to see if other issues surface. To that end, we first share the rich history of *Heather Has Two Mommies* before sharing the research on picturebooks featuring LGBTQ characters. Then we share findings from our analysis on the visual narrative in the newest edition of *Heather Has Two Mommies* (referred to from this point forward as *Heather 2015*). We close this chapter with suggestions for teachers who might like to use *Heather 2015* in their classroom instruction.

Sociohistorical Context of *Heather Has Two Mommies*

In 1989 Lesléa Newman authored the ground-breaking story of *Heather Has Two Mommies* after an acquaintance asked her to write a book about a family with same-sex parents. Newman penned the story of two women, Jane and Kate, who fall in love and decide to start a family. The story explains how Mama Jane conceives Heather through artificial insemination and follows Jane's pregnancy from conception to birth. As a toddler, Heather "spends lots of time together" with Mama Kate, a doctor, and Mama Jane, a carpenter (Newman, 1989, n.p.). Tensions surface in the story when Heather attends a play group and discovers that she doesn't have a father like some of the other children. Tensions get resolved after the children draw pictures of their families and learn that "It doesn't matter how many mommies or how many daddies your family has ... The most important thing about a family is that all the people in it love each other" (Newman, 1989, n.p.).

Newman found illustrator Diana Souza "through the lesbian grapevine" (Peel, 2015, p. 473). At first glance, Souza's black-and-white illustrations seem to lack appeal. However, her generic-style drawings depict a wide range of emotions, with pencil lines and shading that highlight the contours of each character's face. Heather and her mother's expressions draw readers into the story and position them to more closely connect with each character. Together, Souza's black-and-white generic-style illustrations and Newman's verbal narrative "hug each other, their shared goal to represent an indisputably happy family" (Ford, 1998, p. 129).

After several rejections from publishers, Newman self-published *Heather* using $10 donations solicited from friends and family members. Approximately 4,000 copies were printed, of which 2,000 were distributed to those who had donated towards its publication. Newman distributed the remaining copies to small bookstores for resale. Sasha Alyson, the publisher at Alyson Publishing, found *Heather* in one of these bookstores. Eventually, Alyson purchased the remaining copies of *Heather* along with the publishing rights for the next 24 years. *Heather Has Two Mommies* was reprinted in 2000 as a tenth-anniversary edition, and again in 2009 as a twentieth-anniversary edition before going out of print around 2013 when Alyson Publishing underwent changes.

Initially, *Heather* received gratuitous praise mostly from lesbian mothers who appreciated a story in which they and their children were reflected (Maughan,

2015). However, controversy over *Heather* began after an article in *Newsweek* mentioned how *Heather* reflects the changing dynamics of families (Maughan, 2015). Some negative responses to the book focused on the detailed description of Jane's pregnancy. "Must we have lesbianism, artificial insemination, and ana-tomical detail too?" (Ford, 1998, p. 129). The resulting firestorm from con-servatives and the religious right propelled *Heather* into the top 10 on the list of *100 Most Frequently Challenged Books: 1990–1999* (American Library Association, 2018). To quell some of the criticism, the eight-page love story including Hea-ther's conception and birth were removed from *Heather* before it was reprinted in 2000 as a tenth-anniversary edition.

Heather also drew criticism from researchers who took issue with the ways the verbal and visual narratives de-queer the story (Esposito, 2009). Critics argue that the story diminishes the original identity of Heather's mothers as lesbian parents to that of same-sex parents engaged in homonormative, binary gender roles that emulate the roles of heterosexual parents (e.g. Esposito, 2009; Huskey, 2002). Flores (2013) describes homonormativity as "a trend that encourages homosexual, bisexual, and transgender individuals to attempt to mimic heterosexuality and all of its created characteristics and assumptions. The key word in this statement is 'created'" (para. 3). When critics read *Heather*, they see the story of a family living the American dream of the ideal heteronormative family. The story features two committed parents raising a child whom they love very much. The mothers have lucrative careers as a doctor (Kate) and a carpenter (Jane) that afford them a house, pets, and the ability to send Heather to a play group in a private home. Time permits them to go on outings together to the park on weekends or to spend time together playing or building things. Robinson (2016) explains that mimicking heterosexuality (as seen in *Heather*) offers LGBTQ individuals a better chance of being accepted into the dominant (heterosexual) society.

In 2015, Newman and her publisher at Candlewick Press revived the con-troversial picturebook. They hoped to breathe new life into *Heather* by revising the verbal and visual narratives to make the story "a lot shorter, hopefully punchy, and more appealing" (Newman in Peel, 2015, p. 471). In the newest edition, Heather still spends lots of time building, baking, and playing with Mama Jane and Mama Kate. However, Heather attends kindergarten (not play group) where she simply wonders (rather than worries) if she is the only student who doesn't have a father. Like the first three editions, Heather and her classmates draw pictures of their families and Heather realizes that family configurations vary from person to person. The teacher, Ms. Molly, delivers the thematic line, "The most important thing about a family is that all the people in it love each other" (Newman, 2015, n.p.).

The visual narrative changed in *Heather 2015* with the change of illustrators, a decision made by Candlewick Press. In *Heather 2015*, award-winning illustrator Laura Cornell used watercolors and gouache to brighten up her minimalist style illustrations. The minimalist style uses only essential brushstrokes to represent characters and objects in illustrations. In an interview, Newman stated, "the new illustrations are very lively, and they really convey how much Heather's mothers love her, and Heather's joy and pride in her family…. we needed to bring Heather and her family and her pets into the twenty-first century" (Newman in Peel, 2015, p. 471). Together, the revised verbal and visual narratives seem to have achieved their purpose, as reviews of the newest edition have been favorable.

Queer Theories Framework

We use queer theories as the lens to conduct a critical content analysis of *Heather 2015*. Queer can be used to categorize a marginalized group of people as well as to understand relationships between traditionally binary categories such as gender, sexual orientation, and normal/deviant (Dilley, 1999). We use the latter description for our study.

Queer theories aim to deconstruct (seemingly) clear and consistent categories of normalcy and deviance achieved through queering readings of texts and by attending to the performativity of characters' identities (Butler, 1990; Linville, 2017). Conversely, queer theorists argue that these categories are inconsistent and complicated, and to demonstrate these discrepancies the existing categories must be deconstructed, or "queered" (Ryan & Hermann-Wilmarth, 2013). Using "queer" as a verb allows researchers to "name identities and practices that complicate or fail to fit the normative, stable formulation of these categories *and* as a way to name the process of that disruption and recognition" (Ryan & Hermann-Wilmarth, 2013, p. 145). Queering a text also allows for the examination of discourses of power that often discourage individuals from performing their identities outside the socially recognized normative categories, such as non-binary gender identities or socialized ideologies which dictate what is considered "masculine" versus "feminine" (Butler, 1990).

When researchers "queer" texts, they move beyond socially accepted sexual diversity frameworks such as the "tolerance/visibility framework," a framework that allows for the acknowledgement of non-normative identities but does not critically engage with these identities (Kim Lin, 2017, p. 25). The tolerance/visibility framework foregrounds characters' differences in terms of representation and visibility, but also minimizes them through discourse that asserts individuals are all the same, regardless of superficial differences (Kim Lin, 2017). Unfortunately, this method of acceptance ultimately does not challenge the system of heteronormativity, which is considered normal; instead it demands that those viewed as deviant restructure themselves to fit into the existing socially constructed categories. Queer theories, in contrast, attempt to challenge or to queer that which is considered the norm. Queering the norm results in the creation of new, non-normative categories of identification such as transgender, genderqueer, and asexual (Butler, 1990).

Queer theories also assert that texts are a form of discourse which involve power relations and themes of dominance that are historically situated and uncritically replicated within society (Butler, 1990; Foucault, 1978). Accepted by queer theorists, this concept connects with literary theory and its use to investigate "the arbitrary kinds of social and political arrangements and hierarchies that structure texts" (Ryan & Hermann-Wilmarth, 2013, p. 148). The hegemonic hierarchies that emerge from the investigations privilege some individuals (those considered normal) and marginalize others (those considered deviant). Emerging from what Butler (1990) calls "the heterosexual matrix," which involves the unspoken rules that govern ideas about males and females, and masculinity and femininity, these ideas privilege heterosexuality even in same-sex relationships (p. 68).

Using themes and concepts derived from queer theories to examine the illustrations in *Heather 2015* helps us consider the presence of homonormativity throughout the story. These themes and concepts include the following:

- Exploring and challenging the way in which heterosexuality is constructed as normal.
- Challenging traditionally held assumptions that there is an oppositional divide between being homosexual and heterosexual.
- Recognizing that categories assigned to humans (such as sexual orientation and gender) are socially constructed and working to deconstruct those widely accepted categories.
- Challenging, or "queering," those categories accepted as the norms.
- Critically examining how constructed categories and power relations intersect.
- Viewing heteronormativity as a form of power and control that applies pressure to both straight and gay individuals through institutional arrangements and accepted social norms.

We assert that the illustrations in *Heather 2015* portray a relationship between Mama Kate and Mama Jane in ways that can easily be read as a heterosexual friendship, thereby denying the existence of a queer family and normalizing their queer (outsider) identities. Through this normalization, we aim to uncover the embedded ideologies of the narrative which use the power of conformity to minimize the need for queer representation in authentic ways.

Studies Framed with Queer Theories

The field of children's literature is replete with studies framed with the lens of Queer Theories. Researchers including Ryan and Hermann-Wilmoth (2013), Taylor (2012), Lester (2014), and Esposito (2009) surveyed sets of children's literature for different purposes. With an eye towards expanding classroom practices, Ryan and Hermann-Wilmarth's (2013) research deconstructs children's literature to "highlight experiences and subjectivities of nonnormative sexualities and gender identities in the hopes of making classrooms more inclusive" (p. 149).

Taylor, Lester, and Esposito's (2009) research focuses on representations of homonormativity found in children's literature that feature LGBTQ children as main characters (acronyms used are taken from the respective publications).

Hermann-Wilmarth and Ryan (2014) conducted two analyses on ten chapter books intended for readers in intermediate grades. First, they mapped the representations of LGBTQ characters in each book based on race and class criteria. They discovered these texts featured "mostly men, middle-class families and whiteness. We also see … individuals without communities, and very little challenge to social structures" (p. 15). In their second analysis, Hermann-Wilmarth and Ryan used a Queer Theory lens to look past the categorical labels into the origins of these categories. In doing so, they uncovered "queer moves around gender, family, institutions/geography" that characters made to disrupt the homonormative representations found in the various texts. This sharing invites readers to consider their personal reactions (i.e. accept, reject, challenge, dismiss) to those representations, an important consideration if readers believe Bishop's (1990) assertation that books serve as windows and mirrors.

In another study, Taylor (2012) examined four picturebooks to determine the role the books play in "deploying a homonormative subject, how that deployment occurs, and what the consequences are of such a deployment for children; lesbian, gay, bisexual, transgender, queer, and intersex (LGBTQI) communities; and the larger society" (p. 136). Like Hermann-Wilmarth and Ryan (2014), Taylor noted characters that were mostly white, middle-class consumers who conformed to normative gender roles. Taylor purports these homonormative subjects "[ensure] the survivability of [the LGBTQI] population by supporting current regimes of practice including consumerism, marriage, family, inequality, military action, and complicity" (p. 147). In his conclusion, Taylor warns of the "dangers" (Foucault in Taylor, 2012, p. 137) that lie in LGBTQI-themed picturebooks that deploy the homonormative subject:

> One, I have suggested that danger lies in the assimilation of some in the LGBTQI community, because it can fracture and weaken the queer community as a whole. Two, the homonormative subject does not contest existing systems of oppression, even heterosexism itself. Three, the process of assimilating some people from LGBTQI communities can further marginalize and ostracize those left behind, since their needs are not taken into consideration across various political, legal, and institutional venues including education.
>
> *(p. 150)*

Lester (2014) used a queer theory lens to survey 68 gay- and lesbian-themed picturebooks from four different countries spanning three decades. She found portrayals of LGBTQ characters as "less queer and more 'normal' which is read as heterosexual, gender conforming, monogamous, white, upper-middle class and reproductive" (p. 247). Lester explains how these portrayals render the characters as less threatening and more acceptable to readers because they uphold the dominant heterosexual social order. Like Taylor (2012), Lester concludes that de-queering and thus upholding homonormativity in children's literature does "more to perpetuate systems of oppression than to subvert them" (p. 247).

Esposito (2009), in her analysis of five picturebooks featuring children with lesbian parents, found four themes that privilege heteronormativity. The first theme, "problematizing not having a daddy," privileges heterosexual parents, leaving the children in the stories to "wonder why [their] mom-mom configuration falls short" (p. 66). The second theme, "dequeering … strip[s] lesbian families of their differences and the social costs of those differences" (p. 69). The third theme, "don't ask, don't tell," emerged in stories where lesbian parents didn't reveal their family structures until an event like attending a school function such as parent night forced them to do so (p. 72). These three themes, according to Esposito, combine to form the fourth theme of picturebooks as a "catalyst for heterosexual growth" (p. 73). Esposito explains how the problems encountered by children with lesbian parents were used to teach others about life in families headed by same-sex parents. Esposito argues that instead of sharing the ways children with same-sex parents grow in their understanding of what it means to have lesbian parents in a heterosexually privileged society, the stories illustrate the ways heterosexual characters grow in their understanding about families headed by same-sex parents. Esposito argues that heteronormativity is privileged through themes and concludes that these picturebooks send the message that families headed by lesbians should be accepted into mainstream culture because they "are just like" heterosexual families (p. 74).

Methodology

As we planned the analysis portion of our study, we were mindful of our positions as teacher/researchers and avid readers of children's and young adult literature. We believe in the transformative power of such literature, having transacted with it in ways that moved us emotionally and motivated us socially and politically (Rosenblatt, 1994). Mary, a former primary grade teacher, approached this study from the perspective of a teacher/researcher, analyzing the verbal and visual narratives for their appeal to young children and for ideologies hidden within that young children might not be able to uncover independently. Tabitha approached this study from the perspective of a queer-identified researcher, analyzing the illustrations for their maintenance and reproduction or disruption of heteronormative imagery within a queer context.

Three editions of *Heather Has Two Mommies* (2000, 2008, 2015) have undergone changes in both the verbal and visual narratives since its first publication in 1989. We read all four editions in chronological order to determine changes in both narratives. For this chapter, we chose to focus on changes to the visual narrative because we believe these have the most impact, especially when we look through the lens of Queer Theory using Painter, Martin, and Unsworth's (2013) analytical tools for image analysis. However, we first briefly present noteworthy findings of our analysis of the changes to the verbal narrative.

The most notable change in the verbal narrative appears in *Heather 2000* with the removal of the content about artificial insemination and anatomical detail featured in the first edition, decreasing numbers across all categories except words per sentence (see Table 13.1). In *Heather 2015*, numbers decrease further except for the number of pages. These changes reflect Newman's goal to make *Heather 2015* shorter and punchier.

Initially, we compared the illustrations in each edition to the next edition, progressing in chronological order. We noted obvious differences between each edition. We recognized that the illustrations in the first three editions hadn't changed except for the deletions from *Heather 1989* (discussed above) and the colorization of illustrations in *Heather 2008*. For this reason, we decided to do an in-depth analysis using *Heather 2008* and *Heather 2015*. During our comparison of the two editions, two research questions emerged. First, we wondered how the changes to illustrations in *Heather 2015* impact the visual narrative. Second, we wondered how the changes in the illustrations of *Heather 2015* influence the queering of the story.

For our analysis we organized the illustrations into sets. A set was comprised of comparable scenes found in both editions of *Heather 2008* and *Heather 2015*. If comparable visual scenes weren't obvious, we used the verbal narrative as a guide, matching the text from both editions to determine the corresponding illustrations. Working with sets of illustrations allowed us to make straightforward comparisons and to go deeper into the analysis because each set could be analyzed independently of the other sets. In this chapter we discuss our findings from two sets of illustrations that contain subtle changes that might not be obvious to readers,

TABLE 13.1 Quantitative Comparison of Verbal Narratives in Four Editions of *Heather Has Two Mommies*★

Category	Heather 1989	Heather 2000 and 2008	Heather 2015
Number of pages	34	25	28
Number of sentences	133	76	62
Number of words	1,549	924	748
Average number of sentences/page	3.91	3.04	2.21
Average words/page	45	36.96	26.71
Average words/sentence	11.64	12.16	12.06

Note:
★The verbal narrative in *Heather 2008* did not change from *Heather 2000*. Therefore, one column contains the data from both editions.

especially children. We situate our findings using visual analytical tools related to interpersonal and ideational meaning systems of pathos and affect, and ambience (Painter et al., 2013). We also address the subtle changes to the icons that represent gender identity within the text.

Findings

Looking across sets of illustrations from *Heather 2008* and *Heather 2015*, we found noteworthy changes to the pathos and affect, the ambience and the icons in *Heather 2015*. Specific changes and the consequences of each are presented here.

Changes in Illustrative Styles

The pathos and affect in *Heather 2015* have changed significantly due to the change of illustrator and resulting change in illustrative styles. Using Painter et al.'s (2013) visual tools as a guide, we focused our analysis on the physical features of the characters in both editions. On the cover of *Heather 2008*, Souza's generic style illustrations add a sense of realism to the story (see Figure 13.1). The lines in Heather's hair and the shading on her clothes add movement and texture, thus creating depth and dimension. Her facial features are relatively proportionate to her head. We note how Souza used additional lines around Heather's mouth and eyes to convey deeper emotions beyond simply feeling happy. The lines in Heather's smile create lips and teeth. The weighted-line eyebrows and the shading in the inner corners of Heather's eye sockets help readers easily deduce that Heather feels carefree and content. Thus, the generic-style illustrations invite readers to more accurately consider the characters' emotions.

In contrast, Cornell's minimalist-style illustrations in *Heather 2015* feature charming, cartoon-like characters. Part of the charm stems from the iconic renderings of characters whose features are distorted in size, shape, and proportion representative of the minimalist style (Painter et al., 2013). For example, Ms. Molly and two students' eyes consist of an iconic white, circular sclera with a black dot representing the pupil (see Figure 13.2). A simple crescent shape represents the eyes of David, Stacy, and Heather where an iconic black dot represents the eyes of Miriam, David, and Joshua. Anatomically, the characters' heads are disproportionately large, and their hands and feet are disproportionately small for their bodies. The children's small, misshapen teeth are depicted with gaps in their lipless, crescent-shaped mouths. These and other cartoon-like characteristics appeal to young children for whom this story is most likely written. Consequently, deciphering the visual narrative in *Heather 2015* requires readers to rely mostly on visual literacy strategies that they, especially young readers, might not have acquired yet (Painter et al., 2013). For example, young readers might need support to recognize that Heather's warm-colored pink, orange, and yellow clothing and her position in the forefront of the

FIGURE 13.1 Generic-Style Illustrations in *Heather 2000* (Newman, 2000)
Source: Heather Has Two Mommies. Text copyright © 1989, 2000, 2009, 2015 by Lesléa Newman. Illustrations copyright © 2015 by Laura Cornell. Reproduced by permission of the publisher, Candlewick Press, Somerville, MA.

illustration signifies that, despite the other children, Heather is still the focus of the story.

Overall, we find the minimalist-style illustrations in *Heather 2015* more visually appealing than the generic-style illustrations in *Heather 2008*. We speculate that children and the adults who read to them will find the illustrations in *Heather 2015* more appealing as well. Nevertheless, our analysis reveals significant consequences that result from the change in illustrative style.

FIGURE 13.2 Minimalist-Style Illustrations in *Heather 2015* (Newman, 2015)
Source: Heather Has Two Mommies. Text copyright © 1989, 2000, 2009, 2015 by Lesléa Newman. Illustrations copyright © 2015 by Laura Cornell. Reproduced by permission of the publisher, Candlewick Press, Somerville, MA.

First, the characters in *Heather 2015* have flattened emotional repertoires (Painter et al., 2013). Their expressions convey happiness or indifference, but nothing more. In fact, Heather and her mothers' expressions convey happiness from the beginning of the story to the end. Because of the "happy-washing" of all the characters, the story sends the message that Heather experiences only happiness living in her "different" family dynamic. *Heather 2015* overlooks the hard-edged emotions of distress, consternation, and marginalization that the generic style illustrations in *Heather 2008* convey. We argue that the underlying commentary misleads readers to believe that the visual narrative honestly reflects the realities of families headed by same-sex parents. The fact remains that families headed by same-sex parents face more and different obstacles along with discrimination and marginalization than heterosexual parents, as they attempt to navigate a society that favors heterosexuality. The consequence of a happy-washed *Heather 2015* is that readers will continue to overlook the complexities that oppress families headed by same-sex parents.

Second, because the characters have flat emotional repertoires, readers may find it difficult to take an "empathetic stance, where common humanity is recognised and [stand] in the character's shoes" (Painter et al., 2013, p. 33). The altered visual narrative in *Heather 2015* positions readers as disconnected observers who can determine the sameness of Heather and her mothers as they engage in typical family activities in seemingly normal (heterosexual) ways. The commentary "de-queers" *Heather 2015* and attempts to convince readers that Heather's life is no different from the lives of most mainstream children (Esposito, 2009; Lester, 2014). The danger with this commentary occurs when readers create a superficial understanding of what it means to be a child with same-sex parents. We argue that readers might conclude that families with same-sex parents live tension-free lives like Heather does—in a big house with two pets, in a nice neighborhood with good schools, and in a family with two gainfully employed professional parents.

We fear that positioning readers as observers of Heather and her mothers' seemingly normal everyday lives creates very few opportunities for them to ask questions that disrupt the homonormativity portrayed in the visual narrative of the story. We argue that readers who stand in Heather's shoes are better positioned to disrupt the misleading visual narrative in *Heather* that says one's family configuration doesn't matter. Esposito (2009) explains,

> Newman does a disservice to children from lesbian families who may face discrimination and ridicule because they have two mothers. This denial is especially harmful when one thinks of the Defense of Marriage Proposal which clearly represents that it does matter what your family configuration looks like.
>
> *(p. 69)*

A third consequence of the minimalistic style illustration is that *Heather 2015* will continue to serve as a teaching tool for mainstream families and their children to learn about those who are different from them. The happy-washing of *Heather 2015* makes it easier for heterosexual families to tolerate families like Heather's, giving them the false sense that all families are alike. The reality is that Heather and her mothers differ from the traditional sense of what family configurations look like and how families come to be (theirs came about because of artificial insemination rather than "natural" sex to procreate). Having two mothers does change the dynamic both in and outside the home, so readers cannot ignore difference. Instead, readers need to note the differences and challenge the notion of what is constructed as "normal" if they want to change the narrative.

Even though we found the illustrations more appealing, we conclude that the consequences are significant. *Heather 2015* lacks depth and the ability to be used as a real starting point to help children engage in critical thinking. We would have liked for Heather and her mothers to reflect some of the complexities present in being part of a non-normative family structure, as is presented in *Heather 2008*. While we understand the significance of presenting same-sex parents in a positive light and demonstrating that there is nothing wrong with any particular family configuration, the reality remains that LGBTQ+ families are susceptible to discrimination and oppression from a society which values conformity to commonly accepted "normal" identities. Therefore, we value honest representations of struggle, such as those that are demonstrated in *Heather 2008*. Happy endings do and should exist, but often there is conflict before that can occur. While *Heather 2015* can be viewed as an excellent pedagogical tool for children from heterosexual families, it does not consider the role of picturebooks as a reflection of the lived experiences of LGBTQ+ children and/or families.

More Appealing Ambience

The most obvious change in the visual narrative in *Heather 2015* comes from the addition of more vibrant, familiar colors. In 1989, *Heather* was first published in black-and-white, most likely for monetary rather than stylistic reasons. It wasn't until 2008 that the original illustrations were published in muted colors. The addition of color improved the quality of the story somewhat, but overall the illustrations still lacked a genuine appeal to audiences of all ages.

Cornell's ambient illustrations in *Heather 2015* add the appeal needed to draw readers to the picturebook. The vibrant, highly saturated colors range from warm yellows, reds, pinks, and oranges to cooler blues, greens, and purples. The warm colors add positive energy and affect to the story, while the cool colors signal calm, peacefulness, or restfulness (Painter et al., 2013). For example, Heather and her mother's cool colored shirts (blue and purple) symbolize their relaxed and contented feelings after playing together in a public park (see Figure 13.3). The warm colors of their peach skin, the red apples, and the green grass generate feelings of liveliness and energy. Readers deduce that Heather and her mothers are enjoying their time together at the park. The colors in *Heather 2015* symbolize real objects (red apples, green grass), evoking a sense of the familiar. Ambient familiarity helps readers connect with the characters while understanding their relationships with each other and with their environment (Painter et al., 2013).

FIGURE 13.3 Ambience Adds Appeal to *Heather 2015* (Newman, 2015)
Source: Heather Has Two Mommies. Text copyright © 1989, 2000, 2009, 2015 by Lesléa Newman. Illustrations copyright © 2015 by Laura Cornell. Reproduced by permission of the publisher, Candlewick Press, Somerville, MA.

In addition to adding appeal, the ambience in *Heather 2015* represents "a visual meaning system for creating an emotional mood or atmosphere" (Painter et al., 2013, p. 36). We say "represents" because color "does what people do with it" (Kress & Van Leeuwen, 2002, p. 351). For the most part, we like what Cornell has done with color in *Heather 2015*. However, because color is metafunctional (Kress & Van Leeuwen, 2002), we must consider how it combines with other meaning systems like the icons added to *Heather 2015*. For instance, we argue that the color of Heather's clothing—her pink tutu, purple cowboy boots and the purple flower in her hair—are stereotypically female. Consequently, the ambience of *Heather 2015* also contributes to homonormativity threaded throughout the visual narrative.

Changes to Icons

Icons in illustrations "look like that for which they stand" (Kucer, 2014, p. 25) and can also represent social constructs including gender (Butler, 1990). With this in mind, we analyzed the illustrative changes to three types of icons in *Heather 2015*: Physical items, clothing, and physical characteristics.

Although subtle, we noted changes in physical items such as the addition of a purse and a ring in the illustrations in *Heather 2015*. Often considered an accessory, a purse is also typically considered a female icon. We see Mama Kate carrying the purse in the illustration on the front cover and again when the mothers take Heather to school. Additionally, we noted a ring with an oval-shaped stone on the ring finger of Mama Jane's left hand (see Figure 13.3). A curved stone, like the oval, represents "endlessness, warmth and protection" (Dondis as cited in Kress & Van Leeuwen, 1996, p. 54). We also noted that both mothers are depicted wearing rings on the ring finger of their left hands in the picture of them talking with Ms. Molly. Because of this particular placement of the rings we might interpret them to be symbols of commitment between Heather's mothers.

Another change was in clothing. Despite having female names and being identified with female pronouns and titles such as "mommy," neither Heather nor her mothers appear particularly feminine in *Heather 2008*. We noted that neither Heather or her mothers wear overtly feminine clothing like dresses nor do they wear clothing with typically feminine features such as bows or ruffles. Their clothes are relatively shapeless, involve mostly patterns and textures, and would generally not be considered "feminine" or "masculine" by most people.

We contrasted the androgynous look of Heather and her mothers in *Heather 2008* with their more modern, feminized look in *Heather 2015*. In the new edition, Heather wears a pink tutu, bright purple cowboy boots, and a large purple flower atop her head. The flower seems to mark Heather's female nature, even when she is depicted wearing more androgynous clothing such as overalls, shorts, and t-shirts. Heather's mothers are feminized as well. They no longer represent the butch/femme stereotypes that were obvious in *Heather 2008*, although neither is wearing particularly femme clothing in *Heather 2015*. Nonetheless, Mama Kate wears hoop earrings, smaller eyeglasses with pastel-colored frames, and a flowy, ¾ sleeve length shirt with scallop trim around the edges instead of the "No Nukes" T-shirt featured in *Heather 2008*. Although not as feminized, Mama Jane wears a scarf headband, fuzzy pink slippers, and cargo pants–perhaps a call back to the "butch" look evident in *Heather 2008*.

Changes to the physical characteristics of Heather and her mothers in *Heather 2015* seem more obvious because of the changes to the pathos and affect that resulted with the change of illustrators. No longer do the characters look realistic. Instead their minimalist, cartoon-style features emphasize smaller noses and less angular jaw lines. Arched, thin-line eyebrows suggest being plucked and red lips hint at lipstick, although we believe the minimalist style added to the creation of these typically feminine features.

Both mothers have longer, more feminine hair styles. Mama Jane is depicted with less angular, chin-length hair that she holds back with a headband when she bakes cookies and builds things with Heather. Mama Kate is depicted with long, curly hair that she styles with ponytail holders and barrettes.

Depending on the perspective, we found that some of the changes to the icons in *Heather 2015* could be problematic while at the same time be positive. For instance, if we interpret the rings both mothers are wearing as symbols of their committed relationship, we might assume that they are married to each other. On one hand (no pun intended), this perpetuates heteronormative values that encourage parents to marry. On the other hand, we might interpret that the rings represent the fact that same-sex marriage is now legally recognized whereas, in 1989 when the story was first written, same-sex marriage was not recognized. Another example of multiple perspective-taking relates to the clothing and physical features of Heather and both mothers. Because lesbians look and dress according to their personal preferences rather than a universally understood standard of appearance, it is possible that both mothers could present themselves just as Cornell has drawn them, with longer hair, stylized clothing, and plucked eyebrows. Conversely, we can also argue that both mothers have been feminized to appear more like heterosexual women. Esposito (2009) argues that more feminized lesbians are less threatening as a whole and more likely to be accepted into a dominant heteronormative society. Clearly, the icons are subject to interpretation.

Final Reflections

Throughout the four editions of *Heather Has Two Mommies*, both the verbal and visual narratives have been revised, leaving the original vastly different from *Heather 2015*. The story now focuses exclusively on the acceptance of all families, regardless of configuration. We concede that Newman and Candlewick Press achieved their goal of making *Heather 2015* "a lot shorter, hopefully punchy, and more appealing" (Newman in Peel, 2015, p. 471). We predict the newest edition has a much better chance of finding its way into many more families, classrooms, and public libraries than the earlier editions.

With that said, we are left to contend with the consequences of a shorter, punchier new *Heather*. Our analysis revealed that the changes to the illustrations impacted the visual narratives, upholding the heteronormative ideology woven into the story from the beginning. We also noted the missed opportunities to re-queer rather than uphold the de-queering of *Heather*. Re-queering *Heather* will most likely be the responsibility of those who share the story with others. To help teachers and parents re-queer *Heather* we offer the following:

1. Create a text set that focuses on families and family activities like the activities featured in *Heather 2015*. Begin by gathering picturebooks from the school and local public library. Expand children's understandings of families by including global and Indigenous literature in the text set. Search the Worlds of Words (WOW) collection by title, country or theme (https:// wowlit.org/). Explore additional resources available through WOW like the *Family Story Backpacks* and a global book list of fiction and nonfiction texts organized around the Common Core State Standards (https://wowlit.org/links/booklists/).

2. Examine stereotypes, expectations and self-perceptions of family configurations. To begin, invite children to name various family configurations (i.e. same-sex parents, foster parents, two-parents, legal guardians/caretakers). Record children's ideas on chart paper or a white board. Ask children to identify with a family configuration that most closely represents their family. Next, working with a partner with a similar family identity, children construct an Insider/Outsider chart (see Table 13.2). Begin with the Outsider perspective. Repeat the process with the Insider perspective. Encourage children to discuss stereotypes, expectations and self-perceptions as they write. Then, as a class, discuss the children's analysis of Outsider and Insider perspectives of various family configurations. Finally, read aloud *Heather 2015*. During the reading, invite children to analyze the characters according to the stereotypes, expectations, and self-perceptions that emerged during children's class discussion about their own family configurations. Repeat the analysis with other picturebooks featured in the text set created around the theme of Families.

TABLE 13.2 Insider/Outsider Chart

Insider/Outsider Perspectives on Family Configurations		
Looks like	Thinks like	Acts like
Outsider		
Insider		

3. Read Ryan and Hermann-Wilmarth's (2013) article about queering books that do not explicitly feature characters identified as LGBTQ. Replicate the lessons with one or two of the picturebooks featured in the text set created around the theme of Families (see 1 above).

Even though we contend that changes in the newest edition of *Heather* do little to disrupt the homonormative narrative depicted in the verbal and visual narratives, we advocate for the inclusion of *Heather 2015* in home, school, and public libraries. With such a limited number of picturebooks written and illustrated for, by, and with LGBTQ folks, we would be remiss to exclude the story that helped pave the way for other authors and illustrators to explore the subject of homosexuality and non-binary individuals in children's literature. Where *Heather* was initially used to illustrate a special kind of family, the story can now be used to start conversations about LGBTQ issues that lie under the surface of children's literature. We hope this chapter has piqued readers' interest and provided a starting point for these conversations.

References

American Library Association (2018). Banned and challenged books. Retrieved from www.ala.org/advocacy/bbooks

Bishop, R.S. (1990). Mirrors, windows, and sliding glass doors. *Perspective*, 6(3), ix–x.

Butler, J.P. (1990). *Gender trouble*. New York: Routledge.

Child Welfare League of America (2017). Position statement on equality for LGBTQ families and youth. Retrieved from www.cwla.org/wp-content/uploads/2017/05/Child-Welfare-Leaders-Position-Statement-LGBTQ-Equality.pdf

Dilley, P. (1999). Queer theory: Under construction. *Qualitative Studies in Education*, 12(5), 457–472.

Esposito, J. (2009). We're here, we're queer, but we're just like heterosexuals: A cultural studies analysis of lesbian themed children's books. *Educational Foundations*, 23(3–4), 61–78.

Flores, J. (2013). An introduction to homonormativity. *Homo normo*. Retrieved from https://homonormativity.wordpress.com/2013/07/03/an-introduction-to-homonormativity-2/

Ford, E. (1998). Why Lesléa Newman makes Heather into Zoe. *Children's Literature Association Quarterly*, 23(3), 128–133.

Foucault, M. (1978). *The history of sexuality, volume 1: An introduction*. New York: Vintage Books.

Hermann-Wilmarth, J.M. & Ryan, C.L. (2014). Queering chapter books with LGBT characters for young readers: Recognizing and complicating representations of homonormativity. *Discourse: Studies in the Cultural Politics of Education*, 37(6), 846–866.

Huskey, M. (2002). Queering the picture book. *The Lion and the Unicorn*, 26, 66–77.

Kim Lin, C. (2017). Changing the shape of the landscape: Sexual diversity frameworks and the promise of queer literacy pedagogy in the elementary classroom. *Bank Street Occasional Paper Series*, 37, 22–39.

Kress, G. & Van Leeuween, T. (1996). *Reading images: The grammar of visual design* (2nd ed.). New York: Routledge.

Kress, G. & Van Leeuween, T. (2002). Colour as a semiotic mode: Notes for a grammar of colour. *Visual Communication*, 1(3), 343–368.

Kucer, S.B. (2014). *Dimensions of literacy*. New York: Routledge.

Lester, J.Z. (2014). Homonormativity in children's literature: An intersectional analysis of queer-themed picture books. *Journal of LGBT Youth*, 11(3), 244–275.

Linville, D. (2017). Introduction. *Bank Street Occasional Paper Series*, 37, 4–13.

Maughan, S. (2015). A second life for Heather has two mommies. *Publishers Weekly*. Retrieved from https://www.publishersweekly.com/pw/by-topic/childrens/children s-book-news/article/65886-a-second-life-for-heather-has-two-mommies.html

Painter, C., Martin, J.R., & Unsworth, L. (2013). *Reading visual narratives: Image analysis of children's picture books*. Sheffield, UK: Equinox.

Peel, K.R. (2015). An interview with Lesléa Newman: A punchy new Heather, Dolly Parton, and orange is the new black. *Journal of Lesbian Studies*, 19(4), 470–483.

Robinson, B.A. (2016). Heteronormativity and homonormativity. *The Wiley Blackwell Encyclopedia of Gender and Sexuality Studies* (pp. 1–3).

Rosenblatt, L.M. (1994). *The reader, the text, the poem: The transactional al theory of the literary work*. Carbondale, IL: Southern Illinois University Press.

Ryan, C.L. & Hermann-Wilmarth, J.M. (2013). Already on the shelf: Queer readings of award-winning children's literature. *Journal of Literacy Research*, 45(2), 142–172.

Taylor, N. (2012). U.S. children's picture books and the homonormative subject. *Journal of LGBT Youth*, 9, 136–152.

Children's Literature Cited

Newman, L. (1989). *Heather has two mommies*. Boston: Alyson Wonderland.

Newman, L. (2000). *Heather has two mommies*. Los Angeles: Alyson Wonderland.

Newman, L. (2009). *Heather has two mommies*. Los Angeles: Alyson Wonderland.

Newman, L. (2015). *Heather has two mommies*. Somerville, MA: Candlewick Press.

14

A PICTUREBOOK AS A CULTURAL ARTIFACT

The Influence of Embedded Ideologies

Hee Young Kim and Kathy G. Short

Literature plays a critical role in the lives of children, providing a means for them to explore their identities and to experience cultures that differ from their own. Thus, the cultural diversity in books for children matters. Even though marginalized groups continue to be underrepresented in children's books published in the United States, the numbers are increasing (Horning, 2018), and educators are encouraged to engage children in discussions around these books. Without critical engagement, however, these efforts can instead affirm prejudice and the status quo, particularly if a book is embedded in a privileged dominant discourse (Nieto, 2017).

Relations of power, domination, and oppression are established and maintained through ideologies as representations of the world. These ideological representations influence texts, so textual analysis needs to be framed in social analysis to consider the relationships of texts to power relations (Fairclough, 2003). This ideological aspect can be overlooked in children's literature, often mythicized as a neutral and innocent text (Nodelman, 2008). Barthes (1964) argues that myths serve the ideological function of making dominant cultural values and beliefs seem like normal common sense. These myths appear to be objective and true reflections of "the way things are," without needing to be interpreted or demystified, and so what is portrayed in children's literature can be regarded as truth unless the embedded ideology is interrogated. Because ideology serves as a mental framework deployed by a social group to make sense of, define, figure out, and render intelligible the way society works (Larrain, 1996), it is a useful social construct for critically examining the social context embedded within literature.

Ideologies are constructions of reality built into the forms and meanings of discursive practices (Fairclough, 1995) and so are hidden and articulated in society and culture. Examining the social context of a children's book to determine how that context is represented is a method of interrogating the embedded ideology of the text. This analysis can reveal how dominant ideology affects a book and provide suggestions for enacting critical pedagogy in classrooms. The purpose of our research was to analyze the ideological representations in a picturebook to explore the influence of dominant discourses.

As a cultural text, literature inevitably reflects social context; at the same time, literature is an artistic genre and has been traditionally studied as a literary text. Content analysis focuses on literature as representations of human experience and takes a theoretical position that frames the development of research criteria for text analysis in social, cultural, and political contexts (Stephens, 2015). Critical content analysis brings a critical lens to an analysis of a text in order to explore the underlying messages, particularly as related to issues of power and oppression. In this study, the critical theory that frames the research is critical discourse analysis.

Critical Discourse Analysis as a Theoretical Framework

Critical discourse analysis (CDA) is the study of language in relation to power and ideology and the struggle against domination and oppression in its linguistic form. Linguistic text is regarded as potentially ideological, and power is conceptualized in terms of asymmetries between participants and their unequal capacity to control how texts are produced in particular sociocultural contexts. Fairclough (1995) argues that CDA is both a critical theory and a methodology of mapping three forms of analysis onto one another—analysis of language texts, discourse practice, and discursive events as instances of sociocultural practice. Each discourse is a perspective on the world, associated with the relationships of people to the world, who in turn depend on their positions in the world. Discourses represent the world as it is and are projective imaginaries, representing possible worlds that differ from the actual world, providing possibilities to change the world (Fairclough, 2003).

Even though critical discourse analysis focuses on language use, the term discourse is a social rather than a linguistic category. Hodge and Kress (1988) argue that the dominance of language in Western culture needs to be challenged by a focus on multimodality as the material means for representation in other semiotic forms. A picturebook, for example, uses both verbal text and visual images as essential to generating meaning.

Kress and van Leeuwen (2006) developed an analysis of visual representations within the theoretical framework of social semiotics, based on Halliday's systemic-functional linguistics. According to social semiotics, participants engaged in social communication make their messages maximally understandable in a context marked by power differences. The interest of sign-makers at the moment of making the sign leads them to choose an aspect of the object to be represented as criterial for representing their meaning and choosing the most plausible, apt form for its representation.

The theoretical tenets that frame this study are drawn from CDA and social semiotics:

- Text as a discourse practice generated from social context.
- Representation as embodied ideology and power relationships.
- Multimodal representations as essential to the construction of meaning.

A children's book should be understood in its social context to provide the basis for critical pedagogy as an ideology and epistemology through which readers see the world and perceive knowledge. CDA provides a tool for interrogating a book as a discourse produced in a sociohistorical context and in relation to other discourses generated in that context.

Critical discourse analysis has been increasingly utilized in educational research, although only occasionally to look at literature as text. Rogers and Christian (2007) analyzed children's books to examine the literary strategies and linguistic techniques used to present whiteness. CDA was used as both a theory and analytical framework to describe and interpret the construction of race and to explain the ways in which the themes in the books connect to larger societal issues. Smith (2014) explored feminism through CDA to examine how society has ideologically positioned men and women. She examined two versions of *Rapunzel* published in different time periods to determine how the text was influenced by the social context. She posits that a text is a product of the contradictory and complex beliefs of society, and, in the case of texts written for children, there is an attempt by dominant voices to reinforce mainstream views for those seen as most impressionable. The linguistic choices of children's authors can serve to promulgate certain points of view.

Maingueneau (2010) posits that discourse analysis considers the reciprocal envelopment of text and context, shifting the core of the analysis. He identified four modalities for linguistics within literary studies, arguing that the analyst should attempt to question the frontier between text and context and the works should no longer be the focus of the analysis. Instead, discourse analysis is an attempt to understand the construction, management, and role of text in discourse practice.

To explore the embedded ideology of a picturebook in this study, we drew on critical discourse analysis as a theoretical framework along with social semiotics and multimodality. This study reflects Fairclough's (2003) argument that text should encompass other semiotic modes, and Kress and van Leeuwen's (2006) work on multimodality of representation and social semiotics. Through these theoretical frameworks, our focus was to examine how an exploration of the social context of a text can reveal the embedded ideology. We also wanted to understand how discourses generated by social factors in the same social context are represented in a picturebook.

Critical Content Analysis as Methodology

This study is designed with a three-dimensional framework of text, discourse practice, and social structure as conceptualized by Fairclough (2003) to examine embedded ideology. Given our focus on the social discourse within a book, the following criteria were used to select a text: (1) a book with a strong relationship to a specific sociohistorical event or context, (2) a book published in a time in which many social discourses were produced, and (3) a book with visual images to examine how ideology is embedded in written and visual modes of representation. We selected *Smoky Night* (1994), written by Eve Bunting and illustrated by David Diaz, which won a Caldecott Medal in 1995, awarded to the artist of the most distinguished American picturebook.

The sociohistorical context of *Smoky Night* is the LA Riots, which occurred in 1992, so the book was written immediately after that event. The book centers on Daniel and his mother, African Americans who live in Los Angeles in an apartment building with their cat, and their conflict with Mrs. Kim, a Korean American, and her cat. During the riots, a fire occurs in their building and they are evacuated to a shelter, where they come to know each other through their cats and resolve their conflict. As in any social event, the LA Riots involved the engagement of many social institutions, including the police, city officials, politicians, media, and academics, each producing their own discourses during and after the events.

The discourses and ideologies in this picturebook were analyzed through Fairclough's three dimensions. First, we examined the sociocultural context of the LA Riots, including the Rodney King event, the socioeconomic structure of the U.S. at that time, the marginalized situation in urban areas, and the relationships between African Americans and Korean Americans. Second, we examined the discourses generated from social factors during the LA Riots, conceptualizing discourse as ways of representing aspects of society associated with different relations of people to the world.

We used this analysis of context and discourse to examine *Smoky Night*. Discourse specifies "ways of representing in terms of a range of linguistic features which can be seen as realizing a discourse" (Fairclough, 2003, p. 129). We examined the visual images based on the work of Kress and van Leeuwen (2006) as applied to picturebooks by Painter, Martin, and Unsworth (2013). The analysis of both the verbal and visual text was theoretically grounded in systemic-functional semiotics. Discourses are distinguished by their ways of representing their relationship to other social elements.

We analyzed the text of *Smoky Night* by looking at representations in a range of linguistic features as a realization of discourse, focusing on the meanings of vocabulary within the situations they described. Rewording with hyponymy or synonymy is a device authors use to structure the world associated with a given discourse. What is important are preconstructed classificatory schemes that can function as unconscious instruments of construction (Bourdieu & Wacquant, 1992).

These systems are taken-for-granted "di-visions" through which people continuously generate "visions" of the world. When discourses come into conflict and specific discourses are contested, what is centrally contested is the power of these preconstructed semantic systems to generate particular visions of the world, which may have the performative power to sustain or remake the world in their image (Fairclough, 2003). We looked at *Smoky Night* to identify how this lexical classification was used for generating discourses and what discourses were generated.

For visual analysis, we used the work of Painter, Martin, and Unsworth (2013) who base their analysis in Halliday's (1978) discussion of interpersonal meaning as the roles and relationships between writer and reader together with attitudes and stances incorporated into the text. Halliday discusses textual meaning as how a piece of text is organized to be coherent in relation to co-text and context through devices for linking, referring, foregrounding, and backgrounding to explore ideological assumptions. The relationship between writer and reader is explored by Kress and van Leeuwen (2006) as social distance, attitude (including involvement of power), contact and modality. Painter et al. (2013) adapt these concepts to visual images in picturebooks to examine focalization, affect, pathos, ambience, and graduation. Through these devices, readers are positioned and invited to share the author's and illustrator's ideologies of the social world. Our specific use of these tools is described in the findings.

Following the procedures of critical content analysis, we identified and coded each verbal and visual representation that appeared to relate to a certain discourse, and categorized these codes depending on their theme. These themes reflect the ways in which the social contexts and the discourses embedded in those contexts influenced the picturebook,

In this analysis, we also need to identify our own positionalities. Hee Young is an academic and global educator who wants to interrogate the influences of racial discourses and national borders in a globalized society. Kathy is a White academic focused on global literature and intercultural understanding, who watched the unfolding conflicts in LA on the news. Both have engaged with children in responding to *Smoky Night*.

Social Context and Social Structure

The first step of our analysis was to explore the sociohistorical context reflected in *Smoky Night*. Although the riots depicted in the book grew out of a specific event, they reflected longstanding social issues and simmering racial tensions and so involved complex factors and societal structures.

Rodney King and the LA Riot

On March 3, 1991 Rodney King was beaten by Los Angeles Police Department (LAPD) officers following a high-speed chase. This scene was video recorded and broadcast through the media, raising public concern about the brutality of police officers. Four officers were charged but acquitted the following year, leading to protests and rioting. Over a five-day period, 54 people died, 2,300 were injured, 4,500 businesses robbed, 1,100 buildings destroyed, and 3,600 fires set (Stevenson, 2013).

As the fires were extinguished, experts from many fields sought to explain this event. Commentators on the right drew on dated "culture of poverty" arguments to explain the behavior of the rioters and fuel public fears about urban Black and Latinx neighborhoods. At the other end of the spectrum, the events were viewed as an uprising, not random violence. Callinicos (1992) argued that the seeds of the riot grew out of the brutal and controlled workings of capitalism. This historical event is labeled with terms that indicate different interpretations, including disturbance, unrest, riot, and uprising. The many intertwined social factors led some to call this event a "political-protest-turned-into-riot" (Chang, 2012).

One striking aspect of this event is the widespread targeting and destruction in Korean American communities, even though the event started as a protest after the acquittals of the police officers involved in the beating of an African American man. Korean Americans incurred great losses; of the 4,500 stores destroyed, more than 2,300 were Korean-owned or run, and nearly every building in Koreatown was damaged. Tens of thousands lost their livelihoods (Lee, 2015). A complexity of societal factors framed this destruction.

Shifts in Socioeconomic Structures

In the 1960s, African Americans were hopeful their lives would be improved by gains in political power and equal rights due to the Civil Rights Movement. However, the economy shifted from traditional manufacturing to high-tech industries, and factories relocated to locations with lower wages and weaker unions, resulting in displacement and unemployment for African Americans as factories shut down. Workers were unable to find full-time jobs that would utilize their skills and provide enough income to support their families (Bluestone & Harrison, 1982). The lower-middle and middle rungs of the American economic structure were at risk, while the top and the bottom grew. High-tech industries and low-paying unskilled jobs grew, and traditional middle-class jobs declined, polarizing class inequality. Because the economic boom of 1980s primarily benefited white Americans and increased the gap, grievances about socioeconomic conditions were viewed as a contributing factor to the racial tension in LA (Chang, 2012).

Marginalization and Conflict in Urban Areas

In the 1980s, South Central Los Angeles, traditionally African American neighborhoods, underwent a demographic shift. With the breakdown of legal and residential barriers, middle-class African Americans moved to suburban neighborhoods. In South Central LA, the African American population increased only by 13 percent, but the Latinx population increased by 53 percent and Asian Americans by 108 percent, intensifying the competition for limited housing and jobs among marginalized groups (Chang, 2012). African Americans voiced concerns about losing political and economic gains from the civil rights struggle of the 1960s as Latinxs demanded proportional representation. The hardening of racial boundaries exacerbated tensions, especially among groups marginalized by the dominant society. For example, racial tension was heightened when several Black youths were killed by a Latinx gang in the LA Harbor area and was evident in African American boycotts of Korean American stores.

The Korean population in Los Angeles (and nationwide) underwent tremendous growth from the late 1960s. In Los Angeles, the number of Korean Americans rose from 8,900 in 1970 to 145,431 in 1990. According to the U.S. Census of 2006, more than 80 percent spoke the Korean language (Chang, 2012, p. 10). Language, cultural misunderstandings, and unfamiliarity with American society put Korean immigrants at a disadvantage, and so they viewed small businesses as an avenue for economic stability. In a 1986 survey of Los Angeles, 45 percent of Korean immigrant workers were self-employed in small businesses, and another 30 percent worked in ethnic Korean markets (Min, 1995).

These markers of entrepreneurial success obscured the daily hardships that merchants and their families negotiated. Many Korean businesses operated with few or no employees and relied on unpaid family labor. They were resented by customers to whom they sold goods while being exploited by the large companies whose products they peddled. Although some had enough money to open a business and live in a suburb, they usually could not run an establishment in a prime location, and so started or acquired businesses in declining, less costly areas. Additionally, many Koreans opened commercial establishments in South Central Los Angeles, an area bordering Koreatown that had been abandoned by large-scale retailers (Lee, 2015).

This proliferation of Korean-owned businesses in African American communities during the 1980s exacerbated conflicts between the Korean Americans and African Americans. Korean immigrants were caught between dominant and marginalized group conflicts. These tensions were increased by many reports of African Americans being watched and treated as criminals by Korean storeowners. Sexton (2010) points out that these attitudes reflect a stance of antiblackness and that non-Black people of color have often taken racist stances towards African Americans, assigning less value and failing to recognize the higher level of racism faced by African Americans on a daily basis. South Central LA was a context of structural conflict among low socioeconomic marginalized groups who shared living spaces and competed for limited economic resources. Each group experienced discrimination and oppression from dominant societal institutions, increasing the racial tension.

Social Discourses around the Conflicts in LA

We also examined the social discourses within these conflicts. In any event, participants from different social groups create discourses that represent the world as it is seen to be, as imaginaries that project a possible world (Fairclough, 2003). Generated discourses reflect an ideology connecting to a group's interest, so the discourses generated around the events in LA are important to examine as a sociohistorical frame to bring to the book.

Depoliticizing Protests around Racism

The conflict between African Americans and Korean Americans extended beyond LA. In New York, the 1990 Red Apple Boycott involved an African American boycott of a Korean American-owned shop, asking for redress for an African American assault victim and exhorting Blacks to mobilize in pursuit of political power and self-determination to protest racial injustice in the U.S. (Kim, 1993). However, mainstream media coverage criminalized the conflict, obscuring its political dimension and attributing the conflict to cultural differences between African Americans and Korean Americans. By depicting the boycott as unfair and illegal, the media performed the ideological function of depoliticizing the boycott and protecting the privileges of dominant society from challenge (Kim 1993).

This depoliticized practice of the media in New York was part of social discourse at that time. When Rodney King was beaten, public concern was raised about the brutality of White police officers and African Americans argued that this incident revealed a long-suppressed history of police violence against Blacks (Jacobs, 2000). Instead, news coverage focused on violence and looting with little or no discussion of police brutality. Against a backdrop of disfranchisement and despair in poor and working-class Black communities, the verdict symbolized more evidence of the systematic inequality and injustice faced by African Americans (Lee, 2015).

Praising Korean Americans as a Model Minority

Asian Americans in general are often called the "model minority," an image that pits Asian Americans against other marginalized groups and fuels resentment. By praising Korean American merchants as a shining example for other groups to emulate, the press implied that African Americans had themselves to blame for their socio-economic status. Both the "model minority" and the "middleman minority" concepts imply racial stratification, creating resentment and tension (Chang, 2012).

Media portrayals of Korean American merchants as a "model minority" scapegoated by the "underclass" effectively denied the rationality, purpose, and political agency of participants in the LA protests (Kim, 1993). The LA riot was viewed as demonstrating that "the model minority was taking a beating from blacks, whites, and Latinos who seemed only too glad to deliver their comeuppance" (Zia, 2001, p. 184). Korean merchants were a buffer between dominant (White) and marginalized (African American and Latinx) group conflicts in American society. Sexton (2010) argues that the merchants were thus both victims of the more dominant White society with political and economic status and the victimizers of their less powerful clientele, resulting from the "local and immediate relation of institutionalized violence" (p. 95). Further, he argues the media portrayals of racism between African Americans and Asian Americans politically reduced these racisms to stereotypes and disconnected them from racial hierarchy.

By the early 1990s, the Korean shop owner was a staple figure of mainstream popular culture. The discourse escalated to a breaking point of intergroup conflict, to a large degree played up by the media. Korean immigrants felt besieged and vulnerable in the face of rising incidents that targeted them for anti-Asian hate crimes (Lee, 2015).

Scapegoating from the View of Mainstream Media

During the Red Apple Boycott, while a few journalists attributed the boycott to cultural differences or language barriers, the majority depicted it as scapegoating, the irrational venting of frustrations on an innocent group (Kim, 1993), even though the boycott grew out of legitimate complaints from the African American community. In LA, two weeks after the video of Rodney King aired, a young African American girl was shot by a Korean American store owner. The store owner claimed self-defense through security video. The LAPD released the video to the media, editing it to show only the shooting. Lee, a reporter for the *Los Angeles Times*, argues that the LAPD used the video to take the focus away from the Rodney King incident. Lee believes that the media portrayal of the shooting contributed to public indignation and fueled violence directed at Korean merchants instead of the justice system (Romero, 2012).

Koreans call the Los Angeles riots *Sa-I-Gu*, or 4-2-9 (April 29), recognizing the events as a way for mainstream America to deflect Black rage (Romero, 2012). Korean American merchants in South Central and Koreatown received little police protection, with most of the police force deployed to block a road leading to affluent communities (Lah, 2017). In trying to rebuild after the riots, the storeowners discovered just how isolated Korean Americans were from the political mainstream when they received little compensation and their perspectives were not covered by the mainstream media during or after the riots (Chang, 2012).

African American scholars point out that Asian American scholars and reporters often reframe accounts of racial profiling by Korean merchants as "mutual misunderstanding," arguing that both African Americans and Korean Americans were involved in stereotyping each other. Nopper (2015) argues that mutual misunderstanding suggests shared status or power, with each group contributing to the other group's vulnerability and suffering. Given this belief, once people from the two groups get to know each other, the problems will be solved. This stance fails to acknowledge antiblackness views and the economic exploitation of African American residents by non-Black people who find urban neighborhoods fertile ground for their social mobility.

Smoky Night as a Cultural Artifact

Our analysis of *Smoky Night* involved identifying verbal and visual representations related to the social context and discourses, and then categorizing these into themes. For each theme, we share both our verbal and visual analysis of the book, but because of our research interests in critical visual literacy, we provide more interpretations from the visual analysis.

The Decontextualization of Smoky Night

Even though *Smoky Night* is based in a specific historical event, the text does not provide an explanation and focuses only on the act of rioting. The LA incident is a multilayered historical event with disagreement on how to name that event, but the book begins with a scene of violence, and "rioting" is used repeatedly as the only term to refer to what was occurring. There is no reference to the beating, trial, or protests of police brutality. Consequently, descriptions of African American anger against systemic and historicized racial discrimination are absent.

Rioting receives more emphasis through terms like "smashing" and "everything" to create a surrounding mood of randomness and destruction. In example (1), "smash" and "destroy" belong to the same classification of meaning and are used in paratactic relation, which increases the mood of destruction within the rioting.

1.   Below they are <u>smashing everything</u>. Windows, cars, streetlights.
2.   They <u>want</u> to <u>smash</u> and <u>destroy</u>.

Descriptions of violence are emotionally exaggerated. The emotional adjective of "angry" is used twice and juxtaposed by the antonym of "happy" in examples (3) and (4). In example (2), the main verb "want" is used to suggest that their acts are emotional.

3.   It can happen when people get <u>angry</u>.
4.   "They look <u>angry</u>. But they look <u>happy</u>, too."

In the book, the actions of people on the street are compared to a football game by using "toss" and "footballs" to describe people throwing shoes from a store. The "rioters" are described as if they are acting for fun, without rational or ethical consideration, stating that they laugh and "don't care what's right and what's wrong."

Within the actual event, the initial actions were protests of the acquittal, but the anger of marchers was structurally related to inequity and socioeconomic oppression. Neither aspect is represented in *Smoky Night*. The event is represented as depoliticized and decontextualized by focusing on violence and emotionally-based actions. Several sentences describe the social context but fail to provide a critical questioning. In example (5), people inquire about arson at the shelter, but switch to an emotional comment. Example (6) alludes to the African American boycott against Korean merchants, but in (7) no detailed explanation is provided, except just "better" because of "our own people," which is attributed to race.

5   They're talking about who did this. "It's a sad, sad night," Mr. Jackson says.
6   My mama and I don't go in Mrs. Kim's market even though it's close.
7   Mama says it's better if we buy from our own people.

Viewers are positioned into a status that determines their relationship to the event and people in the visual image. According to Kress and van Leeuwen (2006), the social distance between viewer and depicted scene is realized by the frame of a close-up or long shot, with a close-up creating a sense of intimacy between viewer and character. In 11 illustrations out of 14, the depicted character's body fills the frame in a close-up view. Their full bodies are partially cut off by the frame, positioning readers in a personal relationship with those characters. Intimate social distance can have a positive effect so that readers feel compassion and sympathy with characters. On the other hand, viewers are positioned to see the character's personal way of life, not their socioeconomic status within broader societal structures. Viewers are blinded from social position through a narrowed perspective of that character as an individual, not as a member of a larger marginalized group or societal structure. This limitation reflects multicultural approaches that only celebrate the way of life of cultural groups without an understanding of broader inequities. Drawing on structuralism, a person or thing is more clearly conceptualized when seen in relation to others in the broader system.

The spatial backdrop of illustrations is a device through which readers view the social context of the story. In *Smoky Night*, most illustrations focus on characters using close-ups with a barely recognizable background. Two illustrations have tall buildings as their backdrop, which can be misleading of the socioeconomic context. On the cover, high-rise buildings with neon lights indicate a glamorous city life (see Figure 14.1). On the other page with buildings, the same ambience of skyscrapers is the backdrop for firefighters. The socio-economic marginalization of urban areas is one of the crucial structural causes for the LA protests, but the illustrations indicate more affluent urban areas and support misconceptions of the protagonists' socioeconomic status.

FIGURE 14.1 High-rise Buildings to Depict an Urban Context (Cover of *Smoky Night*, Bunting, 1994)

Source: Illustrations from *Smoky Night* by Eve Bunting, illustrated by David Diaz. Illustrations copyright © 1994 by David Diaz. Reprinted by permission of Houghton Mifflin Harcourt Publishing Company. All rights reserved.

Racialization and Racial Formation

The events in LA are considered a racial conflict, but no explicit racial denotation is used in *Smoky Night*. The antagonist is Korean American, but is depicted only by her last name, Mrs. Kim, a generic last name for Koreans. Other characters are referred to in similar ways with "Mr. Jackson" for an African American man and

"Mr. Ramirez" for a Mexican American man. Even though there is no explicit reference to the characters' race or ethnicity, readers can make inferences from their last names.

The social context of Korean Americans running a small business is represented in that Mrs. Kim runs a grocery store and does not speak English, differentiating her from other people. Mrs. Kim yells in the same way and in the same words at both the cat and people, portraying her as an aberrant person. Along with depicting her way of speaking the Korean language as problematic, Mrs. Kim is also shown as isolated and passive with little agency. The woman leading people to the shelter is described with active verbs such as "look back," "call," and "tell," while Mrs. Kim is depicted with "nod." No voice is heard from Mrs. Kim, even when she is invited to say something by Daniel's mother.

The cats are used as an analogy for the relationship between Daniel and Mrs. Kim, representing conflict at the beginning and reconciliation at the end. Mrs. Kim's cat is also used to depict Mrs. Kim's personality. She identifies her cat as orange in color, while Daniel describes the color as carrot, saying to himself that the cat is "fat and mean."

The visual representation of Mrs. Kim also reveals racialized discourses. Early in the book, Mrs. Kim is depicted in a close-up as large, holding up her hands and yelling at rioters (see Figure 14.2). Her body is not drawn in proportion. Her eyes are red, and her skin color is dark with thick black hair, revealing her as a scary angry person. Her skin color, in fact, is darker than anyone else and she is the only person with thick black hair. Omi and Winant (2015) assert that race is socially constructed and is a fluid and flexible social concept. Phenotypic differences are necessarily understood in the same consistent manner, but they nevertheless operate in specific social settings. In *Smoky Night*, African Americans are not represented with generic skin and hair colors. Rather, the generic characteristics are used to represent Mrs. Kim's anger and scariness as an association with blackness. This seems to be an example of the complicated practice of racialization, an extension of racial meaning to a previously racially unclassified relationship, social practice, or group (Omi & Winant, 2015).

Verbally and visually, Mrs. Kim is represented as an angry person, similar to the social discourses of pop culture about Korean merchants, and she is racially conceptualized as aberrant. This social practice could also be an example of racial formation, the sociohistoric process by which racial identities are created, lived out, transformed, and destroyed (Omi & Winant, 2015). While blackness is associated with anger, whiteness is associated with peace. At the end of the story, when the conflict between Daniel's family and Mrs. Kim is resolved, her skin color turns to white with a straight posture and proportionately balanced body shape.

To focus the reader's attention on Mrs. Kim, one semiotic device is the visual placement of objects. The center of the picture is the most effective place of attention and signals the nucleus of the information to which all other elements are in some sense subservient. The margins are the ancillary dependent elements

FIGURE 14.2 Mrs. Kim Standing in Front of Her Market Yelling at Rioters (Bunting, 1994)

Source: Illustrations from *Smoky Night* by Eve Bunting, illustrated by David Diaz. Illustrations copyright © 1994 by David Diaz. Reprinted by permission of Houghton Mifflin Harcourt Publishing Company. All rights reserved.

and are often identical or similar to each other (Kress & Leeuwen, 2006). On the page describing the rioting, the verbal text says, "two boys are carrying a TV." However, in the illustration a TV takes up the center of the image and the boys are positioned around the TV with only their faces and lower bodies visible. The TV is the biggest object in the illustration. The centered TV is presented as the nucleus and the boys are in the margins as ancillary elements. The marginal objects are identical and similar, so they have less meaning and decrease the weight of the act, giving attention to the TV. If the visual image were converted to verbal text, the sentence would be passive in which the thing receiving the action is optionally included near the end of the sentence. The visual is saying "a TV is being carried."

The term "carry" is used for the act of looting even though carry does not refer to looting at a literal level. The verbal text uses the term "dragging" and later "stealing" to refer to people taking items from Mrs. Kim's market. These terms are not synonymous and do not reveal actions within the actual LA events. In comparison to these mild expressions for looting, the visual image on the recto depicts Mrs. Kim's entire body in the center, taking up a large space with her arms held up high, thus amplifying her emotional anger and scariness.

Disengagement for the Reader

Daniel uses first-person narrative to tell readers about the events, and readers are positioned by his narration to be invited into the story. Daniel and his mother live on the second floor in an apartment and physically look down to see the riots. Connotatively, the words used in depicting their stance implicitly position the reader to engage in the story through "I" and "standing well back from our window," so readers also are directed to stay back, thus being distantiated from the event.

The historical context is depicted in an exotic ambience, not reflecting the tragedy of an event in which many people died. Through the words used in describing this event in Examples (8) and (9), readers do not feel the urgent emergency; rather, it feels like a dreamlike illusion, not reality, or at least not something that is the reader's responsibility.

8. Smoke <u>drifts</u>, light as <u>fog</u>. I see the <u>distant</u> flicker of flames.
9. <u>Outside</u>, the sky is <u>hazy orange</u>.

This distantiating discourse is also represented in the illustrations. In picturebooks, when the image is not framed and extends to the page edge, the depicted characters are less constrained and the story world is opened up to the reader. In comparison, a bounded image demarcates the story world as more distinctly separate from the reader's world (Painter et al., 2013). A distinctive technique is to use a rough black frame to bound all illustrations.

Another device for signaling interpersonal relationships between viewer and image is focalization, the way in which the depicted person is looking at the viewer (Painter et al., 2013). When a depicted person gazes directly out at the viewer, that person is inviting participation by the viewer. By contrast, an image without such a gaze is an offer of information for dispassionate perusal (Kress & van Leeuwen, 2006). In *Smoky Night*, most of the characters do not gaze at the reader. Even though the frame uses close-up shots so that readers are positioned in close social distance, readers are not invited into active engagement with characters but remain removed within dispassionate perusal.

The artistic style of depicting characters is a device to show pathos and affect. One way to categorize illustration styles for depicting characters is the degree of detail and realism, referred to as minimalistic, generic, and naturalistic, and serving as a system of reader alignment (Painter et al., 2013). Through this visual device, readers are invited to engage with characters in varied degrees. The artistic style of facial expression in *Smoky Night* is unique, with eyes, nose, and mouth unrealistically drawn in bold black lines that are powerful and strong (see Figure 14.3).

FIGURE 14.3 Artistic Style of Facial Expressions (Bunting, 1994)
Source: Illustrations from *Smoky Night* by Eve Bunting, illustrated by David Diaz. Illustrations copyright © 1994 by David Diaz. Reprinted by permission of Houghton Mifflin Harcourt Publishing Company. All rights reserved.

Although artistically stunning, because this style is so far from a realistic depiction, viewers are strongly alienated from reality. The use of edges and strong contrasts of light and shade can create an eerie unreality (Painter et al., 2013), in this case creating alienation so that viewers feel the otherness of characters instead of empathy.

Ideological Complex

In *Smoky Night*, the author writes a dedication, "For the peacekeepers," and the book is often reviewed as conveying the universal importance of human interaction. While the plot centers around the conflict between an African American child and a Korean merchant, the broader social context is not evident. The book uses a comment by Daniel to imply that conflicts between two groups can be resolved when they decide to "know each other." The embedded ideology in the discourse of *Smoky Night* thus seems to be the importance of keeping peace through the human interaction of coming to know each other. Ching (2005) argues that this book substitutes racial harmony for systemic critique, with the two cats as a metaphor for interracial harmony through empathy and knowledge of each other.

In the book, when people go to a shelter to escape the fire, a volunteer leads them and takes care of Mrs. Kim, while another woman takes care of the cats. The figure of the woman, who appears to be white, is drawn in an overly large size at the center to invite the attention of viewers. The represented discourse seems to be a dominant societal stance of protecting and caring for people, a different representation from what occurred for many Korean Americans in their interactions with officials during the events in LA.

These discourses are represented again with the firefighter as a protector. When the fire breaks out in the next building, the firefighter arrives immediately and evacuates everyone before the fire reaches Daniel's building, showing concern for the residents. The firefighter is depicted in a large size at the center of the illustration. The firefighter also rescues and brings the cats to the families. He is again depicted at the center in a large size, holding two cats in his arms, surrounded by Daniel's family.

The represented social discourses of *Smoky Night* differ from what African Americans and Korean Americans experienced during the protests. African Americans protested structural racial injustice and economic marginalization. Korean Americans experienced abandonment by governmental authorities and felt they were not protected as their stores burned down. In *Smoky Night*, governmental authorities are depicted as a caring and strong protector.

The discourse and ideology of dominant groups are reflected in the book along with a silencing of the discourse and ideology of marginalized groups. According to Hodge and Kress (1988), ideology displays an image of the world as it ought to be, as seen from the vantage point of the dominant or the dominated group. This functionally related set of contradictory versions of the world, called an ideological complex, is coercively imposed by one social group on another on behalf of the former's own distinctive interests, or subversively offered by another social group in an attempt at resistance in its own interest.

Final Reflections

Children's literature is a representation of discourses that, in turn, are the projection of ideologies. Often these imbedded ideologies of children's literature are not examined, due to the view of children's literature as a neutral text. In this study, we investigated ideology by examining a picturebook as a discursive practice and cultural artifact.

In any social event, many social groups are engaged, each producing their own discourses, constrained by their social situations and positions. Their interests and demands are embedded in the generated discourses, that is, their discourses are a projection of their ideologies. The generated discourses are put in the "order of discourses," which are not neutral from the power relations to which each group is associated (Fairclough, 1995). Through this process certain discourses build hegemonic blocs to preserve and maximize their dominance. Consequently, in the process, the dominant discourses are legitimized as truth.

Even though *Smoky Night* refers to a specific sociohistorical event, the represented discourses do not provide the background through which readers can interrogate the social context; instead the social event is portrayed as a decontextualized and personalized act focusing on emotionally-biased violence. The portrayal of Mrs. Kim positions readers to disengage from the social event, legitimizing dominant ideologies. Authorities are represented as saviors who protect the powerless; what is not represented is the perspective of marginalized social groups who felt racial injustice and abandonment. Without tools for critical visual and textual analysis, children and teachers are unknowingly influenced by these ideologies and discourses. Embedding a book within an examination of the broader sociohistorical context provides a critical lens for the reader.

This study interrogated an ideological aspect of children's literature through the representation of dominant social discourses. When the ideological aspects of texts are overlooked, the represented dominant ideologies are naturalized and mystified. Locating children's literature in the social context and interrogating the represented discourses in relation to generated social discourses uncovers the ideological aspects of the literary text as a cultural text.

References

Barthes, R. (1964). *Image, music, text*. Trans. S. Heath. London: Cape.
Bluestone, B. & Harrison, B. (1982). *The deindustrialization of America*. New York: Basic Books.

Bourdieu, P. & Wacquant, L. (1992). *An invitation to reflexive sociology*. Chicago: University of Chicago Press.

Callinicos, A. (1992). The meaning of the Los Angeles riots. *Economic and Political Weekly*, 27(30), 1603–1606.

Chang, E. (2012). Confronting Sa-i-gu: Twenty years after the Los Angeles riots. *Seoul University American Studies*, 35(2), 1–27.

Ching, S. (2005). Multicultural children's literature as an instrument of power. *Language Arts*, 83(2), 128–136.

Fairclough, N. (1995). *Critical discourse analysis*. New York: Longman.

Fairclough, N. (2003). *Analyzing discourse*. New York: Routledge.

Halliday, M. (1978). *Language as social semiotic*. London: Arnold.

Hodge, R. & Kress, G. (1988). *Social semiotics*. Cambridge: Polity.

Horning, K. (2018). Publishing statistics on children's books about people of color. http s://ccbc.education.wisc.edu/books/pcstats.asp

Jacobs, R. (2000). *Race, media, and the crisis of civil society*. London: Cambridge University Press.

Kim, C. (1993). "No Justice, No Peace!": The politics of Black–Korean conflict. *Trotter Review*, 7(2), 12–13.

Kim, R. (2012). Violence and trauma as constitutive elements in Korean American racial identity formation. *Ethnic and Racial Studies*, 35(11), 1999–2018.

Kress, G. & van Leeuwen, T. (2006). *Reading images*. New York: Routledge.

Lah, K. (2017, April 29). The LA riots were a rude awakening for Korean-Americans. CNN. Retrieved from www.cnn.com/2017/04/28/us/la-riots-korean-americans/

Larrain, J. (1996). Stuart Hall and the Marxist concept of ideology. In D. Morley & K. Chen (Eds.), *Stuart Hall: Critical dialogues in cultural studies* (pp. 47–70). London: Routledge.

Lee, S. (2015). Asian Americans and the 1992 Los Angeles riots/uprising. *Oxford Research Encyclopedia of American History*. Retrieved from http://americanhistory.oxfordre.com

Maingueneau, D. (2010). Literature and discourse analysis. *Acta Linguistica Hafniensia*, 42(1), 147–158.

Min, P. (1995). *Asian Americans: Contemporary trends and issues*. Thousand Oaks, CA: Sage.

Nieto, S. (2017). *Language, culture and teaching*. New York: Routledge.

Nodelman, P. (2008). *The hidden adult: Defining children's literature*. Baltimore, MD: Johns Hopkins University Press.

Nopper, T. (2015). On terror, captivity, and Black–Korean conflict. *Decolonization: Indigeneity, Education and Society*, 4(1), 1–6.

Omi, M. & Winant, H. (2015). *Racial formation in the United States*. New York: Routledge.

Painter, C., Martin, J.R., & Unsworth, L. (2013). *Reading visual narratives: Image analysis of children's picture books*. Sheffield, UK: Equinox.

Rogers, R. & Christian, J. (2007). "What could I say?" A critical discourse analysis of the construction of race in children's literature. *Race Ethnicity and Education*, 10(1), 21–46.

Romero, D. (2012, April 26). L.A. riots. *LA Weekly News*. Retrieved from www.laweekly. com/news/la-riots-lapd-tried-to-displace-its-racism-problem-and-put-it-on-a-korea n-merchant-says-former-times-reporter-john-lee-2391941

Sexton, J. (2010). Proprieties of coalition: Blacks, Asians, and the politics of policing. *Critical Sociology*, 36(1), 87–108.

Smith, A. (2014). Letting down Rapunzel: Feminism's effects on fairy tales. *Children's Literature in Education*, 46, 424–437.

Stephens, J. (2015). Editorial: Critical content analysis and literary criticism. *International Research in Children's Literature*, 8(1), v–viii.

Stevenson, B. (2013). *The contested murder of Latasha Harlins: Justice, gender, and the origins of the LA Riots*. New York: Oxford University Press.

Zia, H. (2001). *Asian American dreams*. New York: Farrar, Straus and Giroux.

Children's Literature References

Bunting, E. (1994). *Smoky night*. Illus. by D. Diaz. New York: Harcourt.

PART V
Final Reflections

15

EXTENDING A CRITICAL LENS INTO OUR CLASSROOMS

Kathy G. Short with the Worlds of Words Community

The insights we gained about critical content analysis of written text and visual image in books for young people has given us confidence as researchers. We feel stronger in our rigor in carefully and thoughtfully approaching our research on literature and in taking critical stances that challenge our thinking to develop new understandings and perspectives. We have developed more in-depth knowledge and understandings of critical theories, and are able to be more explicit about how those theories frame and guide our research in systematic and intentional inquiry. We have also developed processes and strategies for analysis that provide a set of options from which we can select when examining language and image in texts. As researchers, we plan to continue our work in critical content analysis of global and multicultural books that matter to the readers with whom we interact. Our new inquiry is to explore what happens when we put the strategies from critical content analysis into teachers' and children's hands,

As educators, we now talk about books differently with readers in university and K-12 classrooms because we have a deeper sense of why particular books are problematic, moving from a vague sense of tension to detailed understandings about the specific aspects that are causing that tension. Those understandings change the types of engagements we create around books with readers and the ways in which we frame those engagements. We also have a deeper sense of the issues connected to cultural authenticity, and to the social responsibility of bookmakers, so we can to raise these issues in interactions with readers.

Our roots as a community of educators are in researching the responses of readers to global and multicultural literature and in understanding how curricular engagements can encourage dialogue and transformation through literature. Our inquiry into critical content analysis of text grew out of several realizations. One was the reminder from Rosenblatt (1938) that the transaction of reader and potential text to create a new text, or "poem," through a lived-through experience must attend to the roles of both the reader and the text. It was clear to us that we had often attended far more to the reader and not enough to the text. The second was our realization that we needed to develop our critical lenses as readers of these books if we wanted to invite children and teachers to become critical readers. Frank Smith (1987) says that teachers cannot invite students to join the literacy club if teachers themselves are not readers who are members of that club. By the same token, we cannot invite our students to take on a critical lens, unless we are critical readers.

Although we remain committed to continuing our explorations of critical content analysis, our inquiry as a community has turned to our teaching in university contexts and our work with teachers, adolescents, and children in schools. We want to explore how our understandings of critical content analysis can inform our classroom practice, assuming in turn that our practice will also change our research. Because we value the learning we do as a community, we met together as a group in the summer to talk about the implications for our own practice. As we brainstormed and dialogued, three main areas of work in classrooms emerged around the use of critical theory as a frame, the significance of sociohistorical and cultural context, and the need for a toolbox of strategies as a critical reader. The thoughts we share here are tentative and part of an ongoing inquiry that will be transformed as we engage in the actual work in classrooms.

Critical Theory as a Frame for Our Teaching

Selecting and exploring a critical theory frame for our research into written text and visual image has been transformative. The lens this theory provides in supporting a critical stance that weaves throughout the research has made clear the political nature of research. In the same way, Freire (1970) argues that teaching is always political, and so we need to explore the critical theories that best support our intentions and inquiries in our teaching contexts. We decided that we would begin that work in our own university classrooms.

As teacher educators, we believe this means examining each course that we teach to determine a critical theory or set of theories that can frame the course and that matches with the purpose and intent of the course. We realized that often theoretical perspectives are mentioned at the beginning of the course and then examined more deeply at the end of the course after students have had a range of experiences with the content. The problem with this approach is that it matches the typical use of theory in research as part of the initial literature review and in the discussion of the findings, rather than to frame the research process.

So our current inquiry is each taking a course we are teaching and considering the purpose and intent to select a critical theory as an explicit lens for us and our students in selecting and examining the content of that class. Carmen and Andrea are both teaching a graduate class on biliteracy/bilingualism, and decided to use postcolonialism as the theoretical frame for the course, particularly the lens of "othering" (Said, 1978; Tyson, 2011). The students will initially explore their own names and identities through the creation of cultural boxes in which they include meaningful artifacts that speak to aspects of their identities. As they share their boxes in class and select one artifact to highlight, they will be asked to make connections to Sonia Nieto's (2009) definition of culture and consider the social, political and economic factors that influence aspects of their cultural identities. This introduction will provide a context in which to introduce the concept of "othering" that frames the course. Throughout the class as they explore children's books on bilingual children and curricular materials and lessons plans for bilingual learners, they will use this lens to consider how particular books or lesson plans reflect othering through colonial oppression or anti-colonial resistance. The lens gives them a position and understandings from which to analyze and make sense of their experiences. This lens is one they can take into their other coursework and their future work as bilingual teachers.

As Mary, Susan, Deanna, and Holly thought about their literacy methods courses for undergraduates, they decided to explore framing their courses around the lens of positioning theory (Davies & Harré, 1990; Harré, 2015; Van Langenhove & Harré, 1994). Their courses involve students interacting with children's books and mandated materials and programs for teaching reading. Positioning provides a critical lens for them to question how these books and materials position children and teachers. The questions they see consistently framing each assignment and class engagement are:

- What are the assumptions about who children are as human beings and as readers?
- What are the assumptions about the teacher's positionality in relation to children and to experts in the field? What are the assumptions of the book-makers in relation to the positions of administrators, school boards, and classroom teachers?
- What are the assumptions about relationships and what it means to have responsibility to others?

The goal is for students to develop a critical lens and set of questions that they can bring to their future teaching contexts as they encounter mandated reading programs. They need a lens from which to view these programs, and the confidence to engage with that lens in new contexts.

Kathy and Tracy are teaching graduate courses, with Kathy teaching a seminar on reader response theory and Tracy a course on teaching with children's literature. They both decided to frame their courses around the lens of critical pedagogy, specifically Freire's (1970) argument that dialogue is the only means of transforming the world, and that this dialogue should be based around generative themes that are significant in the lives of learners. They began their courses looking at different kinds of talk and the way in which dialogue differs from discussion or sharing (Peterson, 1992), before introducing students to Freire (1970), focusing on his belief that dialogue is based in love, humility, faith in others, trust, hope, and critical thinking. Kathy is noticing that as graduate students read Rosenblatt and consider her beliefs about dialogue, imagination, and democracy, their reflections include connections to Freire and critical pedagogy because of that framing. Tracy found that the framing around dialogue and critical pedagogy was effective for moving into reading Leland, Lewison, and Harste (2017) on teaching children's literature through a critical lens.

Several others who are preparing to teach undergraduate children's literature courses are considering a lens of intersectionality (Collins & Blige, 2016). This theoretical frame focuses on the overlap of social identities, such as race, gender, sexuality, and class, and how that overlap, or intersectionality, of identities contributes to systemic oppression and discrimination experienced by an individual. By asking students to first identify their own multiple cultural identities and consider which of these combine to "label" them in some way by society, a context is set to introduce this theoretical frame. Questions generated from the frame of intersectionality can then provide a lens that weaves across the course. As students read children's books, they will be encouraged to consider how a particular group of people are represented in a novel, what are the sites of oppression or privilege in the novel, and how the intersections of identity, power, and privilege operate in the novel for specific characters. These questions are adapted from the ones that Charlene Mendoza is currently using in her work in Tucson with high school students in reading literature.

These explorations are tentative and in process, but we are excited by the possibilities of framing each of our courses within a critical frame. Instead of teaching *about* critical theory, our goal is that students *experience* a critical lens in much the same way that Rosenblatt (1938) talked about transaction as a lived-through experience. Students have the opportunity of trying on a lens in a thoughtful and in-depth way across multiple experiences in a course. They can then decide whether that lens becomes part of the way in which they live in the world, but they understand the lens well enough so that it's an option for their thinking. Actually living a critical lens in an explicit and systematic way within a course is a different experience for students. As teacher educators, critical theory has guided our teaching but not in the explicit ways we are envisioning now, nor in ways that so carefully involve student awareness of this frame.

Trying on a critical lens can also be integrated into elementary and secondary classrooms. Angelica Serrano engaged her Grade 4/5 Latinx students in trying on the lens of childism, prejudice against children, telling them about the basic tenets of that theory. They talked about how adults question whether children have the right to participate in decisions that affect their lives and are viewed as competent to make contributions in society. This critical theory frame was one that children immediately connected to and used to talk about the many examples from their lives where their voices were not heard or considered in interactions with adults. Angelica shared a set of picturebooks she had gathered in which teachers and children interact at school. After initial reading and response to the books, students met in pairs to try on the lens of childism with a book. One major theme that they found across the books is that children who advocate for themselves are often labeled as engaging in "bad behavior" by teachers and that teachers often use fear or threats to scare children into "behaving." Childism was an effective critical lens because it connected to and gave voice to tensions already present in children's lives.

Sociohistorical and Cultural Explorations as Context

As researchers, we search for sociohistorical and cultural sources that will help us understand the broader social context within which a book is embedded. The increasing significance of these understandings for our research has led us to consider how we might encourage these explorations with students without a return to transmission models of teaching background knowledge.

In an undergraduate course on global citizenship that involved many small group literature circles where students read and discussed young adult global literature, Kathy asked students to do internet research on an aspect of a book that they wanted to know more about. Students started their literature circles with sharing that information and then moved into the book discussion, often resulting in major shifts in their transactions with the book and their dialogue. For example, one group read *Sold* (McCormick, 2008) about a girl from Nepal who is sold into sexual slavery, a book they found compelling. Their initial written responses reflected feelings of superiority and pity, with comments about how glad they were to have grown up in the U.S. and in loving families. As they came together to share their internet research before talking about the book, one had researched Nepal, a country she knew little about, several had looked into the sex trafficking of young girls in Asia, and one had researched sex trafficking of girls in Tucson. Her research challenged the others' responses of pity and superiority and led to an in-depth dialogue around the book and the larger issues.

Another effective strategy has been to never read a book alone, but instead to always read a book alongside other books. When students read a book within a larger text set, they have a range of texts to explore and to build their understandings of that context. We also pair books to read against and with each other, for example a global picturebook with a book set in the U.S. that have similar themes or a fiction novel with an information book. Particularly with global literature, these books are often the first they have read set in a specific global community and, unless surrounded by other books from that community, they bring a very limited perspective to that book and culture. Adichie (2009) notes the dangers of reducing a person to a single narrative of who we think they are. When we see an event or a person as one thing, we see that person or event in a limited way as a commonplace narrative. That danger is always present in reading global literature from unfamiliar cultures.

Explorations of context also involve considerations of the author, illustrator, and translator and their positionalities in relation to a book. In working with K-5 students in Tucson, Kathy found that reading the book jacket information on the bookmakers before reading the book aloud provided children with a context from which to interpret the book. Making a quick comment about that information, such as saying this author grew up in this culture or lived in the culture for a period of time or visited this global community and did many interviews, provided a lens for children and a context for understanding the book. This context became so important to the children that when the librarian did read-alouds, they stopped her to ask for that information about the author before she started the book. At the university, asking undergraduates to do quick internet research on the authors of books they are discussing in literature circles was a quick way to establish some context.

Holly asks university students to consider their own cultural locations in relation to a book, particularly when their own cultural location is a mismatch with the culture highlighted in a book they are reading. Raising this awareness to a conscious level encourages students to take an open-minded perspective and not to immediately leap to judgement by using their own culture as the norm against which to view all other cultures (Johnson, Mathis, & Short, 2016).

Analytical Tools as Critical Reading Strategies

One of the most exciting aspects of our inquiry into visual images has been finding a set of tools that we can use as researchers in examining the meaning-making processes of the visual images in illustrations. We thought we understood art as a meaning-making system, having explored the role of the elements of art, such as color, line, shape, space, and perspective, along with style, media and technique, and composition. These concepts, however, did not provide us with the tools we needed to look at images through a critical lens. As we shared in Chapter 1, we explored Kress and van Leeuwen (2006) but found their work difficult to apply to picturebooks and graphic novels because of their focus on a single image rather than a sequence of images that work together to tell a story. Finding the work of Painter, Martin, and Unsworth (2013) was an exciting moment and started a new inquiry that resulted in this book as we each engaged with their visual tools to analyze the images in books.

We are eager to introduce these tools to undergraduate and graduate students in teacher education classes and to children in classrooms. With children, our focus is on introducing tools that are relevant to their discussions of read-alouds, commenting on gaze or social distance as connected to the meanings we are exploring together. Another possibility is to create short mini-lessons much like those that occur in a writing workshop, around a specific tool that is relevant to students and their current inquiries.

In examining the tools we used in our research, the ones that we are most interested in exploring with students, teachers, and children are those related to the interpersonal metafunction (Painter et al., 2013), particularly the following:

- Gaze—the direction of a character's eyes in relation to the reader/viewer.

  a   Direct gaze is when a character looks out at a reader, inviting the reader into the situation or sending an appeal to the reader.
  b   An indirect gaze invites an observer stance from the reader.
  c   A reader can also be positioned to look over the shoulder of the character to see from the same angle as the character at what is being observed, inviting empathy with that character.
  d   Positioning also includes power dynamics in whether the reader's angle of vision is looking down at the character from above (giving power to the reader) or looking up at the character (giving power to the character).

- Social distance—the distance of the reader from the characters in the illustration.

  a   Close-up indicates a close, intimate relationship with the reader.
  b   Mid-range indicates a friendly distance and relationship with the reader.
  c   Distance creates a physical space between the reader and the character.

- Proximity and attitude—the closeness or distance between characters and their orientations to each other to indicate different power dynamics.

  a   The amount of distance between characters indicates the closeness or distance of their relationship to each other.
  b   Orientation also can indicate the nature of characters' relationships with each other, ranging from whether they face or touch each other as well as whether one stands above the other or towers over the other to reflect a power dynamic.

- Drawing style—the ways in which the faces of characters are drawn.

  a   Minimalistic or cartoon-style lacks detail and shows little emotion, so that readers are kept as detached observers of the characters.
  b   Generic style has more detail, especially around the mouth, but could be any person and so readers are positioned to see themselves in the characters, to stand in the character's shoes.
  c   Naturalistic style is nuanced and detailed to look more realistic, allowing for more emotion and reader engagement with that character as a distinct individual person, as an actual person who has actual life experiences.

- Color choice or ambience—the use of warm or cool colors and the familiarity of the colors.

a   Warm colors, such as reds and yellows, evoke an emotion of warmth and connection.

b   Cool colors, such as blues and greens, evoke more subdued and toned down moods.

c   Familiar colors that are close to those found in the world invite the reader to connect with the image as a familiar one, while a reduced palette of only a few colors signals a removal from reality or a reduced certainty for the reader about that context.

• Weight or graduation—what is given "weight" or dominance in an illustration to emphasize importance and to pull in the viewer's eye.

a   Size of a character in relation to others.

b   The extent to which a character fills up the page or takes the least amount of space.

c   Numbers or high/low repetitions of a certain image.

In Chapter 2, Painter includes charts that note the full range of tools identified in her work and shows how diagrams can be created to understand how a specific tool plays out within an image. More information and examples of these tools are found in Painter et al. (2013).

These visual tools combine with tools to examine written language that we explored in *Critical Content Analysis of Children's and Young Adult Literature* (Johnson, Mathis, & Short, 2016). These tools are described in greater detail in the final chapter of that book, but include:

• Focalization—considering whose story is being told and from whose point of view.

• Closure—examining how a story is resolved and by whom, as well as what assumptions are made in that closure.

• Power and agency—asking who has power and who has agency in a book.

• Identifying key scenes or passages in the text or in the visual images for a closer look.

• Identifying key words, sentences, or phrases for a close look.

• Identifying a cornerstone or exemplary book and the way that book approaches a theme/issue and then using intertextuality to compare other books on the same theme to that cornerstone book.

Final Reflections

In reflecting on the power of taking a closer look at written text and visual images in a book through the lens of a critical theory, we are reminded by Rosenblatt (1978) that this reading encourages readers to take on an efferent stance. She argues that the analytical reading of a book is interesting and meaningful for a reader *only if* the book itself matters to them, and that involves a first reading where the focus is the experience of the book from an aesthetic stance. Readers need to care about the book, and that caring grows out of immersing themselves in the story world of a book as a lived-through experience that provides them with the opportunity to construct their own connections and thinking. After giving voice to that experience through dialogue with others or through written reflection, readers can then stand back to distance themselves from the experience and to critique both their response and the text.

Without the lived-through experience of a story, the kind of analysis shared in this book becomes an academic exercise, one that many of us know well from high school and college literature classes. Sometimes those classes took the form of New Criticism, where the teacher had the "correct" interpretation which was conveyed to us through lectures or painful discussions where we tried to guess at that interpretation. Other times, a literary theory such as feminist criticism or postmodernism was taught, and we were required to read a book through that lens. Neither of these experiences were positive and fall into what Dewey (1938) called non-educative in that they were painful, uncomfortable experiences that we did not want to continue in the future. We are aware that critical content analysis could become a negative experience for students in teacher education and K-12 classrooms—clearly not our intent.

Although we are committed to working with students to develop their critical stances as readers, we recognize that this stance cannot develop unless readers have lived their own experiences within a story world. That experience is the basis for dialogue with other readers and is what they critique to examine how the text and their own cultural locations shaped their interpretations. Hurrying readers past their experience into a critical lens results in another teacher-imposed interpretation of a book. Our goal instead is that readers try on a critical lens to change their position in the world and, hopefully, to consider how to change the world.

Our focus on readers immersing themselves in a story world and entering another time and place is based in our belief that story is more than a book. Story is the way our minds make sense of our lives and world (Short, 2012). We work at understanding events and people by constructing stories to interpret what is occurring around us. In turn, the stories we create from our lives become our world views and the lens through which we construct meaning about ourselves and others. This understanding of story as a primary act of mind expands the significance of bringing a critical lens to the stories we construct from books as well as from our lives. The experience of story through a critical lens has the power to direct and change our thinking and actions if we have the time and space necessary to fully experience their role in meaning-making and to engage in transformative dialogue within a community.

References

Adichie, C. (2009). The dangers of a single story. TED talk. London, July. You Tube.

Collins, P. & Blige, S. (2016). *Intersectionality*. New York: Polity.

Davies, B., and Harré, R. (1990). Positioning: The discursive production of selves. *Journal for the Theory of Social Behaviour*, 20, 43–63.

Dewey, J. (1938). *Experience and education*. New York: Collier.

Freire, P. (1970). *Pedagogy of the oppressed*. South Hadley, MA: Bergin & Garvey.

Harré, R. (2015). Positioning theory. In T. Sandel & C. Ilie (Eds.), *The International Encyclopedia of Language and Social Interaction*. doi:10.1002/9781118611463.wbielsi120

Johnson, H., Mathis, J., & Short, K. (2016). *Critical content analysis of children's and adolescent literature*. New York: Routledge.

Kress, G. & Van Leeuwen, T. (2006). *Reading images: The grammar of visual design* (2nd ed.). London: Routledge.

Leland, C., Lewison, M., & Harste, J. (2017). *Teaching children's literature. It's critical!* New York: Routledge.

McCormick, P. (2008). *Sold*. New York: Hyperion.

Nieto, S. (2009). *The light in their eyes: Creating multicultural learning communities*. New York: Teachers College Press.

Painter, C., Martin, J.R., & Unsworth, L. (2013). *Reading visual narratives: Image analysis of children's picture books*. Sheffield, UK: Equinox.

Peterson, R. (1992). *Life in a crowded place*. New York: Scholastic.

Rosenblatt, L. (1938). *Literature as exploration*. Chicago: Modern Language Association.

Rosenblatt, L. (1978). *The reader, the text, and the poem*. Carbondale, IL: Southern Illinois Press.

Said, E.W. (1978). *Orientalism*. Harmondsworth, UK: Penguin.

Short, K. (2012). Story as world-making. *Language Arts*, 90(1), 9–17.

Smith, F. (1987). *Joining the literacy club: Further essays into education*. Portsmouth, NH: Heinemann.

Tyson, L. (2011). *Using critical theory: How to read and write about literature*. New York: Routledge.

Van Langenhove, L.V. and Harré, R. (1994). Cultural stereotypes and positioning theory. *Journal for the Theory of Social Behaviour*, 24, 359–372.

CONTRIBUTORS

Editor Bios

Holly Johnson is a professor in the Literacy and Second Language Studies program at the University of Cincinnati. She teaches courses such as literature for the middle grades, international literature, and language arts methods. She currently chairs the NCTE Standing Committee on Global Citizenship and has served on USBBY's OIB Committee. Her research includes critical content analysis of texts for adolescents, the impact of positioning theory in middle level classrooms, and how visual images can position readers.

Janelle Mathis is a professor of Literacy and Children's Literature at the University of North Texas. Her research, publications, and instructional interests focus on international and multicultural children's literature in supporting greater insight for readers to the global community and are centered at the intersection of critical content analysis, the transactional theory of reader response, and multimodality. She is past president of USBBY, the U. S. national section of the International Board on Books for Young People, and currently is co-editor of *Bookbird, A Journal of International Children's Literature*.

Kathy G. Short is a professor in Teaching, Learning and Sociocultural Studies at the University of Arizona with a focus on inquiry, dialogue, intercultural understanding, and global literature. She is the Director of Worlds of Words, a center on global literacies and literatures. Her most recent edited books include *Teaching Globally: Reading the World through Literature* and *Critical Content Analysis of Children's and Young Adult Literature*. She is a past President of NCTE and USBBY.

Author Bios:

Seemi Aziz is a visiting/adjunct professor in the Department of Teaching, Learning, and Sociocultural Studies and a lecturer in the department of English at the University of Arizona, Tucson, Arizona. She has taught a range of children's literature and literacy courses. Her research includes studies on critical content analysis of global and international children's literature, including global immigrants and diaspora's representations in children's literature especially those of Muslim origin.

Wanda M. Brooks is an associate professor of Literacy Education in the College of Education at Temple University. She teaches graduate and undergraduate courses related to literacy research, theories and instruction. Dr. Brooks' primary research interests consist of examining the literary interpretations of urban middle school youth as well as conducting analyses of contemporary African American young adult literature. She has published in journals such as *Reading Research Quarterly, Children's Literature in Education, Research in the Teaching of English, The Urban Review* and *The English Journal.*

Tabitha Parry Collins received their doctorate in Education from New Mexico State University (NMSU). Their scholarship focuses on queer issues in education, social justice issues in education, and adolescent and children's literacy. They currently teach multicultural education courses for pre-service teachers at NMSU.

Susan Corapi is an assistant professor in the Division of Education at Trinity International University where she teaches classes in literacy methods, diversity, and children's and adolescent literature. Her research interests stem from her years of living internationally, and focus on the development of intercultural competence through interactions with global literature.

Desiree Cueto is an assistant professor in the Department of Elementary Education at Western Washington University. She is the Director of the Pacific Northwest Children's Literature Clearinghouse and teaches courses in children's literature and language arts methods. She also serves as Chair of the NCTE Charlotte Huck Award for Outstanding Fiction for Children and Section Editor for the *AERA Handbook of Research on Teachers of Color.* Her research has been published in the *Journal of Literacy Research* and the *Journal of Children's Literature among* others.

Denise Dávila is an assistant professor in the Language and Literacies Studies program at the University of Texas at Austin. Her research focuses on the inclusion of Latinx and diverse works of children's literature in both formal and informal learning spaces. Her research has appeared in journals such as *Research in the Teaching of English* and the *Journal of Children's Literature*

Deanna Day weaves her passions of art, technology, and children's literature into all the literacy courses she teaches at Washington State University in Vancouver. Currently she is studying apps for elementary writing and reading instruction.

Mary L. Fahrenbruck is an associate professor in the School of Teacher Preparation, Administration and Leadership at New Mexico State University in Las Cruces, New Mexico. Her research focuses broadly on access to literacy and specifically on comprehension strategies, on children's literature in the classroom and on the ways children develop as literate beings. She has published articles in journals including *Journal of Adolescent and Adult Literacy*, *WOW Stories: Connections from the Classroom* and *Talking Points*. She teaches courses in multicultural education at NMSU.

Jeanne G. Fain is a professor and lead faculty of Multilingual Learners at Lipscomb University. Her research agenda includes a focus on early literacy and literacy in K-8 classrooms, critical conversation around global, culturally responsive, and social justice texts in local school partnerships. She teaches literacy, language acquisition, and research courses.

Angeline P. Hoffman is the Student Support Service Director, Teacher Assistant Team Coordinator, and After School Program Coordinator for Dishchii'Bikoh Community School in Arizona. She is interested in multicultural literacy and Indigenous children's literature, both in the United States and internationally, and their roles in the lives of children and teachers in the classrooms.

Hee Young Kim is a doctoral candidate in Language, Reading and Culture at the University of Arizona, previously teaching elementary school in Seoul, Korea. Her research focuses on visual analysis and discourse analysis of children's literature, along with reader response and literacy instruction, within a globalized context.

Julia López-Robertson is an associate professor of Language and Literacy at the University of South Carolina. Her scholarly agenda is built on a commitment to working with children, families, teachers, and preservice teachers in public schools, universities, and communities for the purpose of advancing understandings about emerging bilingual/multilingual students and their families and on the transformation of teacher education to support equitable teaching for all children, particularly English Language Learners.

Carmen M. Martínez-Roldán is an associate professor in Bilingual / Bicultural Education at Teachers College, Columbia University. Her research focuses on bilingual children's literate thinking–the various ways Latinx children construct meanings from texts and the contexts that mediate their interpretive processes and discourses. She co-authored *Visual Journeys through Wordless Narratives: An International Inquiry with Immigrant Children and the Arrival* (with Arizpe and Colomer).

Megan McCaffrey is an assistant professor in the Division of Education at Governors State University. She teaches undergraduate developmental reading methods, and language arts methods in the Elementary and Middle School Education Program. She also teaches graduate courses in the Masters of Reading program. She focuses her research on children's literature and the reading process.

Clare Painter is an Honorary Associate in the Dept. of Linguistics at the University of Sydney. She has retired from the University of New South Wales, where her teaching and research interests included children's language development, children's literature, systemic-functional linguistics and visual communication. Her most recent book, co-authored with J. R. Martin and L. Unsworth, is *Reading Visual Narratives: Image Analysis in Children's Picture Books.*

Janine M. Schall is an associate professor and department chair of Bilingual and Literacy Studies at the University of Texas Rio Grande Valley. She teaches literacy courses and conducts research in the areas of multicultural literature and children's literature with LGBT characters.

Junko Sakoi is the Coordinator of Professional Development and Multicultural Integration for the Tucson Unified School District in Tucson, Arizona. She develops multicultural curricula for the district and provides implementation support to the district's K-8 teachers. Her research interests include children's literature, popular culture, and visual storytelling, Kamishibai.

Yoo Kyung Sung is an associate professor in Language, Literacy and Sociocultural Studies Department at the University of New Mexico in Albuquerque, New Mexico. She teaches a range of children's literature courses. Her research includes studies on critical content analysis of global and international children's literature, including global immigrants and diaspora's representations in children's literature.

INDEX

Critical Content Analysis of Visual Images in Books for Young People: Index.
Locators in **bold** refer to tables.